HUGH
JOHNSON
Sitting in the shade

From ten years of Trad's Diary

Foreword by
Alan Titchmarsh

MITCHELL BEAZLEY

First published in Great Britain in 2021 by Mitchell Beazley,
an imprint of Octopus Publishing Group Ltd, Carmelite House,
50 Victoria Embankment, London EC4Y 0DZ
www.octopusbooks.co.uk

An Hachette UK Company
www.hachette.co.uk

Distributed in the US by Hachette Book Group
1290 Avenue of the Americas, 4th and 5th Floors, New York, NY 10104

Distributed in Canada by Canadian Manda Group
664 Annette St., Toronto, Ontario, Canada M6S 2C8

ISBN 978-1-78472-707-9
A CIP catalogue record for this book is available from the British Library.
Printed and bound in the United Kingdom.
13 5 7 9 10 8 6 4 2

Editor: Diane Pengelly
Art Director: Juliette Norsworthy
Senior Production Manager: Katherine Hockley
Illustrations by Simon Dorrell

I started writing Trad's (or Tradescant's) Diary as the Editorial column of *The Garden*, the then-new Journal of the Royal Horticultural Society, in 1975. Thirty-odd years later Trad, anxious to keep up, went online and started print publication in the quarterly *Hortus* (www.hortus.co.uk). This is Trad's third anthology, following *Hugh Johnson on Gardening* in 1993 and *Hugh Johnson in the Garden* in 2009.

I have to thank many gardening friends, many colleagues, many books, my publisher Denise Bates, Simon Dorrell for the delicate decorations and above all Diane Pengelly, my cherished editor since 1989, for inspiration, encouragement and even a modicum of discipline.

CONTENTS

You can find an index to the topics in this volume online at 'tradsdiary.com'. Type any topic you wish into the search bar, top right.

Foreword

'See how the fates their gifts allot', wrote W S Gilbert in *The Mikado*, alluding to Nature's unfair distribution of her favours. Hugh Johnson always reminds me of that song, having been gifted not only with a perfect combination of aptitudes, but also with the ability to share them in the most generous way.

He is a brilliant and perceptive writer not just about wines but also about gardens, gardening, trees and all life-enhancing cultivation. His musings, shot through with common sense, are provocative, poetic and revelatory. They convey beauty and joy in nature, they (re-)introduce forgotten and undiscovered pleasures, and at times highlight petty bureaucracy and gross injustice.

It is not easy to remain fresh and relevant, but *Trad's Diary* never stales, I suspect because its author continues to be fascinated by his subjects, to study them and wonder and look again, and to articulate his discoveries in endless stimulating ways.

I can number on one hand – well, perhaps two – the gardening writers whose work I look forward to reading, knowing I will come away fired with enthusiasm or stirred by opinions I might not otherwise have considered. Hugh Johnson is one of them, and *Trad's Diary* is a delight.

Alan Titchmarsh

Introduction

The first garden I remember had all the prescribed qualities of a great design: unity, proportion, ecological soundness and fitness for purpose. My father made it on half an acre by the sea, using a single species: the bramble.

The tip of Selsey Bill, in the centre of England's south coast, was where, at least in the apprehension of the locals, Hitler planned to step ashore. Our summer house there was commandeered for the war years. Giant cubes of concrete were put along the beach at the bottom of the garden, and miles of barbed wire. I don't know what the garden contained in 1939, the year I was born, but by 1946, when we got our house back, the answer was brambles. Was there a purple lilac in April? Perhaps. One or two twiggy tamarisks were a dowdy pink. Otherwise the whole plot, a rectangle with the beach at the bottom and the house at the top, was a thicket of brambles five feet high.

Fuel was rationed and time was short. My father took the positive line. He saw plant material rather than weeds. He wouldn't have recognized such designer's jargon, but he recognized an opportunity. He spent his weekends with his bagging hook, the Sussex sickle, carving his plant material into the streets round his City office: Watling Street, Queen Victoria Street, Bow Lane and Bread Street. Queen Victoria Street led obliquely down to the blocks and the beach where Father gave me half a crown for learning to swim. Watling Street (his office was at number 60) branched off to the right at 45 degrees towards St Paul's. First left took you into Bow Lane and back to the main road; right and you dog-legged by St Mary-le-Bow into Cheapside. Various culs-de-sac on the way represented bomb-sites where the Blitz, still a recent memory, had left holes in place of massive stone offices or churches. They made snug places to hide from my brother and sisters.

Brambles are the worst plant material to keep in order. They stretch out painfully prickly shoots a foot a week in summer. The bagging hook was never put away, but the streets took more and more solid shape, their façades in late summer clustered thick with purple blackberries: sweet, staining, pippy heaven.

That was Garden One: easy to remember, easy to understand, simple, decisive and economical (except in effort). The great landscapers would have approved. Clarity of vision, appropriateness for its site; it ticked all the boxes. Above all it had a sense of place. I hope its subliminal lessons are still with me.

I have made or remade half a dozen gardens since then, and visited hundreds. The perfect one is either where I'm sitting, shaded from the sun, at the moment, or will forever stay out of reach. Searching and sifting, though, have kept me happily busy for half a century, passing on my observations and thoughts to my friend Trad. There is a great deal to be said, for a writer, for having a second persona. Trad is the old tweed jacket I slip on when I head out with my fork and my secateurs into an area of the mind, not without its problems, but with infinite promise. I first slipped it on in 1975. The elbows may be out, the hems frayed, but the promise is still there.

2010

January

FRIEND OR FOE?

Is moss friend or foe? I'm never sure whether to apologize for my apple trees or admit to my pride in them. At the end of a wet winter their branches are thickly coated on their upper sides with an emerald-green fabric like baize crossed with velvet. It is thicker on the trees on the shadier side of the garden, and thickest, covering much of the trunk too, on the tree in the southwest corner that gets the most shade.

Our trees have been pruned into open goblet, or even parasol, shapes to let light into their canopies, cutting off the year's new growth but leaving fists of old wood on snaking stems; hardly a classical method but wonderfully energizing to flowers and fruit. The combination of gnarled and writhing grey wood and the emerald moss gives me enormous pleasure. Visitors gasp and get their cameras out. Serious fruit-growers give me recipes for moss removal. Should I be worried?

It was in Japan that I first appreciated moss as a plant that could transform a garden. Saiho-Ji, the monastic moss garden, is only the most notable of many where the moss on rocks, paths, on the banks of streams and the trunks of trees, feels like a spell cast by an old green witch. In winter it is almost lurid green, in summer, shades of green and brown, but the muting, softening effect is permanent. There are no sharp edges: no ultimate focus except the textures, the (rather rare) shock of pure clean petals, and the contrasting polish of water.

In this garden, moss has crept up on me. It must be cumulative in the whole garden, endemic (and increasing) in the lawns, overwhelming on the abandoned tennis court, and presumably finding its perfect perch on the apples.

PRIVATE PRINCEDOM

Snowed up, the sun painting sharp blue shadows on a ground of silver gilt between my window and the churchyard wall. It is too cold to enjoy being outdoors. Time to look through a drawer of old papers about the house and garden accumulated over nearly 40 years. One is an inscription I never got round to putting in the garden temple:

> *Every man's proper Mansion House and Home, being the*
> *Theatre of his Hospitality, the Seat of Self Fruition,*
> *the Comfortablest Part of his own Life, the Noblest of his Son's*
> *Inheritance, a kind of Private Princedom, nay, to the Possessor thereof,*
> *an Epitome of the whole World, may well deserve, by these Attributes,*
> *to be Decently and Delightfully Adorned.*

This is Sir Henry Wotton, in 1624, introducing his *Elements of Architecture* in the manner of Bacon. He does not speak directly of gardening, but his lapidary language spoke strongly to me when I was younger. Does it sound absurd today? No more, I suppose, than the whole idea of a garden temple.

February

SKETCHED FROM LIFE

It was a regular customer who suggested I should change my nom de terre to Treedescant. You're always writing about them, she said.

Touché. But it's largely a winter habit. At this time of year they are the only thing in the garden to look at – and this is the time when you really can see them; they're not all covered with leaves. It is the intricacy of their frameworks that I love to see, and the intimacy of their just-swelling buds. The comparison with people, with and without clothes, did occur to me – but you never know where these things will lead.

Certainly there's nothing outside the window so well worth study as the Siberian crab that rises like a wind-blown fountain a hundred yards down the drive. Its lopsided silhouette perfectly expresses its experiences over 60 years or so; the constant shove of the west wind inclining it to the east, the perennial effort to find more light for its leaves ....

An artist who could draw such a telling design would be rightly celebrated. Every tree out there is a drawing of an autobiography, expressed in a different medium and a different style. Call me Treedescant if you like.

March

THE CUSP OF SPRING

A weekend in North Wales (let's say Merioneth, for the poetry) to see how the winter has treated the woods. Kindly, is the answer. The grass on the hills is still sere, snow hangs in the high gullies and dusts Cadu Idris again in the night. The larches, pines and spruces stand impassive, a few leaning, a few prone, but no mass casualties in a winter with no strong gales. It is catkins that provide the excitement, close up where the hazels are clouds of yellow down-strokes, and here and there pussy willows flash like shards of mirror, and in the distance where they begin to paint the hills.

The brilliant colours of massed twigs always surprise me: oaks pale buff, birches purple, ashes the colour of bone and hazels en masse, as their catkins ripen, bright orange. Spruces are dull green with silver flashes if the wind shows you their petticoats. European larches are pale custard colour, Japanese larches pinky-orange. In forest land the colours are laid on in random brushstrokes. The silver slash of a waterfall (there is very little water after a long dry spell) hangs from a hilltop.

Ponds and puddles are fecund with frogspawn and loud with froggy noises, sharp croaks above a long soft purr like a contented cat – the sound of spring warming its engine.

Home to a quite different scene. What unit of energy do you use for a spring garden getting going? Kilojoules? Megatonnes? The energy driving the buds on every bush and tree, driving the crocuses and daffodils and fritillaries, driving every blade of grass (not to mention every weed and bramble) is immeasurable. If knotweed can split concrete, the concerted force of this garden could reach the moon.

May

LITTLE AFRICA

I'm lucky enough (and that's very lucky) to be intimately engaged with a garden on the Riviera. More precisely, looking down on the Riviera from a hillside called La Petite Afrique. In this mildest of climates, sheltered by the Alps and insulated by the sea, this plunging slope below vertical limestone cliffs is the only one to be compared with Africa.

We started work on the ancient terraces five years ago. They were originally farmed for olives and vines, and latterly, when the railway was laid along the route of the Roman Via Aurelia, for early flowers for the markets of Lyon and Paris. There are still flower-fields terraced up the hills at Villefranche, and many plastic tunnels once you cross the Italian border. Beaulieu-sur-Mer has no terraces wide enough; it was colonized as a fishing village by the late Victorian English. Prime Minister Salisbury had a villa here, the Duke of Connaught helped to build the Anglican church; there may be a reconquista by the French one day, but it hasn't happened yet.

We have parts of the four top-most terraces before it becomes a steep scrub of Aleppo pines and wild olives, then cliffs. Across the bay, 150 metres below, we look down on the eastern cape of Cap Ferrat. From the western end of the top terrace the view takes in the whole garden, the cliffs above and the bluffs leading to Cap d'Ail and Monte Carlo, crowned by three perilously perched castles you only notice at night, when they are disneyfied by floodlights.

The terrace rises in steep steps to the western end, backed by high stone walls. We have given each step a corresponding cascade, so you walk up to follow the glinting water-spouts to their source under a monster olive tree. This is where the gazebo offers you the full view, after you have reached a platform of orange and lemon trees and another more severely furnished with a box parterre under an umbrella pine. The sea is hidden, until you reach the top, behind an iron pergola of roses and grapevines.

Then looking back you see that the uppermost terrace, or the central 30 metres of it, is a tunnel of grapevines and a wisteria, a cutting from one on Cap Ferrat that covers a quarter of an acre with flower streamers that start above your head and almost reach the ground.

On this visit we were not lucky with the weather. The cold wet blast that had hit England two days before followed us there. There was plenty to do, weeding and trimming and planning future planting, but none of that contemplative lazing such pampered gardens are supposed to be for.

June

SOFT HUMMOCKS

The most fragrant job in the garden today is pulling the goose grass out of the Scots briars. You have to stand chest-deep in them and their prickles to get a good straight pull, steady or they break off. The roses are right under your nose, and does any rose have a sweeter smell?

Scots briars are hardly the height of fashion now, but if they have ever grown in your ground they are probably still there. They are the roses of, among other places, the sort of sand dunes that become links; thrifty, low-growing with slender stems, advancing gradually by root-suckers to colonize new ground with soft hummocks of tiny leaves.

They are the prickliest of all roses. Their name, *Rosa spinosissima*, describes the dense fuzz of spines and bristles up every stem, which certainly call for gloves but are not quite substantial enough to wound you.

Their other name (do they really need two?) of *R. pimpinellifolia* points out the resemblance of their leaves to salad burnet: *Sanguisorba major*, or indeed minor. Burnet is yet another old name for the rose which the French, incidentally, call pimprenelle (or sometimes pimpernelle); nothing to do with the scarlet pimpernel, which is *Anagallis arvensis*, or indeed Sir Percy Blakeney.

You smell the genes, as it were, of Scots briars in some excellent hybrids. The tall pale-yellow 'Frühlingsgold' has a fragrance that seems related, and so does 'Stanwell Perpetual', a seedling of unknown parents that seems to have popped up in the 1830s at Stanwell on the outskirts of Colchester. 'Stanwell Perpetual' is a soft pale bush with complex pale-pink flowers and again that swooning-sweet smell just tinged with lemon.

At one point in the 19th century, I read, there were many hundreds of Scots briars and their near relations listed in catalogues. Does anyone collect them now? The little white-flowering original is good enough for me.

If weeding their thicket is a particular pleasure, guaranteed to be repeated every spring (how can you definitively clean the ground in a thicket of thorns?), it is not alone. The weeding season is going well. There was enough rain last week to loosen up the roots of many old adversaries. Deadnettle and goose grass have been surrendering with little struggle. Ground elder never surrenders, but a bunch of its fibrous roots at least feels like a minor trophy. One warm dry spell, though, and they will be locked down. Hard ground makes them unassailable.

THUMBNAIL

I'm not sure what it would be called if you did it to a sentient being, but I'm certain it would be against the law. In so far as a plant has instincts and urges, they are controlled and expressed by its hormones. Can it be legitimate to frustrate them?

At this time of year, when plants are in active growth, their messages are plain to see: the priorities of one bud growing before another, the rationing of vigour between one shoot and another; the election, as it were, of a leader (or the equal energy of several branches) are all determined by hormones. And we, superior beings, seeing how they are programmed, can outwit and re-direct them as we please with our forefingers and thumbs.

If you wait until the plant has obeyed its hormonal instincts and grows its branch or its truss of flowers, you call it pruning (a verb, oddly enough, with no apparent roots or relations). You then have the wasted effort, the amputated stems and leaves, on your hands, your compost heap or your bonfire. Better, surely, to take the initiative and pre-empt unwanted developments.

A florist disbuds to get bigger and better flowers, choosing to concentrate the energy into one flower rather than two. I bully my young trees and shrubs in the same spirit, examining them to see what buds have opened, with what consequences, and what buds are next in line. If a new shoot has set off in a direction I don't approve, I look for another with ideas that more nearly match my own and eliminate the first. At this early stage my thumbnail is usually the ideal tool.

There are plants with such simple and deliberate ways of branching that errors are obvious. Fir trees put up one leader surrounded by incipient branches like a ring of spokes. So strong is the hormonal drive to keep going north, as it were, that when a pigeon lands on and snaps a newly grown and still-green leader (its wood unripened and fragile), one of the spokes gets a hormonal command to take its place.

How does this work? The growing cells on the underside of the chosen shoot (chosen by whatever mysterious form of election) begin to multiply faster than the rest. The shoot bends upwards as a result. Very soon its terminal bud becomes the highest point of the tree, the leader and hormonal dictator. It even develops buds all round in readiness for a new ring of spokes next year.

Intervention is pointless with such a clearly programmed plant. When a rather splendid fir in the garden here lost its leader to a bird in the usual way I did try to help it, from a ladder, tying a light bamboo to the top of the trunk and hoisting one of the side branches into the leadership position, secured with string. When I came back two months later the tree had ignored my advice and produced a new leader from a spare top bud lurking among the needles.

There are deciduous trees that seem to share the fir's philosophy. Alders often have the same simple spoke-like rings of branches; many poplars, too. You can count the age of trees of this persuasion: it is the number of rings of branches – up to the point where circumstances take over: breakage or uneven light and shade modify the simple pattern.

It is oaks that keep my thumbs busiest. *Quercus* is quirky. An English oak rarely leads with an end bud pointing straight ahead. It has buds in clusters that seem to leave all its options open, to grow into whatever space offers most sunlight. In a crowd of seedlings this will usually be straight up, but an oaklet with equal illumination all round will hesitate, first prefer one direction and then another, and soon become a tangle of zigzag branches with buds pointing in all directions.

Welsh sessile oaks are worst; herding cats is straightforward compared with directing a vigorous little Welsh oak tree. It may seem obvious which branch or shoot is dominant and should be encouraged. There are never less than four buds on each shoot, though, ready to surprise you. I suppress three with my thumbnail, or snip little shoots with my secateurs, favouring the one nearest to vertical. I'll come back weeks later, to find all the tree's energy has gone into a bud I didn't notice, heading for Machynlleth.

It's a curious hobby for a grown man, I'll grant you.

IN BOTTOM GEAR

I have never known such a slow and steady build-up to summer. Everything has conspired to put the brakes on the garden. The cold winter, the welcome soak of February and March, the total drought of April and May (less than an inch of rain in four weeks) and a mild(ish) and rainy (so far) June seem to have answered every plant's needs. There is a prodigious amount of leafage in the garden; ramparts of green in the borders with fat buds just beginning to open all around.

Some plants have got their timing wrong. What was a delphinium doing opening its first flowers at the end of April? Most have held back for a grand splurge in late June. And I know why. It's Lucy's wedding on the 26th.

Our first daughter's wedding, on May 31st 2003, coincided with the warmest May day on record, after a cold month. We were congregating in what shade we could find in a garden with precious few flowers.

This time all the roses will be out at once. The forerunners, 'Maigold' for example, may have finished, but the main battery, which in this garden is mainly hybrid musks and ramblers, will be firing salvo after salvo. On our sunniest wall 'Paul's Lemon Pillar' has joined 'Maigold', white after orange, with the orange *Lonicera tellmanniana* and the pale blue of *Clematis* 'Perle d'Azur' scrambling over a philadelphus already smothered in white.

In the borders, cream thalictrums and my favourite goat's beard (why goat's beard?) with its almost-white spikes are the main background to the erupting roses. The full-flowered French fire first: 'Comte de Chambord', 'Jaqueline Dupré', 'Baronne Prévost', 'Belle de Crécy'; all tones of pink and purple. Best of all with 'Madame Alfred Carrière', just-blushing white, high in a holly tree.

Round two, just under way, includes 'Felicia', 'Iceberg', 'Cornelia' (who should be kept away from Felicia – her coppery pink shouts at Felicia's silvery pink), the custard-coloured 'Buff Beauty' and the cooler, creamy, 'Autumn Delight'.

Round three looks perfectly timed for wedding day. Indeed it starts with 'Wedding Day', high in a pear tree, and 'Rambling Rector', covering a shed, and culminates in 'Wickwar', occupying three Christmas trees – with 'Paul's Himalayan Musk' scattering pink bouquets through a rather jaded old Chinese pine. 'Treasure Trove' and 'Mrs Honey Dyson' are still alarming us with 12-foot shoots. Will they make it to the wedding?

WEDDING DAY

If no good deed goes unpunished, perhaps no bad deed goes unrewarded. What else can account for two daughters' weddings in the garden, seven years apart, being blessed with days of a perfection I didn't dare imagine?

What has conspired this year to deliver a garden greener, more full of flowers in first flush, when sprays are still fresh, spires upright, leaves unblemished, than it has ever been before? Did the seasons hit a magic sequence, a royal flush of perfect measurement of temperature, sunshine and rain? Certainly after cleansing winter cold there was a good topping-up in February and March. Then no rain for two months meant (among other things) no slugs. And here (though not elsewhere) little damaging frost.

Elbow grease has not been wanting. We watered and deadheaded down to the wire, but the buds had to be there in the first place, and nothing but providence can explain the timing. The Monday before wedding day our showpiece climbing rose, 'Wickwar', 50 feet (no, just remeasured: 60 feet) into the trees, opened its first bud. On Saturday there were 10,000.

It's true I cheated a little. I packed the beds with mid-summer flowers. Thalictrums of various persuasions are important, along with the delphiniums and emerging campanulas (*C. persicifolia* the star, both blue and white, both herded into clumps and scattered where it seeded). The golden oats of *Stipa gigantea* are already waving in the sun with the cool blue leaves of *Macleaya* in contrast. White foxgloves and blue delphiniums. *Clematis durandii*, tied into hazel wigwams, in deep indigo (though not so deep as the neighbouring *Baptisia*). *Salvia nemorosa* repeats the dusky theme in purple against the greys of *Artemisia ludoviciana*, *Lychnis chalcedonica* with bright magenta flowers and *Phlomis italica* with the gentlest pink. *Nepeta sibirica* and blue *Tradescantia* are rather irrelevantly punctuated by the silver of Miss Willmott's Ghost. *Yucca flaccida* is still just phallic spikes before its ivory bells appear. *Lilium regale* is raising its trumpets to blow. Alliums are fading and penstemons preening, lavender a forest of pale-green tentacles, alstromeria flecked with tentative colours. Pale roses shine so bright at dusk that the others almost disappear. 'Iceberg' above all, but also 'Buff Beauty' and 'Penelope', with 'Paul's Lemon Pillar', fading on the wall, filling up with a violet *Clematis viticella*. *Euphorbia palustris* is more important than ever as a bulwark of brilliant green. Geraniums, pale pink and 'Johnson's Blue' (an easy name to remember) surge over the grass. As for paeonies, a full frilly white and the absurdly formal 'Bowl of Beauty', I have never seen so many flowers, let alone so many standing up straight.

The paths are frothing with valerian, here white, there pink, and the unstoppable little paving (or Spanish) daisy (or fleabane), *Erigeron karvinskianus*. At dusk the honeysuckles breathe out (is early Dutch the six o'clock one and late Dutch the follow-on at seven?)

Can a garden feel, and proclaim, the happiness of a wedding? So it seems.

July

MAGIC MEADOWS

To supper on a June evening with Tom and Sue Stuart-Smith in their garden near St Albans. We were talking about garden eye-catchers; objects that represent conclusion or resolution in the same way as a predictable final chord. I can't resist them. But am I, as it were, talking down to my visitors, saying 'look over here', rather than trusting them to see things in their own way?

This seems to be pretty much what Tom thinks. His garden makes theatrical use of tall beech hedges pierced with openings, some of them surprisingly narrow, that inevitably engage your curiosity. You are bound to go and see what lies beyond. Some lead your eye on to another opening, some to a rich patch of planting, some to relative vacancy: a plain boxed-in lawn you can mentally furnish as you wish.

The main axis from the terrace leads invitingly on through such hedge-gaps, repeated several times, to more green space beyond. It's hard to tell how far beyond because the end is left blank: the distance is just green. It would be fun to put an urn there, or a gate or an obelisk or any of the conventional conclusions. Tom would prefer to leave you wondering.

In June the generous blocks of herbaceous planting ('borders' gives the wrong idea) were like magic meadows – as though the shire had an endless flora of tall, short, feathery, gesticulating, creeping, aspiring, pale, dark, transparent or solid herbs in generally complementary colours.

More than anything I was reminded of Beth Chatto's celebrated stands at Chelsea in the 1970s. The unusual (her term) plants she put together always spoke quietly to one another. It was an intelligent conversation among flowers that had no need to show off. She was making you look at what till then you had passed over: the ingredients of a hayfield, a streambed or the early flowers of a coppice that disappear in summer in drought and shade. Her lessons gave many of us a permanent distaste for the cosmetics of the nursery business. This is Tom's taste too, I fancy – with significant exceptions when a perfect peony, shall we say, is called for.

Beth Chatto had a quiet celebration, an open day for friends, on June 28th; 50 years to the day since she opened Unusual Plants at Elmstead Market, near Colchester. I have watched nearly 40 years of its evolution, from an unremarkable stream under some senior oaks to a landscape emulated wherever people garden. Beth's dry garden, never watered, come what may, is an extraordinary one-step lesson in ecology. Her bog gardens around shining ponds are the same. Perhaps in her writing I discern most love of all in her description of the woodland she developed later and the plants that flourish before oaks cast them into shade.

Eye-catchers? I think I know what Beth would say about a statue.

THE DRY SKY

It begins to grind you down when gardening is reduced to one question: where to carry the can or lug the hose to next. We've had the best of the weather here, alright, in the infuriating phrase the fore-casters use, for the past four months. The rainfall figures are: April 7 mm; May 28, June 17, July (with five days to go) 7. Total 70 mm (or nearly three inches). The same period last year, reckoned dry at the time, gave us 140.

It is cold comfort to know that Cambridge had a downpour. Week after week the promises are broken. Up the road, perhaps a shower. Down the road, a nice little soak. Across the valley, rain last night. Here, on this sand-coloured grass: zilch.

There has been no question of planting anything since April; no new plant has a hope of putting roots beyond the circumference of its pot. Most plants, in fact, have simply stopped. They must be transpiring, in emergency mode, and their root hairs finding mois-ture somewhere in the dust, yet new growth, or anything but a tiny travesty of a flower head, is simply put on hold. What surprises me most is how few plants are obviously losing turgidity in their veins and wilting.

I am taking a can to this year's new trees (luckily there are only half a dozen) daily. I might as well be pouring it into a hole in the ground: it all disappears as fast as I can pour it. I mentally map the rootscape underground: the soil must be full of tiny roots from big trees compet-ing for moisture. What happens when they meet? Does the big horse chestnut challenge the cedar of Lebanon for the last remaining drops? Are some root hairs bigger bullies? Miraculously they seem to get by without destroying each other.

There is one clue, though, to what is going on out of sight. With the grass merely ticking over, the deeper-rooted lawn weeds come into their own. And trees prone to suckering send up a forest of sprouts. We haven't had to mow for weeks; instead I hand-pick the succulent shoots of acacias, cherries, the wingnut and above all the prolific cedrela, *Toona sinensis*, before it obliterates the grass under a groovy toona grove.

--------------------- *August* ---------------------

SUSPENDED ANIMATION

We all know the joke about the man who dug up a plant to see how it was doing. But have you, seriously, never been tempted? Something you have planted with all proper precaution inexplicably malingers. You water and feed, examine its leaves, its buds, its neighbours. You watch and wait: it doesn't budge.

I'm thinking about a vine I planted 18 months ago on the front of the house to replace a 50-year-old one that died (Aha! Clue! Cause of death?)

It is Furmint , the excellent Hungarian variety that gives the fiery spirit to Tokay. It came home with me in a pot; a bonny plant with splendid roots. I planted it with some ceremony, between the Wrotham Pinot (aka Pinot Meunier or Dusty Miller) and the Chasselas.

Come to think of it, why Wrotham? What is the connection between one of the champagne grapes and the North Downs – apart from chalk? Was there once a vineyard there (Wrotham has the remains of a Bishop's Palace)? Now Google has put a stop to such airy speculations. It was Edward Hyams, whose pioneer vineyard at Oxted was the ancestor of the English wine industry, now so flourishing, who identified an old vine with dusty leaves as peculiar to Wrotham. Others, bolder in their speculation, have claimed it as a relic of the Romans who paused, as we all do, to admire the view of the Weald from Wrotham Hill.

My Furmint has six leaves. Last year it had seven. They are green and healthy, rather small, and show no sign of growing. There are no swelling buds or incipient tendrils. If I don't dig it up, how will I ever know what's wrong?

SUMMER BREAK

I missed the moment the garden relaxed; when the tension of water-stress eased under proper penetrating rain. We were away for a week on a Solent salt marsh, in a garden under a different sort of stress – always. It is totally exposed to wind and salt sea-air; nothing but the grasses, gorse, brambles and goat willows can take the punishment.

I said 'garden' because it is the setting for a house and in summer the scene of endless entertaining: ball games, races, dinghies on chocks, picnics, trampoline, barbecues. Oh, and golf croquet, where the rabbits make interesting bunkers in the sandy turf.

The house is a '30s bungalow with iron windows and a big verandah overlooking a creek endlessly washed by the tide. The colourful clutter of boats at their moorings is almost at eye level one moment, only, when you look again, to have sunk below the sea wall.

A gardener's urge, of course, is to stick in a few plants that will survive, or even profit by, the unusual conditions. Escallonias have been tried at some time, but just look tatty. Hydrangeas are the default decoration for the summer holidays. Their muddle of pale colours, like washing left too long on the line, expresses the time and place better, perhaps, than any other plant. Someone once planted a birch in the waving brown grass: the wind has made it aerodynamic; a vegetable slipstream as it were. (Willows, curiously, seem to grow upright despite the wind.) We have planted two or three Scots pines to join, or succeed, the couple that have become gnarled in the line of duty, but the wind and the rabbits will always prevent a gardener from doing anything so foolish as to garden here.

SIGH OF RELIEF

The garden that welcomed us home had had a personality change in the week we were away. The borders are looking blurred compared with the rather stark, if bright, stressed-out look they wore: new growth has rounded and softened them, and new colours and new scents clearly mark the change of season.

Phlox, long delayed by lack of water, is now a major player. 'White Admiral' jostles with deep-purple monkshood under a golden veil of the irreplaceable *Stipa gigantea*. Pink and white Japanese anemones are opening. *Salvias bethellii* (magenta) and 'Guanajuato' (piercing blue) are clocking on for duty. Now it's the turn of agapanthus, deep blue and washed-out grey, *Geranium wallichianum* 'Buxton's Variety', the slender spires of *Veronicastrum* and the flopping stems of willow gentians with their sumptuous sapphire flowers. A few rosehips are just turning colour, grapes have become smooth little green globes, *Clematis flammula* in white sheets has overwhelmed a *Choisya* and scents the corner by the garden door with sweet almond.

It is all potential and excitement again. Until it rained there seemed no future. Now autumn is on the horizon the garden has a point and a purpose – and the mower a job to do, though it will be a while before the burnt brown patches, the fairy rings and the eager suckers (above all from the cedrela, *Toona sinensis*) give way again to an even green.

So the sights and scents of mid-summer postponed and early autumn advanced paint the garden in unfamiliar combinations of colour. When we come home again – this time from Wales – there will be another change of regime.

RATE OF CHANGE

A noble one-stone henge greets us as we descend into our wooded valley in North Wales. We extracted the thick slab of brown granite from the roadside and set it up at the entrance to the forest when we arrived 15 years ago. This time, though, we had a shock: some anonymous artist has defaced it with a huge white eagle – at least I think that's what it is. At first sight it looked more like a swastika.

We have washed off what we can of the paint but the shape is still there. I'd like to know more about it, but no one seems to know. Is it the sign of some Welsh anti-English underground? I've never seen it before, and neither have our Welsh friends and neighbours. Perhaps it is just the invention of the artist faced with a tempting blank stone surface; in which case chapeau to him for an icon combining the Prussian eagle of the First World War with the swastika of the second. If we ever meet, I'll know him by his tattoo.

It won't be too long, though, before the rain and the lichens erase his work. Speed of change is the thing that always strikes me most in the timeless sheltered world of the forest. Saplings double their height while your back is turned. Paths grow over in a season with grass, rushes, bracken, brambles, gorse and birch. Moss covers tree trunks and conceals rocks. Our latest contribution to the cycle of alteration is a new track to give us access to a steep part of the hill planted 50 years ago with a tree now considered pretty much a weed; a strain of lodgepole pine from California that is neither fast, nor handsome, nor useful, but is unfailingly fertile with its seedlings.

There are ten acres or so of it interspersed with larch and spruce on the steep bank facing west towards Cardigan Bay. Before we made the track we had never seen either the trees or the view. Wyn and Arfon, the bulldozer brothers we rely on for heavy machine work, have contrived a route crossing the contours of the hill at the gentlest, most insinuating angles. When I first saw the prospect their work had revealed I wanted to live there, right there between the trees and the sea, for ever. Prospects here, though, are almost as evanescent as paths. Even on land left unplanted first birch blocks them, then rowan, then, faster than you would believe possible, the deep-shining-green native sessile oak.

September

FIAT LUX

'What the eye don't see the 'eart don't grieve over' (for full effect, say it in an Aylesbury accent circa 1930). It was the first rule of life I remember Nanny teaching me, as she wiped a bit of no-matter-what off the nursery floor with the hem of her apron.

I often repeat it as I go round the garden, rejoicing that a good percentage of it comes into the 'eye don't see' category. Maybe ten percent, maybe 15. It lies under old shrubs, at the backs of borders, under the skirts of trees, or where ivy has covered the ground with an impenetrable carpet. Occasionally, and often in autumn when the need for hacking back is most obvious, I poke my nose in, hoping not to find a body, and peer through the gloomy tangle to see what's going on. I have been rewarded with useful, even interesting, seedlings. But sometimes the reward is an idea for something better. Even for abolishing the 'don't see' zone altogether.

There is a proper mean between a judicious mingling of plants and each one having its own space. We have a rather splendid old Judas tree, a good 40 feet across, two of its branches supported by props. It was planted in 1959, in an enthusiastic fit of planting by our predecessor at Saling. Over 50 years many good trees and shrubs have united in one canopy, the Judas tree included. Once I had decided it was time to let the light in, the cutting back would have done credit to the Tories and the piles of branches were prodigious.

An amelanchier has been cut down to the stump, a photinia the same, also a Chinese privet; a clerodendron abolished altogether and a score of bottom branches lopped from a *Cryptomeria* and one of those Lawson cypresses that seem to droop with exhaustion. We have taken perhaps ten feet off the diameter of the Judas tree, letting the light flood in to its handsome undercroft. At the same time we have de-ivied the adjacent teahouse. The effect is revolutionary. I see the components of the scene as mature individuals framing delicious glimpses instead of a 'don't see' zone. And there is a glorious bonfire waiting.

NO JOKE

A few summers ago I proposed a competition to find France's funniest *rond point*. It was the early days of a gardening fashion that has done nothing but expand. It started with concrete planters of the most durable shrubs wasting valuable space in shopping streets. It flourished in more and more exotic concoctions of the most emphatic flowers anywhere the municipality could find to perch them, seizing on roundabouts as empty spaces where excesses of horticulture could be committed in the fullest public view with little likely retribution.

We soon had golfers, astronauts, vignerons, fishermen and of course cyclists and their habitats represented, often on a huge scale and in unmissable materials. This year a mélange of banana plants, tall blue grasses, cannas and camphor plants and every brilliant daisy have been in play – and of course a gazillion petunias. No street lamp, meanwhile, has been without its hanging basket. Today a ville fleurie, to gain even one star, must mortgage the mayor's chain to splurge on flowers.

All this is harmless, summer-seasonal, gaudy, potentially comic, and fun. Not so a newer tendency: to let the spirit of horticultural gaiety invade the sombre rhythm of an avenue.

The Avenue de Champagne in Épernay was once described by Winston Churchill as France's greatest address. For a mile or so it is lined with the rather comely factory buildings labelled Perrier Jouët, Pol Roger, Moët et Chandon, their courtyards protected by gilded gates. Now, in the spirit of the times, the street has been dug up and relaid at half the width as an anti-motor measure. On either side is a broad strip of granite setts to prevent smooth walking, and in the setts, instead of an avenue, is a sort of linear arboretum; an omnium-gatherum of the most ill-assorted trees you can imagine: maples, cherries, ginkgos, pines, oaks, larches .... There is nothing so unsuitable for street planting that they haven't popped one in. The effect, young, is simply demented, like a building put together with whatever materials came to hand. Long term, if it is allowed to remain, it will become more and more grotesque as the habits and proportions of the trees become more assertive and more different.

What does this tell us about public taste in the country that invented the *allée* and gave us majestic gardens in harmony with majestic buildings? Do they really have to relearn the lesson that repetition is the essence of harmonious planting? An avenue works by repeating the form and scale of a perfectly chosen tree without hesitation or deviation.

Twenty years ago Westminster City Council committed the same solecism, putting planters with such trees as birches and spruces along Pall Mall and St James's Street. Public ridicule got rid of them within half a year. The trees of the Avenue de Champagne are not in planters, though, and where is the ridicule to undo this ignorant and tasteless folly?

───────────── *October* ─────────────

A LA RECHERCHE ...

Back to our old French property, after an absence of two years, to see how my trees are getting on. A tree you've planted yourself is always yours, whoever else may be its legal proprietor. I am always happy to take credit, and there was plenty to take in the ranks of pines – pale Scots and dark Corsicans – the fluttering files of poplars and the battalions of young oaks, wonderfully wayward in comparison, mobbed by brambles and wild roses: an impenetrable mass of prosperous native vegetation.

When you set out a new plantation and watch anxiously over its first few years, every rabbit is a threat and a deer a disaster. Only 15 years later do you realize that if one tree in four is spared to make serious growth, your wood will be overcrowded.

In all our time in France I never saw a squirrel. Deer, boar, hares, badgers, foxes, martens (and once a wildcat), but no squirrels. This time, to my joy, I saw two red squirrels attacking 'our' walnuts. Can they be on the increase in France? At last Europe is waking up to the threat of greys spreading from Italy (where they are proliferating) through Piemonte into the Alps, and through the Alpine beech woods into France.

It is almost 20 years since we found our place in France: at exactly the same time as two Paris architects found an abandoned priory 25 miles away in the Cher and started what is now a famous garden, Le Prieuré de Notre-Dame d'Orsan.

Orsan today has an air of long establishment. Some of its visitors are convinced that it has always been like this, that it really was monks who planted and shaped the intricate hedges and espaliered apples and pears. We have nothing like this in England, and I wonder whether it has ever been in the English psyche to create a whole landscape on the theme of sustenance.

There is a vineyard in the middle, the vines trained on hurdles copied from the 1471 Augsburg edition of Petrus de Crescentius. In the first compartment, surrounded by tunnels of hornbeam, the autumn crops are leeks and cabbages, all perfect, steely blue against the green-brown of the hedges. Beyond the vineyard, which has a simple stone fountain at its heart, are compartments of soft fruit, of roses (sustenance spiritual), of pumpkins in waist-high osier beds and of espaliered pear trees forming a circular maze. The next room has tall apples, the next pears, the next service trees ... until finally you come to alleys of perfectly trimmed oaks, an archery ground, and coppiced woodland.

Calm vegetable geometry like this seems timeless. But then so does the forest. Neither takes as long as you think.

November

WINDING DOWN, HEATING UP

There has hardly been a really dark night for a month. When I part the curtains after midnight, the lawn has been painted in tiger stripes by the moon shining through the poplars, and The Plough has been diamond-bright above the pond. So little or no cloud cover – and yet no frost. There has been ground frost on several mornings, but no air cold enough to crisp and brown the leaves of poplars, even, or ashes. Border flowers may be dying away, but their plants are standing green and unscathed, while roses keep offering limp efforts.

It is the slowest-moving autumn I remember, the fullest in volume of mellowing leaves and the brightest for the roadside hedges, as the maples move from green to a medley of yellows. Since the elms went, field maple has become our principal hedgerow tree, and nothing in the countryside holds more consistent and enduring gold. Norway maple is brighter yellow, and wild cherry glows with a pink-blushing light. The oaks are undecided, all the chromatic possibilities of slow decay still before them.

I always reckon on having the most candle-power in the first week of November – and always from the same trees. Japanese maples are the latest. First to turn are varieties of *Acer japonicum*: 'Aconitifolium' is reliably orange-scarlet, at its best now. *A. j.* 'Vitifolium' is following it hard in a paler set of colours; yellow, scarlet and pink. *Acer koreana* has turned an even pillarbox red with no variation, a little matt compared with the best. *A. mono* is quite different: taller with shiny three- (sometimes five-) lobed leaves rather like starfish, that hesitate between green, scarlet and purple. 'Osakazuki' is celebrated as the best and brightest of all, starting green, now deep maroon, eventually traffic-light red with bulbs that are definitely not energy-saving.

But to me the ultimate performance is from the big bush of tiny fretted leaves called *Acer palmatum* 'Seiryu'. It starts the autumn by fading from fresh green to a darker shade that modulates into purple and maroon, even within one tiny segmented leaf. Then current starts to run through it, the filaments heat up, glow and begin to burn. Scarlet brightens to orange, then flecks with gold. Eventually – and there are still two weeks to go, given fair weather – the bush becomes a burning fiery furnace, hottest of all, it seems, as dusk fills the garden.

EYEWASH

Spontaneity. Is it more than a positive gloss on indecision – or indeed on a mistake? Positive it certainly is; it suggests warm-hearted effusions. Spontaneous malice is just conceivable, I suppose, but Iago and the ugly sisters seem to have the monopoly. No: if spontaneity gets into a review it counts as a plus – even in gardening.

So how do you recognize it? There is no forethought in spontaneity, but nor is it a synonym for afterthought. Afterthought: you stand back, survey your handiwork, and decide that a splash of orange would set the blues and purples singing. Spontaneity can't undo; to move something out of the picture would be an afterthought. But spontaneity implies more: it is self-created, like combustion in a haystack. The elements present reach a point in their relationship where equilibrium breaks down, or fizzes up, with surprising results. It is sudden, inevitable and unarguable. It is also a quality desired by the Dutch Wave school being celebrated at the moment in an exhibition at the Garden Museum.

Says its leader (or one of them), Piet Oudolf, 'Inside I want to be spontaneous. But I know I must control.' The resulting tension is the attraction of the Dutch Wave style – even if its influence on this country is still only recognized among the hortiscenti. And perhaps in the number of grasses offered in garden centres. Christopher Woodward, the Garden Museum director, has published an excellent little booklet to accompany the exhibition. While in this country, he writes, we 'languidly elaborate on old patterns', Oudolf and company 'wash their eyes' to see everything afresh. How true.

Working as they mainly do on the modest scale of Dutch domestic gardens, their medium is usually restricted to herbaceous perennials – or indeed annuals – with hedges playing a vital structural role. The essence is focus on plant details (they love, for instance, the structure of umbellifers) and above all colour. They evoke watercolours, with their transitional wash-passages – if there is such a term – and their interwoven patches and bands of grasses and astilbes and thistles and knotweeds. In his contribution to the booklet, Stephen Lacey says he originally found the new Dutch planting 'wild and scruffy' – before he realized it could be 'revolutionary, highly refined'. 'Scruffy', 'spontaneous': could they amount to the same thing?

The style began in the 1980s in nurserymen's gardens in Holland, inspired, at least in part, by the work of Jacques Wirtz ten years before in Belgium. Wirtz re-invented the hedge to make memorable, even monumental, landscapes for the Belgian haute bourgeoisie. He used grasses and massed perennials to powerful effect. But Wirtz gardens belong in Belgium's most prosperous neighbourhoods. The Dutch school were humble nurserymen, starting with little money and working on a small scale – just as the Impressionists did. And it was the Impressionists' little canvases that found a worldwide market.

December

A (COMPLETELY) NEW FOREST

It is not only autumn colour that has got into a muddle this year. Pigments have not developed in leaves as we expect, but neither has the abscisic acid that seals off the stalks of leaves and lets them part company with their branch. I am looking out of the window at a *Stachyurus praecox*, which by now should have turned its special bright-parchment yellow and dropped its leaves. They are still green, frost-rimmed but neither colouring nor falling. The only colour is below them where *Iris foetidissima* has opened its pods and bared its scarlet seeds, among prostrate bergenias, their prone leaves a mournful sight.

Last weekend we were in the New Forest for our son's wedding in Beaulieu parish church, the converted refectory of the abbey destroyed by Henry VIII. Beaulieu is one of the loveliest spots in the South of England, isolated on its tidal river by the wilderness of the New Forest. Crossing Beaulieu Heath in deep frost (it was -7° C) was like Hobbema's Holland. They were skating on Hatchet Pond (and have been able to for the past three winters; a hat-trick without precedent, they tell me).

The road to Brockenhurst from Beaulieu winds through a grove of ancient oaks and beeches which were still full of leaf. Even the golden birches, sparkling with rime, were holding their leaves. A fine layer of snow on the upper side of every branch turned wide-spreading trees into dancers, gesticulating with outstretched arms. With such movement and such colour the forest became fantastical: a mythological tapestry, sparklingly clear in some places, veiled in others by patches of low mist, and stained, at sunset, with pink and purple light.

SCENTS RESTORED

When the thaw, sudden and complete, gave us back our garden this morning and I walked on green grass again, I had a flashback to arriving in harbour one summer morning after a week at sea, when I could hardly believe that the earth and its plants have such an all-pervading smell. It was still cold and misty, very different from the balmy summer air that almost chokes you with the scent of hay and honey, but the green/brown scent of growth gave me a surge of joy, and the sight of leaf, twig and bud in all their intricacy, after the dull shroud of snow, made me rush to touch them.

This is what I garden for: the infinity of familiar forms, the sense of potent, complex life in every plant, even in winter-dormant twigs. Already the elasticity of branches that were prone under snow is restoring their old posture. A few have snapped. The principal swooping bough of an old arbutus in the walled garden has split, and the weight of snow has levered its bole half out of the ground so that six feet of its trunk is lying on the bare brown border. The cinnamon sheen of the trunk is the main attraction of this tree. Its leaves attract mould in spring and most of its flowers fall off. This is my invitation to do away with it. But no, in its truncated shape I can see the promise of a new tree, more compact and vigorous, possibly even layering itself and forming a splendid strawberry-bearing bush.

Can that be the smell of crown imperials already permeating the sodden soil, or did a fox brush by, or is it just the box hedges? The cold air is sweet and heavy; mist has risen from the grey ice covering the moat. Three pigeons clatter out from the grey flint church tower. The grey sky in the west is gashed to reveal its apricot silk lining.

BLEAK MIDWINTER

'The English landscape', said Horace Walpole, 'is best appreciated framed and glazed' – a thought never more apt than when snow still covers the trees two weeks after the blizzard, and the ruts on the drive have frozen into unbreakable ridges. Only a long memory can bring to mind a freeze like this one.

The ground was frozen when the snow fell. The first covering, the transformation of green to ghostlike, the printless revelation of the first morning, was a theme for poetry. The magic doesn't last long. Is there a more dismal subject for gardeners than the block on all activity while unknown damage is happening unseen?

Better unseen, some argue: at least the snow insulates plants and the ground from the lowest temperatures. But the thermometer dropped before the insulation arrived. What is trapped in there is not exactly snug. Winter closed in on an unconsummated autumn. There were so many leaves still on the trees that the snowy woods look strange: carpeted here, spotted there with leaves, some brown, some still green. Nor did the earthworms get even halfway through their work of gathering leaves and tugging them underground. They must have dived for cover in relative warmth when the soil first felt the chill.

It doesn't do to count your losses prematurely – let alone to cut away plants that still lie half-buried. Spring is too soon to write plants off, too. There will be shoots from the base of things that will surprise you. The leaf-damage is evident enough – from abelia to yucca. I don't like the look of ballota, camellias, drimys, embothrium, fuchsia, garrya, hoheria, indigofera, lavenders, myrtle, nerium, olearia, penstemons, rhamnus, salvias, trachycarpus, vitex .... Some will surprise us, but I fear a lengthy list of disappointments.

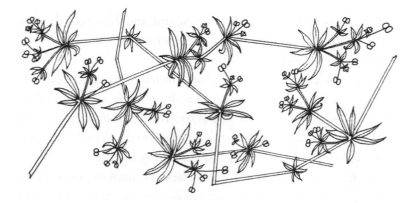

2011

January

BLOODY BEIGE

It's been going on too long. It's too long since a fashionable dress shop dared to put any other colour in its window – except black. And now I read that every one of the six five-star hotels opening in London this spring is settling on beige and brown as its colour theme.

What are hotels doing in Trad's Diary? Eyes are eyes. A sense of visual appropriateness and stimulus is basic (or should be) to us gardeners. Where are the chintzes, the mad Indian floral hyperboles that tell you it's England?

Chintzes come from the Far East, it's true, but then so did half our favourite garden plants. What if the passion for beige should invade our flower borders, too? Too late, I'm afraid – it already has. Grasses are doing to our borders what beige curtains on taupe walls are doing to our rooms: condemning them and us to the tedium of good taste.

Yesterday was our grand-daughter's first birthday. Her friends came to tea – dressed, I was thrilled to see, like wild flowers in a meadow, medleys of pink and red and blue. How long must we wait until Prada and Armani and Nicole Farhi wake up to the full spectrum of colour, and our hoteliers rediscover the orient?

PS I just walked up Bond Street to check on the colours, and in fairness I should add grey, sand, drab, slub, grunge, mud ... and, of course, many more shops.

February

FRONT DOOR

Here's another of those 'What sort of gardener are you?' tests. How do you feel about plants seeding themselves in the gravel of your drive? I mean desirable plants, probably ones you put in the bed by the door or under the windows. One Essex neighbour of ours has the art to perfection. Annie Turner (she lives at Helions Bumpstead, and sometimes opens her immaculate garden for charity) has, to my mind, the world's most alluring front door. You pick your way to it among plants you long to touch, scattered with artful abandon from under the windows to halfway across the drive. Cars? They take another route.

There are obvious candidates that enjoy the shelter of the wall: cistus (*C.* 'Silver Pink' for one) and rosemaries, including the marginally tender ones. *Euphorbia wulfenii* in its best forms is almost too happy here; they need discipline – and echiums, their perfect companions, love the conditions. The variegated *Sisyrinchium striatum* stands up perkily in its pale fans. Hollyhocks can be overwhelming and block the house windows. Alstroemerias are not advised: they eventually push up through and flop over everything else. Alliums are hard to control, too. Nerines for October, of course.

The prickly green-and-white-leaved *Silybum*, the far-spreading fretted leaves of *Geranium palmatum* (it has survived this winter unscathed), wallflowers in their element, seeded between the bricks and hanging down the wall. Almost too much of the daisy-froth of *Erigeron karvinskianus*, some gracefully arching *Dierama pulcherrimum* ... the tide of 20 different plants flows over the gravel, seeding and rooting. In reality Annie is always editing it; most of the plants will come up with a simple pull (which means giving them to visitors is easy). My latest acquisition (I must be careful what I admire) is a knee-high weeping caryopteris. I called Annie to check a name. What had I forgotten? Only the Corsican hellebores, the white valerian (loved by hummingbird hawkmoths), the *Verbena bonariensis*, the saffron crocuses, the cerinthes, the pinks, the *Daphne odora*, the early dwarf irises ... (you do reach the front door eventually).

I was first attracted to the idea of a drive swamped by seedlings at Keith Steadman's Wickwar nursery near Chipping Sodbury, many years ago. But then his whole garden was swamped by plants too rampant for their space, yet too precious to touch. It was hard to find even the garden walls. When I let the tide advance too far at Saling I was firmly told that cars (it is a turning circle) have precedence. 'Why can't they share the space?' was my question. The wheel tracks would look good where they discouraged the tapestry of growth. I often claim that untidiness is interesting – and don't always get away with it.

March

EASTWARD IN EDEN

Back from China, excited and jetlagged. Beijing was still grey with winter, raw, yellow-hazy and smelling of pollution, but throbbing with life. The Chinese seem to live faster, louder, more Italianly than other races. You see more smiles – or am I just a romantic traveller?

At last, on a second attempt, I saw The Forbidden City. Versailles, Schönbrunn, the Kremlin ... eat your hearts out. There is no palace to compare. The scale, the spaces, the wide sky, the variations in a consistent style of building deserve the word awesome, however you pronounce it.

The colossal rectangle, within its two miles of stone-built moat an arrow-shot wide, progresses from larger courts to smaller ones. The first vast space, the Outer Court, is traversed by the meandering Golden Water River, crossed by five stone bridges and lined with pale stone culminating in carved bosses. In the centre is the Hall of Supreme Harmony, 125 feet high. There are no trees, no plants, no shade, nothing green. The floor is brick.

The Inner Court is smaller and more complex, with more buildings and more subdivisions, but still no trees. It must be a punishing place in summer to parade and process, or go emperor-visiting.

You penetrate further, more marble steps and ramps, more pavilions: still no green. At last you come to the emperor's residence. Behind it, cloistered and gated, lies his garden.

The impression it gives is that the intimacy and luxury of a garden are something private, reserved for family and friends. I have always found the freakish contorted rocks of important Chinese gardens hard to enjoy. Where the Japanese choose stones softened by the ages and deploy them (not always, but usually) in harmonious naturalistic groups, the Chinese try to evoke the crags of the Yangtze gorges that figure on so many painted scrolls. Without, it seems to me, much success.

But suddenly, in the palace garden, the pavilions grow gorgeous, their roofs elaborate, their eaves gilded. Beds of paeonies line the walks under ancient trees. There are pots of flowers, and flowering trees, and trees sculpted to look like embroidery. There is joy in artifice, and joy in nature. In all the pomp of ultimate power, the garden is the ultimate pleasure.

SHOWER POWER

Can birds see through windows? It depends, I suppose, on light and reflections. The pigeons pecking the buds of the sophora in the churchyard opposite our bedroom window certainly see me in the morning with my air rifle, making to open the casement.

Can they hear noises inside the house? The mating ducks seem to love the courtyard under the bathroom window. This morning a pair of mallard were fussing energetically about until I turned on the shower. Then they stopped on the edge of the grass, looking up, heads cocked, and went on looking and listening all the time the water was running. When I picked up my towel they started squabbling again. I wonder if Gilbert White noticed the same thing. But no, of course, he didn't have a shower.

April

DON'T DITHER

'Faites simple' (was it Voltaire who said it? Or Escoffier?) is often quoted as the soundest, the most essential, stylistic advice. Keep it simple. What does it mean to a gardener? I picture spaces in perfect proportion, a theme of brilliant relevance, an ideal triad of colours, a single tree, or urn, or rock placed precisely to balance a distant spire or crag.

Simplicity – and boredom. How often can you admire the designer's judgement? The greatest designs have authority, true, which rarely comes from over-complication. You remember a decisive garden better than one made by a ditherer. What Voltaire (or Escoffier) meant, or I hope he meant, is not 'cut out the fiddly bits', but 'know what you are aiming for and go for it.' Evident intent, consistently pursued, is the winning formula. Decide what you want and, if side-tracked, clamber back to your original plan as quickly and as gracefully as you can.

May

WATER FIGHT

Each time the rains dry up in spring, just as the plants push out their sappy shoots, I puzzle over what must be happening underground. Is it the big fat powerful-looking roots that elbow weaklings aside and suck up the dwindling moisture in the soil, or is it the fine thread-like roots in their masses that win the lion's share? I suspect the threads, with their much greater surface area, do better in separating what water there is from its adherence to soil particles.

How they can keep supplying multiplying leaves with the liquid they need is beyond my imagination. The suction in each stem is transmitted to each minute rootlet – which has its own needs to keep it growing, too. The forces at work to keep every shoot and leaf turgid and functioning are astounding.

There has not been a millimetre of rain here since the scattering we had in March: the five weeks of the year with the greatest demand for water have been supplied entirely from moisture held in the soil by surface tension – and yet I hardly see a limp or drooping shoot.

Certainly growth has been slowed down. I started watering perennials a week ago. *Aruncus sylvester* (already with flower buds) quickly shot up to three times the height. Delphiniums looked as if they were about to flower at knee height; watering has made things a little better. A young *Magnolia* 'Star Wars', which always seems to overdo its flowering, had scarcely a leaf two weeks ago but 15 flowers. A can of water a day and it presents a much more balanced picture of flower and leaf. Does localized watering with cans create bedlam below as every rootlet smells water and heads into the damp zone?

SECONDS OUT

Gardening never features on the sports pages, yet there is a competitive element in most of us, and looking back on my most active garden-making years I realize I was often really gardening against one friend or another.

Mostly it was John Hedgecoe, an alarmingly creative photographer who in due course became the first Professor of Photography at the Royal College of Art, and sadly died late last year. His last and most ambitious gardening enterprise was at Oxnead Hall in Norfolk, but 30 years ago we were neighbours in Essex and battling it out, tit for tat.

John planted an avenue; I responded with a grove of trees. I built a 'Japanese' cascade; back came a fountain. Roses: John used to tip on neat pig manure for bigger flowers.

John introduced us to the architect Sir Freddy Gibberd, who was creating his wonderfully theatrical garden at Marsh Lane on the outskirts of Harlow New Town (for which I fear he must take a great part of the responsibility). Freddy was miles ahead, in time and in resources. (The Corinthian columns from Coutts Bank in the Strand ended up in his garden, and huge rocks from a Welsh reservoir became available to line his little river.)

Gibberd's wife Patricia had a brilliant eye for sculpture, which led in turn to more and more garden incidents – made, incidentally, with the quickest materials to hand: a poplar avenue takes a fraction of the time a lime one does. Ideas came so thick and fast that Freddy would take up the stones of a path he had just laid to make a different one.

It was the right atmosphere for pressing on with one's own ideas, however half-baked. (I'm sure my garden would be much duller without the lurking spirit of competition.) And now I'm just home from another garden that started my fingers itching to do something foolish – if that's the definition of a folly.

MIND GAMES

I give myself one point for an English name and two for a Latin one. Names of weeds, that is. I play silly mind games in my weeding time, or recite poems – or even sing songs. One of the games is categorizing my fellow gardeners into tribes or tendencies – of which those who enjoy weeding is, or so I'm told, one of the rarest. I don't believe a word of it. Weeding is the very essence of gardening – and in May, when leaves are at their most aromatic, it's a most sensuous task.

There is, though, a clear division between those who relish perfecting an already orderly picture and those who are only happy tackling chaos. It is partly, of course, a matter of how many acres you command, but those whose idea of heaven is rearranging granite chips around a *Lewisia* are likely to be daunted by my idea of a great afternoon: pulling nettles, digging docks and gathering great sticky armfuls of goose grass (cleavers for one extra point, *Galium aparine* for two).

I worked my way this afternoon to an isolated and overgrown rose bush, a tall dome spangled with dishevelled pink flowers in a wide

skirt of cow parsley (Queen Anne's Lace, *Anthriscus sylvestris*). The
scent reached me yards away, achingly sweet. I picked a flower (it is
R. californica 'Plena') and asked a visitor what it reminded her of. 'My
mother', she said.

No, weeding is the wrong word for the springtime editing of the
flora that distinguishes a garden from a meadow.

June

THE PEAK

'Roses at their peak' is one of the notes I write in my diary every year
– but never quite as early as this. Twelve months ago we were actually
anxious about them: our daughter was getting married and roses were
the main theme of the party décor. They peaked on cue: June 26th,
while this year the entry went in on June 2nd.

The 'peak' is a pretty artificial concept; to me it means the moment
just before we have to start deadheading the bush-roses, when the
major climbers are just revealing how far they have scrambled with
outbreaks of colour high in the trees. You can see and smell the flowers
on a bush more easily, but the ultimate rose picture is one of swags and
flying sprays far out of reach, sending down showers of perfume and
petals as you stand wondering below.

The peak of the garden here, its most thrilling spot, has migrated
from the concentration of its walled centre, where roses make a
patchwork with a score of other flowers: alliums and thalictrums,
campanulas and day lilies, *Aruncus* and poppies and delphiniums, to
a secret corner of the wood. Standing there, bathed in sweet perfume, I
look up through an arch of a 'Felicia', never pruned and stooping from
12 feet or so, mingling with 'Natchez', a tousle-flowered philadelphus.
The grey/pink *Rosa glauca* has somehow infiltrated above head height,
carrying my eyes up to 'Wedding Day', ascending in plateaux and glacis
of cream and white through a pear tree into the flowering branches
of an acacia.

Most soul-melting of all, though, glimpsed through the flanking bushes, are the apricot-fleshy-white flowers of 'Treasure Trove' surging over a little bower of the purple clematis 'President'. This is Eden, and words cannot express its beauty.

GARBURE

Here's another funny thing about the French. They have the world's most beautiful, best kept, most photogenic, most productive and various, most orderly and desirable vegetable gardens. But where does the veg go? It never turns up at table.

The mystery deepens. French markets are a wonder. There can be as many photographers as customers around the jewel-like trays of fruit and veg in the dappled light of a summer marketplace. The restaurant across the way? It gives you a few radishes and, with your Suprême de Whatever, a little plate of sticky rice.

I exaggerate of course. But we're just home from a few days' journey, in perfect early summer weather, from the Côte d'Azur to Burgundy. We went back, 46 years later, to the hotel at Lamastre in the Ardèche that Elizabeth David sent us to on our honeymoon. Chez Barattero no longer has rooms, but the restaurant is still in the family, and still offers its famous Pain d'Ecrevisses Sauce Cardinal and Poularde de Bresse en Vessie. Vegetables? There were a few pretty little carrots. Barattero may be in a time warp, but we then stayed at a château known for its table d'hôte and distinguished for its potager. A deep terrace on the south side of its hotel is a model of generous cultivation. An old orangery is now a prolific potting shed, where the rotovators and sprays crowd in among enormous benches of seedlings ready for pricking out, the seed packets on sticks promising every known variety of succulent leaf and root. Raspberry canes are trained along the walls, irresistibly ready to pick. The tomato patch is the size of a small vineyard. And the deep crumbly tilth ....

Dinner? A little lettuce salad with mushrooms and croutons. Then Blanquette de Veau with rice. You could just detect carrots: red dice in the veal sauce. Never a green leaf, no potato, no courgettes or beans.

But in the gastronomic temple of Dijon, Le Pré aux Clercs (you'll think we do nothing but eat), things got worse. The melting and mega-rich piece of beef in red wine sauce was accompanied by ... a spoonful of rhubarb purée. That was the nearest we came to a vegetable in the whole evening.

I have a theory. The grander the meal, or the more the cook wants to impress, the less chance you have of seeing the produce of the potager. In my dreams I see the Potage Garbure I ate years ago in a hotel in the Franche-Comté. Cabbage, beans, peas, potatoes, turnips, onions, carrots, kale, tomatoes, nettles and herbs could all be seen and tasted in the translucent broth. The tureen was tall, the ladle battered silver.

Oh France, why do you hoard your true riches?

July

MINUTE PARTICULARS

He who would do good to another must do it in Minute Particulars.
General Good is the plea of the scoundrel, hypocrite and flatterer.

Blake might have added (and probably meant) the politician.

I love reading Blake. He is the hippy's Samuel Johnson: trenchant, terse, and often deep. These lines came to me in a context that might surprise you: reading the Annual Report of the Metropolitan Public Gardens Association. The MPGA does good, horticulturally, in minute particulars. Since it was founded in 1862 to transform derelict sites in London into green oases for recreation, it has touched hundreds of little-known corners and turned them green. Often only the locals notice, but a tree or a bench or a planting of bulbs can be a very worthwhile contribution. This is basically what the Association does: it gives small grants where they are keenly appreciated.

A long-established and respected body can be useful in other ways: its moral backing can put gentle pressure where it can do good ... carefully, though, and never General Good (see Blake above). I was delighted to be asked by the chairman to succeed my friend Michael Birkett as President of this modest body, and of course accepted.

FOOLHARDY

The outdoor trial of our aspidistra, planted out in a bed through one of our coldest winters, with a minimum temperature of -12° C, ended in disappointment. It survived.

PLUVIOPHILY

I'm such a pluviophile (and with so few opportunities to practise my passion) that I find myself watching the rain, or at night listening to it, and trying to calculate how many millimetre marks it is filling in the perspex cone in the kitchen garden. I picture the big juicy drops making the tiny water surface jump, or the minuscule misty ones accumulating on the sides until a nice fat teardrop tumbles to the bottom. We need rain, almost always, and we sure do enjoy it when it comes.

Last night it was forecast. The BBC weather maps were spot on with light brown, darker brown and light and bright blue amoebas floating across, representing clear, cloudy, drizzly and wet patches (almost always from left to right, on the prevailing wind).

I was swimming when the first little drops made themselves felt, from a merely light-grey sky. When rain comes on slowly you know it is the real deal. The merest pitter at 8pm became a patter by 8.15. By now I was in the conservatory. By 8.30 it was a steady hiss punctuated by urgent tapping. The fishscale panes of the conservatory roof were delivering constant rivulets down the centre of each bay. I went out into the yard; yes, there was the gutter overflowing, splashing and spattering on the paving. It always does this after a dry spell; moss from the roof blocks the downpipe. But I love taking a kitchen stool out, climbing on it and reaching to clear the moss, and the subsequent slosh into the drain.

The smell of the soaking garden is best of all. How does rain release so much scent into the air?

GARDENERS' DELIGHT

The opening of the tomato season is not quite the red-letter day it used to be. The first bite of the first 'Gardeners' Delight', the little scarlet globe exploding on your palate in a rush of sweetness and greenness, was a moment as important as the first asparagus, broad beans, sweet corn .... No, more important – it ushered in a long late-summer season of perfumed salads and stews, tomato sharpness with bacon and eggs, the red tomato signature everywhere.

That was before the supermarkets woke up to the variety of tomatoes. There used to be just one on their shelves. It was red, round, watery and tasteless. It still has a public – and still appears at breakfast in Greasy Spoons. I started writing about its inadequacies 25 years ago or so, and pestering the press departments of Tesco and Sainsburys. I remember the hallelujah day when one of them called me to say that their purchasing board was in shock. Tomatoes had overtaken bananas in turnover.

In the past three years new varieties have been pouring in, even from growers in England. We started seeing good ripe tomatoes, in pretty funny shapes, some of them, as early as February. It is a wholly benign development; who could not be thrilled? And my tomato plants? As iffy as ever. But I still nip down to the greenhouse for a surreptitious 'Gardeners' Delight'.

THE SMELL OF RAIN

John Grimshaw (Director at The Yorkshire Arboretum) has responded to my coinage of Pluviophily as a word for the love of rain with one for the scent of it: 'petrichor'. Petrichor combines the Greek for stone and the blood of the gods. Two Australians coined it in 1964 in the journal *Nature*, explaining that the smell derives from oil exuded by certain plants during dry periods, then absorbed into clay particles. Rain releases it into the air along with another compound, geosmin. These are what we smell – or at least what Australians do.

We have different plants and different soils. Having looked up geosmin (literally 'earth smell'), I am more inclined to think it is its associated microbes that give me so much pleasure. Although the long-range forecast suggests the novelty will soon wear off.

A HACK AT WORK

'Pruning' is too polite a word for what I am doing in the garden at the moment. 'Hacking back' describes it more accurately – and it is one of my favourite annual jobs, comparable with weeding, and with the same essential purpose: to rebalance the growth of the past weeks and months in favour of less vigorous plants that I prefer.

I am usually as sentimental as the next gardener, but this is no time for soppiness. People say 'I can't cut that, there's a flower on it.' Let it alone and you'll have fewer flowers next year. Stragglers go in the buttonhole while I get hacking.

I set out with my favourite Japanese secateurs in my belt and with some particular plant in mind. This morning it was a philadelphus with long new shoots shooting up vertically from its drooping, flowered-out branches. They were pressing down on and shading out whatever grows below.

I haven't finished with the first philadelphus, cutting off all the old stuff and bringing light and air to a young golden *Cotinus*, a stylish but slow-growing *Trochodendron araliodes* and a thicket of epimedium, when I remember another. Then I remember a deutzia, which needs exactly the same treatment to rescue the geraniums underneath. Zigzagging with my barrow from one to the other I suddenly realize that it is two years since I tamed a *Mahonia* 'Charity', now bending its shoots soaring like palm trees above a hapless *Viburnum davidii*. I clamber into the thicket; the half-inch *Mahonia* trunks snap easily under my secateurs, revealing their bright yellow wood.

I pass a corner where *Viburnum tinus* is thrusting its dull and dusty branches through a pretty white-variegated buckthorn, a form of *Rhamnus* I can't find in the books. It is worth spending time choosing its best feathery sprays to show off against the dark background. A vine maple is invading and shading out the bottom of my Syrian juniper, *J. drupacea*; more branches join the heap on the barrow.

It is not a methodical process. I look about me, sometimes in the middle of a bush where I have never stood before, and lay about me with my blades. I'm afraid hacking back is the proper expression.

August

BRIGHTNESS AT LAST

Why does the sun come out as it goes down? It has happened so many times this summer that I am looking for an explanation. It is happening as I write.

Is it a local phenomenon? Obviously it depends on your viewpoint. There have been pesky grey clouds all day. It is too cold and breezy to sit outside. Then, just as I start wondering where I left the corkscrew, the garden floods with light.

It could be a weather front moving on at the end of the day. Sometimes it clearly is; the cloud formation shows it. Not this evening, though, with what appears to be an equal covering of cloud everywhere except this window in the northwest where orange light is streaming in. It sets light to the old red bricks of the Tudor chimney above the conservatory. It gilds the grey flint of the church tower, evening after evening.

The redness of the evening sky can be explained by the fact that sunlight at an oblique angle passes through more of the earth's atmosphere than when the sun is overhead. The opening of the sunset window is what puzzles me. Is it a meteorological fact, or do we just live in a lucky spot?

TAKING THE LONG VIEW

Back from a week in Snowdonia. Chilly for August, but ideal for long, steep walks. Our favourite, starting from our woods overlooking the Mawddach Estuary, follows the ancient Harlech road from Dolgellau, more or less straight uphill (which is why hot weather is not ideal) to a ridge at 550 metres.

You are walking through heather and reeds, with low gorse here and there; the track often a glittering rivulet under your feet. The gate in the wall at the top opens on a panorama of Snowdonia and Cardigan Bay, from Bardsey Island at the tip of the Lleyn Peninsula to the west, to Snowdon itself almost due north. On the western horizon the hills of Wicklow are a faint line. To the east rises the smooth shoulder of Diffwys, to 260 metres. Turn around and the long leonine ridge of Cader Idris forms the southern horizon, with our dark woods and the silver arrow of the Mawddach far below.

We took a rough scramble down a too-steep path last week, arriving at the woods hot enough to plunge straight into our pine-fringed tarn. But not for long; there has been no summer to take the chill off the black water.

The pace of growth in these woods, with 150 or 180 cm of rain a year, is constantly surprising. A great deal of the forester's job is to discourage over-vigorous interlopers that take space and light from the main crop, whether it be spruce, larch, fir or the long-term goal and point of the enterprise, oak and beech. I have a kill list, with the most pernicious weeds at the top: rhododendron and the invasive lodgepole pine, mistakenly planted (it is useless timber) in the 1960s and self-sown everywhere ever since. Next come Lawson cypress (a similar story) and, sadly, western hemlock. Hemlock is one of our most beautiful trees, pale green, graceful, drooping, with a formidable straight trunk. The trouble is no one wants its timber.

Birch needs weeding because it comes up everywhere, fast, and its slender twigs can unfold and stifle the far slower oak. In fact nurturing oak, even pruning young trees (they have precious little sense of which way is up) is my most time-consuming job. I can spend all morning moving slowly through bracken and brambles liberating little trees, with a deep sense of doing good.

WHO'S BATS?

Is it guilt that makes us, or at least our legislators, so absurdly over-protective of badgers? No creature has so many walls of regulation, euro- and home-grown, keeping it from harm. Guilt for what? They should be feeling the guilt, not us, if the disappearance of our hedgehogs is their doing. We haven't seen one of our spiky friends all summer. Or do we feel guilty for preferring furry things that can't answer back to the young of our own kind, which resoundingly can?

And if badgers are molly-coddled, what about bats? The bat lobby is so powerful that at least one ancient church (St Hilda's, at Ellerburn in North Yorks) has become unusable; its congregation is rated irrelevant while bats leave their messages on the altar and the stink of their urine in the air.

I had a letter recently from the bat authorities that left me worrying about their belfry. 'You have a cave on your property', they wrote. (This is true.) 'You have closed it with a gate made of vertical bars.' (Also true: to keep people out. The bars are four inches apart.) 'You may be unaware that bats prefer horizontal bars.' I admit I'd never asked. Nor can I imagine why my money and yours is being spent on civil servants asking bats their preferences.

Bats are our ecological allies. They eat lots of insects. Some are rare, even endangered. The lesser horseshoe bat, though, is abundant, and if it suffers some inconvenience in barrel-rolling to fly through my gate, I shan't beg its pardon.

September

AUTUMN MUSIC

Who on earth is chopping down a tree this beautiful autumn morning? It must be a big one, to judge by the demented racket of the saw. But there is no tree, and the random roaring corresponds to no pattern of felling and logging. The noise fills the neighbourhood, obliterating the peace of every garden, annulling anemones and making roses irrelevant. There is an oily smell with it, too.

Yes, it is a leaf blower: an infernal contraption designed to cost 50 times more than a rake without fulfilling its purpose. Every autumn the nuisance gets worse. We were woken at five in a French hotel the other morning when the council sent a man round to blow the leaves off the pavements into the path of the almost equally noisy street-scrubbing lorry that followed at six. Would a 200 percent VAT rate put a stop to it? I doubt it.

November

PATINA

It's a simple question, but not easy to answer: why am I so drawn to old gardens, old houses ... anywhere palpably old? What is the appeal of history? What does it matter that (let's say) a garden has been growing, in more or less recognizable form, for a century, or centuries?

To people who think or feel as I do, age gives a sense of validity. I am easily seduced by the word 'authentic' – although who is to say that what's left of the past is more authentic than what has just been created? It's hard to argue rationally that Dickens's London is more authentic than, let's say, Canada Square.

Surely what speaks of today, made and inhabited by living people, is more real than anything remembered – let alone reproduced? Yet scraps of grey brickwork or stone that have, as we say, 'seen a lot of history', somehow offer reassurance. I see new buildings, or new planting, as something provisional, as though it were waiting for some sort of authentication that comes only with passing time. Patina adds a vital dimension to the actual. It lets imagination get to work, 'authentic' or not.

Do you remember Stanley Holloway in the Tower of London? 'It's 'ad a new 'andle, and per'aps a new 'ead, but it's still the original axe.' It's what you might call an existential question.

TRUE BLUE

I get self-conscious when the time comes for winter bedding plants. It's probably the snob in me that recoils from popping in the same blue-and-yellow pansies that you see for sale on garage forecourts at this time of year. Surely I should be more original?

But whereas I blithely plant perfectly routine perennials (in what I hope will be original and ravishing combinations), I never get round to sowing anything for the winter. I hope my wallflowers will do it for themselves. Indeed I spent half a morning in the summer slipping seeds from a self-sown wallflower in a wall, deep in all the gaps in the brickwork around it. There followed ten weeks without rain. I hosed down the wall once or twice when I remembered to, but none of the seeds germinated.

So here I am with trays of pansies and wallflowers from Springwell Nurseries, a jolly spot on the road from Saffron Walden to Cambridge, deciding how to deploy them casually, as if they had volunteered. That is not how they will look, but nor should they; at least not the pansies. Their wonderful satin extravagance needs a more or less formal frame. There is a new one (to me) this year; not bright yellow but pale primrose. I will speckle it with the one called 'True Blue' in the bed behind the cottage where the rugosa roses stand gaunt in winter.

My favourite wallflower for years has been the old cultivar 'Scarlet Bedder'; a gauge, I'm sure, of my deep conservatism in choosing flowers. This year there is an F1 hybrid called 'Treasure Bronze' which is so much healthier looking, stockier and more compact that I am planting that instead. Sadly there is no chance of a true F1 seedling in a wall.

Heaven knows what the pansies' provenance may be. 'True Blue' is a strong colour I would have called violet until I checked in my old RHS colour chart. The name is right: it corresponds, making allowance for its lustrous texture, with colour 95A: Cornflower Blue. The colour chart originated in the 1930s with the British Colour Council, now long defunct. Another of their publications was a *Dictionary of Colours for Interior Decoration*, in two volumes, which goes to the length of having three samples of each colour: one matt, one glossy and one a piece of carpet. My copy belonged to the decorator Anthony Denney, who gave it to me when I started to garden. His message: texture is as important as hue. And light, of course, decides everything.

December

IN FOR A BIG SURPRISE

To Wales for a walk in our woods, on a day as clear and glowing as only winter can offer. Summer is just a distraction in this wild upland country; only in winter do you see the real thing, the flesh and bones of the countryside painted in its deepest, warmest, most varied colours.

As a forester I try to look at the woods from a business point of view. This block of trees (black, in this low light, gothic, jagged and aggressive) is due to be felled next year. How much will it fetch? The price of timber is right down (this is the stuff they use for homes – only they're not building any). The trees will safely grow on for a couple of years, but perhaps the euro will die, and then who'll build houses?

My natural interest, though, is what the view will be when they're gone. Cader Idris is straight ahead, and over to the right shall we just catch a glimpse of Cardigan Bay? There will be a dreadful mess for a couple of years, then new plants will start to give it a pattern; timid lines of green. I hope to see at least a low cover of new trees in my lifetime: but then what?

This is the nearest a forester comes to a gardener's perspective: weighing the impact of the different possibilities on the fallow land-scape. One is to leave it fallow, or at least parts of it, and watch the first-year foxgloves and the gradual return of the heather and bilberry, and gorse and brambles and bracken, the inevitable birch and rowan seedlings, volunteer spruce and larch, and hopefully a smattering of oak. Leave it two hundred years and, theoretically, oak will be the climax vegetation – at least in sheltered spots and gullies where soil has accumulated over the ungiving granite.

I have planted a lot of oak. It struggles. Local Welsh oak has no sense of direction: mostly it goes sideways, with a nudge of course from sheep. In autumn its patchwork of colours is wonderfully wayward: one tree is copper, one gold, its neighbour jade and the next as dark as an Amsterdam front door.

Larch I love; its pale seedlings brighten the woods as fast, even, as birch. But there is a threat hanging over it: the same *Phytophthora ramorum* that threatens our oaks. It has reached South Wales, apparently travelling north. No one is planting it around here any more. Our tall stands of larch, planted in the 1960s and now 70 feet high, straight poles to a thin canopy, are the most graceful parts of the woodland, and their pale spring green and autumn gold two of its principal delights. If we see trees browning in summer we have to call the authorities, and they will say 'Fell'. I remember the elm disease, 35 years ago, and I tremble.

But now, in the short days with long shadows, I can spend time on the details, see the work that nature puts in to arranging heather and rock and bilberry, gorse and bracken and long-jumping brambles; none of them, not even the brambles, quite destroying the magical equilibrium. I can prod little freshets into new courses, promote them to streams, yank a ponticum from a path, play the gardener on a domestic scale within the implacable macrocosm of the forest.

CONSTRUCTIVE NEGLECT

I suppose I used to assume that moss and damp went together; that our mossy bits were just shady and badly drained (as they may well be). I had no intention of cutting down the trees or installing new drainage, so too bad; let's enjoy the moss.

But here we are, after one of the driest years of our times, and there is more moss than ever, so it can't be rain. Anyway it looks marvellous. If I hadn't read so many lawn-care articles I'd say I prefer moss to grass. The Moss Garden in Kyoto (the result, they say, of ages of neglect) makes me want to take up neglect as my retirement hobby.

Why is our moss shameful, where theirs is a matter of pride? Because, I fear, Japanese summers have plenty of rain, and ours, in spite of folklore, not nearly enough – or only during Test Matches.

We have to keep tipping the balance in favour of grass, because grass is our default ground cover. Even if the evidence, in large parts of this aging garden, points in the direction of ivy as nature's choice.

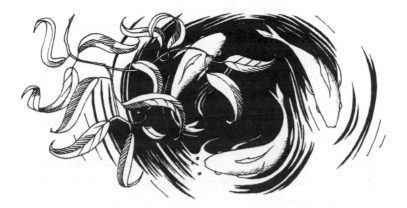

2012

January

A DREAM OF PONDS

There is a landscape I have never seen that has been haunting and inspiring me for 20 years. It is a chain of ponds in a painting: a retreating procession of silver surfaces that took hold of my imagination and still won't let go.

Wherever I first saw it, presumably in a book, it went with me to France when I was trying, with laughable over-ambition, to impose my will on 200 acres of deep bocage. I set about channelling the stream that issued from a generous spring in the hillside to form three oval ponds descending into the valley so that from the track at the top they formed a gleaming chain.

It was a struggle. The soil was so *filtrant*, to use the French term, that as soon as I cut into the marshy streambed as it meandered down the hill, the water immediately carved itself a channel and disappeared in the coarse sandy ground.

Eventually, using a piece of pipe here and a primitive bridge of logs there, I persuaded it into my little ponds. For a few summer weeks I had my picture. Then the deer identified them as drinking troughs; their hooves broke into the lip of each carefully excavated hollow and the water found another way downhill. Cattle joined them from another field and a general swamp began to form.

You would be amazed how soon goat willow seedlings spring up, reeds multiply, and the muddy mix is a pond no more. As for the swamp spurge, *Euphorbia palustris*, I optimistically planted; the azalea mollis in bold groups, the bluebells and ferns and the red-stemmed willows, their trashing was almost instantaneous. Do you know how much deer love stropping their velvet on young willows? Does the aspirin in the bark cure their headaches?

The picture stayed in my mind though, and came thrillingly to life when Lady Salisbury apparently dreamed the same dream at Hatfield House. Using the spillway over the dam that forms the lake, she remade the identical scene – but solidly in sensible material, and with an abundant supply of water: three shining discs descending, in this case, into an ancient wood.

Did we share the same inspiration? Indeed we did. And last weekend I saw it, in its frame, for the first time. It hangs in the wonderful little gallery in Christchurch Mansion in Ipswich. It is Gainsborough's painting of the park at Holywells. The water, apparently, served a brewery.

NATURE, NOTICED

Ever since Picasso declared war on beauty, especially feminine beauty, mocking it or jumbling it up, artists have fought shy of it. 'Major' artists, at least. Lucian Freud, as major as they come, found ugliness in the human flesh that should, surely, evoke our warmest feelings. It is perverse to say, as some critics do, that he was loving the blotchy flab he painted so precisely. What he was loving was paint.

No wonder, then, that David Hockney's paintings of trees in his native Yorkshire landscape are causing queues round the block at Burlington House. Here is a major artist daring to admit that he loves nature and wants us to share his feelings. The point of his huge canvases of the most humdrum of woods and lanes is that they are worth studying in minute (or rather magnified) detail. These are not beauty spots, sublime scenery or sunsets. Not the faintest memory of Turner. His Yorkshire Wolds (or the corners he chooses) are interchangeable with the bottom of your lane – or indeed my daily Essex walk.

Loving trees as I do, I find endless details to admire even in my 40 minutes to the bridge, over the stream and back: the alders, the oaks, the bat willows and the hazel bushes (their catkins are starting to lengthen). Their winter colours, in sun or shade, or rain, form a palette of extraordinary richness and beauty, and their tracery against the clouds is infinitely fine.

Hockney is celebrating precisely these things, and giving us permission to do the same. He uses strong colours partly in celebration, out of sheer excitement at what he sees. Partly, perhaps, to surprise his metropolitan viewers into looking at something they would otherwise take for granted. Does it sound smug to say that I could never take a tree for granted, that I am right up there with the painter? Not many, I fear, are as lucky. This is the importance of what Hockney has done: an old man with the eyes of a child is making nature mainstream.

February

DANGER ZONE

Our friends' little gardens between the houses in the middle of the village are noisy with birdlife already. Tits, chaffinches, sparrows, robins and blackbirds are hopping and swooping everywhere.

Here in the seclusion of a much bigger garden, there is near-silence. A couple of blue tits come to the peanuts in the feeder, a woodpecker cackles and a pheasant shouts. One blackbird sings in the weeping willow but there is hardly any movement in the bushes. I wonder why. And then I realize. There is nowhere in this garden, literally nowhere, that a squirrel can't reach. Our trees have given them a monopoly; total control. Birds have to go into the village to nest.

THOUGHT-BYTES

I have embraced my iPad as eagerly as anyone, but have so far refrained from twittering. It's not that I disdain brevity of expression. Indeed for almost 40 years my *Pocket Wine Book* has tried to encapsulate the essentials of its field in far shorter phrases than the 140 characters allowed in a tweet. That's what I call verbosity.

No, it's not the language I feared for. It's our minds. Once we had, and thought we needed, a variety of ways to learn the contents of each other's minds. Surely this is the whole point of literature. The power and delight of a library is that each book you open is a glimpse into another's consciousness. Lectures, essays, sermons were formal means of exposition. And the highest means of all was poetry.

Now we have Twitter; the thumb-jerk expression of fleeting thoughts. It is pure chance if they have any significance beyond their moment of conception – and transmission. Will some future Jobs or Zuckerberg find a way of validating second thoughts – even third ones? Could there be a shiny new format for joined-up thinking?

March

INNOCENT PURSUITS

The Murdoch family has had such a bad press recently that I keep remembering a visit to Dame Elisabeth, Rupert Murdoch's mother, at her garden south of Melbourne, it must be ten years ago. Ten years ago she was only 93; at 103 she remains a central figure in the cultural and charitable life of Melbourne – and a passionate gardener.

We were introduced to her at a garden festival at Hatfield House by Marchioness Mollie. We went to tea with her a year or two later at Cruden Farm, the house her husband Keith gave her when they married in 1928. There was nothing formal about our visit; she put the kettle on and fetched a cake tin, then told us that she had just been to Melbourne and back (she drove herself in a small car) to chair a meeting of one of her charities. The garden, she said, was too big to walk round, so she drove us in her buggy, stopping every few yards to point out a plant with evident knowledge and relish.

You reach Cruden Farm down a long curving alley of *Corymbia citriodora*, the gum-tree equivalent of *Betula jacquemontii*, but whiter of trunk and more sinuous. A rugby goalpost, as it were, with hips. Tall trees shade the white clapboard house, one of them an oak I have never seen before or since, an evergreen with leaves rather like *Quercus* × *turneri* but immensely tall and as deeply drooping as a weeping beech. Its name is *Q. Firthii*. I want one. Hydrangeas are stacked in tall banks round the house, their feet in a lush bed of agapanthus; blue and white the predominant colours.

But any memory of the planting is hazy beside my memory of the woman who was brought home here as a bride at 19 and has reigned in the garden (and in Melbourne) ever since. The innocent pursuits of philanthropy and gardening have occupied her for 80 years.

TURNED INWARDS

Reading an article on the gardens of Suzhou by John Dixon Hunt in the excellent *Historic Gardens Review* reminded me of my one visit to this capital of classic Chinese gardening in 1989.

Then it was called Soochow. I took a train (with some difficulty) from Shanghai and hired a bike to join the thousands who pedalled sedately, like a steady humming river, along the avenues of this historic town. There is a flavour of Amsterdam about its canals (which were kept impeccable, at least in the centre, I remember, by men and women in punts with nets to scoop up the slightest litter).

In its concentration of gardens it could be compared with Kyoto – except that Kyoto is a city of temples and palaces in a naturally beautiful valley, while Soochow (do you say Kolkata?) is a commercial centre on a river plain. Its gardens therefore have no prospects, no interest in the world beyond, but concentrate your thoughts on the ingenuities and intricacies within their high circling walls.

The gardener's art was how to make a short stroll satisfying, even exciting, within these limits. Rule one, it seems, was to keep pricking the visitor's curiosity, raising his expectations and then frustrating them. Each garden is a complex of elaborate low buildings (their roofs and eaves are very much part of the picture: curved and convoluted and decorated with dragons and creatures of all sorts). A great deal of the space between is filled with great grey rocks, as craggy or water-worn as possible. They are utterly unlike the calm solemn boulders of Kyoto; these gesticulate as though they want to move around and change places.

Often you find yourself squeezing through a claustrophobic chasm between high stones with nothing but stone to see, then emerge beside a little pool full of technicolor carp. A lacquered pavilion in the midst contains the master's desk, scrolls and pens; an icon of tranquil schol-arship (or, for that matter, petty-fogging bureaucracy). He cannot, you imagine, sit there long without succumbing to one of the insistent invitations to walk: over these stepping stones, into this rockery to admire the peonies or through that moongate where the skirts of a willow – and perhaps other skirts – are beckoning.

You pass a bamboo screen and glimpse another pool, or flurry of rocks, mysteriously inaccessible. Your steps are frustrated, your exploration interrupted, your expectation raised at each turn. As John Dixon Hunt points out, it is the art of delay, of delicious foreplay. Even a moongate is a means for making you step on alone (or bow your companion through before you). But I don't think these are companionable gardens. A drinks party would be a solecism, almost an outrage. As, indeed, are the crocodiles of visitors, both here and in Kyoto. Such gardens are turned inward to the point of obsession – or is it me obsessing?

A TASTE OF HONEY

I was ambushed by a blast of honey just now; an overwhelming jar-full of scent, clear, golden, sweet and even waxy. I jumped like Winnie the Pooh. The trees around are bare, a few willow catkins are opening, maples are just showing points of promise where their buds will be ... where are the flowers?

Then I saw, behind a screen of the fine twigs of Japanese maples, some modest spots of dull yellow. It is *Lindera obtusiloba*, a Chinese bush I love for its waywardly three-lobed leaves, no two quite the same, memorably bright yellow in October. The leaves are slightly scented too. One to plant.

YOUNG PROMISE

Tidy people with orderly minds are excluded, I'm afraid, from the sort of pleasure I had the other day rummaging in the potting shed when I noticed, buried in old seed packets and balls of string, a thick little black book.

It is our garden diary for 1975, a year when we planned and planted with an energy I only half remember. The notes are half in my handwriting, half in another, much neater and with more complete sentences and many references to nature, as well as this kind of thing: 'April 25th. Made second sowings of lettuce, spinach, beetroot. Planted Helleborus corsicus behind cottage with R. rubrifolia, Hosta glauca, Asters, yellow foxglove, hebe, Viburnum fragrans. Piptanthus flowering.' (Most of these were still here.)

Who was my co-diarist? His observations grow sharper: 'Potted geraniums in greenhouse. There are more in flower every day, particularly Catford Belle, which seems more dwarf than miniature. The ferns are doing well, Adiantums especially fine and the effect in the shaded corner is almost subtropical. First strawberry flowers out; fed with liquid fertilizer.'

Then the penny dropped. This is the last volume to record our first proper gardener, Christopher Bailes. The entry for September 13th reads 'Chris left today to go to Merrist Wood College. He has been here three years and three months.' We had suspicions then that this studious young man would go far, if not quite as far as Philip Miller's old job at the Chelsea Physic Garden, which he now adorns. (Since when he has been curator of Rosemoor and Hyde Hall for the RHS, has written a number of books, and has recently been awarded the Victoria Medal of Honour, the highest honour in gardening.)

FAST FORWARD

I try not to let this diary become too meteo-centric, but there is no avoiding the topic du jour. Magnolias are going over, and horse chestnuts are in leaf, and we are still in March. The spring of 2011 was pretty alarmingly warm, and excessively dry, but this fast-forward eruption of a season makes it moderate in comparison. We have a blackthorn summer instead of winter. The daffodils in the royal parks had the shortest flowering in memory: there will be none for Easter. If this sort of spring becomes a habit there will be less and less reason to grow them: a week in flower and a month looking miserable is not going to keep the popular vote.

ALL ALONE

There may not, I suppose, be many records of the birthdays of goldfish, but mine has passed his 35th, and we are quietly celebrating together. What's more, he has passed more than 30 years of his life swimming alone, the only inhabitant of his (lead) tank in the conservatory. His companion died and I hesitated to introduce a stranger into his placid life.

I am no judge of a goldfish's state of mind; he may relish his independence, he may be lonely and depressed (or indeed he may be a she), but there he is every morning basking peacefully among the leaves. A few flakes of fish food give him obvious pleasure – but what he likes best is the hose; a jet dropped from high enough to bubble oxygen into his water. Each time I do this he swims a little jig.

His name is Diogenes, after another loner who lived in a tub – although I like to think my Diogenes is more of a philosopher.

April

LOOKING BOTH WAYS

Is this a moral dilemma, or an aesthetic one – or is it a dilemma at all? You possess a building which all agree, monotonously, in describing as 'iconic'. One view of it, from a public road and across a riverside meadow, is as well-known (all right, then: iconic) as any view in the country. The catch is that the reverse view, from the building and its surroundings, is the public road, emphasized by traffic lights and the resulting line of waiting cars' brake lights. Is the proprietor obliged to leave the view open, both ways, or would he be justified in planting appropriate trees to screen the road from his own viewpoint?

The building, you may even have guessed, is King's College chapel in Cambridge. Coach parties of tourists make an inevitable stop to photograph the view. Members of the college learn to accept the traffic across the summer view, softened by leafy trees. In winter it is different. From teatime on there is only one thing you see across the Cam from the college: winking red lights.

There are worse problems, I know. But there is also the hope of a solution, at least in part. The college has just succeeded in 'respacing' (which means felling) half the trees between the road and the river. Italian alders planted 40 years ago as a nurse-crop for oaks (this was the plan when we lost all the magnificent elms) have finally gone – in the nick of time: the oaks they were 'nursing' were almost shaded to death. In their place are planted more oaks, lots of hawthorn, and an entirely new feature for the Backs: a crowd of Chinese dogwoods, which will make a mass of white flowers at May Ball time in June, and (I hope) colour up in an orange/harlequin way in October.

Flanking the rather stark and lonely stone Back Gate of the college we are planning to plant a pair of weeping willows· the first step in screening the intrusive traffic lights. In other words, no obvious move; just slow and sensitive improvements.

——————————— *May* ———————————

DREAMING

A reverie is a comfortable place to be. I have just spent ten, 15, I'm not sure how many minutes watching *Berberis* petals float over a weir: tiny flakes of gold on black water, drifting slowly, with a growing sense of purpose, over the surface of my little rock-rimmed pond.

The weir (the whole thing is tiny: a foot across) acts like a magnet, mysteriously setting the surface in motion. Petals settled in the centre of the pool begin almost imperceptibly to move, gradually, gently organizing themselves to head towards the fall. Little groups of four or five move together, as though some force (could it be surface tension?) held them in formation. Individuals feel the same pull and move at the same speed.

I switch focus and look deeper, through clear water to snail trails (if that's what they are); paler tracks on the leaf-littered bottom. It has always baffled me how we can switch our vision from reflections to the surface, and through the surface to what lies below, with only a change of thought.

Three feet from the weir the petals change course, reset their sails and pick up speed. They keep in their flotillas, but now there is urgency in their drift, they collide, form bigger squadrons, then coalesce into a pool of gold to hurry through the gap between the rocks. They fall perhaps an inch, perhaps two, but just enough to break the surface into silver glints.

As a way of seeing the whole world it is much more interesting than a grain of sand.

MR MELDREW

Plain simple degrees, and lots of them, are what the garden needs this miserable May. Fahrenheit or Celsius; it won't mind. The plants are in as much of a muddle as I am, not so much early or late as all over the place and not going anywhere. Oak has never been so far before ash, but magnolias are just sitting, their flowers half open, some petals frosted, others effectively drowned. And my favourite winter-flowering cherry has caught that nasty fungus and lost all its leaves.

And yet. When I splashed out this morning in my winter coat to see what could be done, I walked into a wall of what to me is the Chelsea smell: azaleas in all their boudoir sweetness. The pale faces

of azalea mollis, soft yellow in the grey light, were gently chiding me:
look at us, you grumpy old fool.

RHODOLAND

To Bowood on a rainy day to visit the Rhododendron Walks, open for
the first time this year. It is almost incredible that England still has such
wonders under wraps, but the Lansdownes have kept this separate part
of the gardens, miles across the estate from their celebrated Capability
Brown lake and spectacular water gardens, as a private enclave around
the Robert Adam family mausoleum.

The woodland garden is sheltered and framed by oaks, and some
of the most venerable beeches I have ever seen, on a series of steep
spring-fed slopes that offer everything rhododendrons could need:
shelter, moisture and air-drainage.

Some of the first collections from the Himalayas were planted here
in the days of Sir Joseph Hooker, by the great-great grandfather of the
current incumbent. Subsequent Lansdownes have added to what is
now a woodland garden of extraordinary beauty, while the present
marquess, the eighth, is a full-time hands-on gardener.

I am no rhododendron expert, and easily impressed by a bush
30 feet high covered in huge pale-pink flowers giving off sweet
scents. When I am told that it is one of the earliest hardy hybrids
with Himalayan blood, and that its name is lost in time, I can only
nod in assent. It is clear why such impressive creations became the
show-flowers of the great, raised and selected with as much care as
their racehorses.

Satiety would soon be reached, though, if they were too densely
planted. It is the beauty of Bowood that there is space and variety,
that glades and rides, pools of bluebells and grass open to the sky
make it a magic wood rather than a rhododendron forest, There is
the delicacy of white dogwoods, the brilliance of *Pieris*, one the size
of a cottage, and above all, here and there among the rich green and
the pale glades, floating over the bluebells, the sumptuous near-blues
and -purples of *Rhododendron augustinii*.

The rain at Bowood, at least in retrospect, was like the creative touch of a great director. The shine and drip (it didn't pour), the grey light and the cool soft air completed the magic and made the exotic (even the ultra-exotic) seem believable.

June

THE LONDON FOREST

The camera zoomed in from an improbable height above the royal Bentley purring back from St Paul's. On the way it encountered the branches of a plane tree and saw right through them, through sadly depleted leaves and sagging shoots, in a way you never can through the canopy of a healthy tree. London's planes are sick, some of them very sick, and the prospect of their decline is too dreadful to contemplate.

Is it a new disease, as some suggest, or the occasional weakness that strikes them under peculiar circumstances? Does it relate to a hot dry early spring followed by a long cold and wet April and most of May – and June? I used to worry about an alley of London planes I planted in central France; in some years, particularly in wet springs, their new shoots died back as we see them doing in London now, but 20 years on they are robust young trees.

Central London has been verging on a monoculture of planes since its elms died nearly 40 years ago. We forget how important they were. Many of the finest trees in Hyde Park, for instance, were field elms, with their crowning fans of branches, their flaring skirts and their pale-gold leaves almost to the end of the year. London has few oaks and not (except in Kensington Gardens) nearly enough limes. The resilience of the plane, its resistance to pollution as well as its majestically graceful canopy and its huge reptilian trunk, have given it the status of *the* London tree.

Local authorities have been imaginative in the past few years with their street trees. We see rowans and alders, ginkgos here and there, many hawthorns in the parks, and so many Chanticleer pears that we have to hope they are resilient too. But the mainstay of our parks and squares is the London plane. Since the 18th century it has defined the landscape of the West End, historically and practically. It is strange that a sterile hybrid should become the climax tree of the London forest – and should certainly be worrying us now.

SEE WHERE YOU'VE BEEN

I may well lose more readers through my enthusiasm for weeding, annually expressed, than by being boring, repetitive, out of touch, living in the past and my many other weaknesses. I can't help it. Weeding for me is the epitome of gardening; the time when every move is decisive and, to use that corny phrase, you can see where you've been. Planting is the other supreme gardening pleasure; the satisfaction of settling roots in soil always gives me a glow. But planting is the work of moments, while weeding is a long-drawn-out pleasure, always (at least in this garden) available.

Why do I love it? Because it calls for total concentration. As I stoop or grovel in the border (or anywhere else where muddle is taking over) my eyes must be fully focused. What appears at first an agreeable jumble of green shapes becomes progressively clear as I start to edit it. There are in-your-face weeds: a dock or a nettle makes no attempt to hide. There are insidious weeds that blend with the background: violas and little balsams that can lurk while they multiply. And there are wily, snaky weeds that infiltrate under disguise.

There are plants that never seem to need weeding, but they are rare. I seldom find weeds in clumps of hemerocallis, and the big leaves of *Phlomis russelliana* are effective at covering the ground. Some geraniums are hard for casual weeds to penetrate, but nothing, of course, smothers bindweed. Nor I fear is there any pleasure in it. In fact, I exclude bindweed, couch grass and ground elder from my enthusiasm. So perhaps I am not so different from other gardeners after all.

MADAME SAUCY

Don't you sometimes speculate about the women whose names adorn some of the most voluptuous roses of the summer? They are nearly all French. I wish we had their portraits. Did 'Madame Grégoire Staechelin' blush (or droop) like her namesake rose? Was 'Monsieur Staechelin' the bristly buttoned-up individual his name seems to suggest?

Can you form a mental picture of 'Madame Lauriol de Barny'? A plump and pleasing, rather artless young woman, I rather fancy, apt to put her foot in it. 'Madeleine Selzer' (marital status unknown) was self-evidently a fizzer. 'La Séduisante' (name unknown) needed careful handling. And what does 'Madame Isaac Péreire' conjure up for you? I see a severe and stately lady in black holding her luscious magenta cabbage of a rose at waist level to avoid being suffocated by its dangerously sweet perfume.

The ladies parade before us, all décolleté and bustle, with no shortage of artful ribbons. Are some lovesick? Is 'Madame Bovary' an unchristened rose? 'When first open on a cool clear day', says Graham Stuart Thomas, 'Madame Pierre Oger is of a soft warm creamy flesh.' The 'Nymphe Emue' even lets us see her blushing thigh.

We know that Caroline Testout was a couturier from Grenoble, and that Madame Sancy de Parabère was a general's daughter and lady-in-waiting to the Empress Eugenie, who would not have been amused by her bothy moniker of 'Saucy de Paramour'. Nor, I fancy, would Madame Alfred Carrière, patroness of the loveliest of pale blushing climbers, have answered happily to 'Mad Alf', the name I heard a gardener give her.

In this rosiest of seasons, in the first warm days after unending rain, the fleshy fragrant presence of these women is inescapable. 'Climbing Lady Hillingdon' is pressing her soft orange globes against my bedroom window. Surely this can't be, as Robin Lane Fox tells us, the Lady Hillingdon who closed her eyes and thought of England?

BOTCH UP

My son-in-law brilliantly described an old house we rented in Wales as representing a hundred years of botching. An archaeologist might have loved the rich evidence of ages past: former décor in curling wallpaper and peeling paint, superannuated plumbing, no-longer -functioning window catches, proof that every room had been converted (but not quite) from some former use.

I am an ace botcher myself. My family calls in a professional if anything needs doing beyond changing a light bulb. They can manage that. A garden, unless I'm kidding myself, is more forgiving. How do you recognize botching unless you know what was really intended?

I don't mean gates tied up with baler twine or roses on old bedsteads. That was the scene here 40 years ago. That style may well be having a renaissance in certain gardening magazines. Old bikes, jam jars, that kind of thing. No, with me it is largely a matter of tools. Some mornings or evenings I march into the tool shed full of resolution, sure that I know just what I'll need. Fork, spade, saw and shears, trowel and twine go in the barrow. I reach the scene of operations and set to when I meet a plant that needs a stake. No stake. Do I retrace my steps? I look around for anything that will serve. I even tie one plant to another, resolving that I'll be back with a stake very soon.

The garden is full of evidence that I've surged through, half-doing a hundred jobs. The mercy is that no one but I will know, and I'll have forgotten.

July

A LIGHT TOUCH

'You garden with a light touch', said a knowing visitor the other day – appreciatively, I hope. Could she have been referring to the complementary campanulas, the aleatory alliums, the volunteer violas and random ranunculus that meet your eye wherever you turn? 'You leave things in; so much nicer than taking them out.'

I do take them out. I've been barrowing opium poppies to the compost for weeks now. The idea is to let them show a first flower or two, decide whether it is a good colour or not, is fully frilly or otherwise desirable, and pull up the ones that have no special quality, in the hope of improving the stock. After years of doing this I admit we aren't getting very far, but I enjoy the process.

The thing to remember is what comes out easily, like the poppies, and what leaves roots in the ground. You can enjoy an allium, even into its seedhead phase, and still get rid of it. Not so an invasive campanula. And violas are the devil to do away with.

But most of the pulling up at the moment is what I think of as busy lizzies of various kinds. I'm not clear about all their identities; only their vigour and the distance they can chuck their seeds. You merely look at the watery-yellow-flowered kind, only a few days old, and it looses off a petulant scatter of seeds. It's lucky I enjoy weeding so much.

August

FISH TALK

We have just moved a dozen mirror carp from the spacious duck pond, which I'm told has far too many, to the much smaller pond with Japanese pretensions, a little rock cascade and a stone lantern, where we can see and enjoy them far better. It has been fascinating watching them deploy in their new quarters. I don't suppose they enjoyed being caught and released. How does a carp convey chagrin? At first they didn't seem to recognize the bread I offered them as an apology. Perhaps they are shortsighted?

Then one of the big ones, perhaps 18 inches long, took a sniff, opened his ugly white lips, gave a noisy slurp and swallowed it. Others paid no attention. The four smallest fish were most timid, staying almost motionless on the bottom of the slightly shallower end. A senior flotilla decided on a station under a bushy willow that shades the deeper part. Sometimes they move to investigate a *Hosta fortunei* whose broad leaves overhang the water, or go and have a sniff at the splashes under the cascade. Their relationships keep me guessing. They can crowd together, swimming at cross-purposes, sometimes bumping but seemingly ignoring one another. They can commune, two or three at a time, evidently in conversation. When one or two of the seniors enter the nursery end, the little 'uns form up and play follow-my-leader for a while.

Considering they were kidnapped at random from a community of hundreds, they are unlikely to have an established hierarchy. They are probably working on that as I write. But there is some sort of organization down there in the murky water. How I'd love to understand it.

BIODIVERSITY

I'm tired of being lectured by every gardening magazine and news-paper article about 'biodiversity'. Most of what they say is frankly patronizing tosh. 'Don't forget to leave some stinging nettles for the butterflies' indeed. I'm afraid it's just not my T-shirt. Mine says: 'Save our planet: it's the only one with chocolate.' Any sense of proportion (let alone humour) has disappeared from the wildlife obsessives who try to scare us into planting 'natives' in our gardens. Is it partly the guilt complex of the urban/suburban gardener who spends 20 times as much on decking and 'water features' than on anything that grows and needs looking after?

Native nature is far from benign. Moorhens are aggressive preda-tors: we no longer have ducklings, and rarely ducks. Herons prey on our fish. Badgers dig us up and seem to have eaten all our hedgehogs. Muntjac, admittedly not native, browse everything up to two feet or so; above that it's roe deer, and above four feet probably red. Pigeons not only eat the crops; they peck the canopies out of trees. Moles destroy the lawns; foxes the hens. Less activity from all these pretty creatures would be welcome – and yet the mantra (in many cases supported by law) is to cheer them on.

Gardening is not a natural activity. It is an effort to take control of nature for a specific aesthetic or economic purpose. To garden well we must learn nature's laws – and then discriminate against the ones that frustrate our purpose. Gardening organizations and publications that put 'biodiversity' first are losing sight of what gardening means.

September

GREEN PROVENCE

It is hard not to worship the vast pale-trunked planes that form an airy canopy over where I am sitting, on the broad terrace of a château in La Provence Verte. They soar up from the croquet lawn 20 feet below, their creamy boles pollarded long ago to divide into five or six great creamy curving limbs, time-stopped fountains of suspended leaves.

A curving double staircase, enclosing a cool splashing water tank, leads down to the lawn. Olive and fig trees screen the vineyards on two sides; on the third the morning light is coloured brilliant apple green by a steep hillside of Aleppo pines.

Stone parapets, box hedges, a few vases of geraniums; those are all the ingredients of a perfect vision of Provence. Or at least of La Provence Verte. What gives this high part of the Var its verdant name? Rolling hills for miles around are clad almost exclusively in the lightest, palest members of the pine tribe. The undergrowth is varied with juniper and prickly little oaks, wild olives and arbutus, rosemary and lavender and spurge. From where I sit I can make out the limestone cliff at the start of one of many limestone gorges – the Vallon Sourn, to give this long craggy cleft in the forest its gloomy name.

Or am I imagining the mood? I always hear the Caribbean 'morne' as 'mourn', when all it means is 'hill'. 'Sourn' may just mean 'deceptive', as the dictionary says. But the sounds of words can colour our feelings, and the shadow of something dire just outside this green heaven seasons its pleasures.

2013

January

DAPHNE ARBORESCENS

There is no light-meter more sensitive than a leaf. Barely two weeks since the shortest day, a mere 12 minutes longer between sunrise and sunset, and there are plants sitting up in their sleeping bags rubbing their eyes. Primroses always seem most alert; their leaves spring to attention as soon as any warmth confirms the change of season. And today, after a frosty night, the air has balm in it and the primroses are opening flowers.

Even if there is proper winter in the forecast, a new year with moderate temperatures gives us a head start. Once the aconites have surfaced, the primroses started, the hellebores pushed up their flower stalks and the snowdrops their spearheads, they won't go back. Catkins are lengthening all around – most spectacularly on *Garrya elliptica* and the proud pyramid of the Turkish hazel, where the first are already a foot long.

We were given a new version of *Daphne bholua* when we went with the International Dendrology Society to Lake Maggiore three years ago; a form simply labelled 'd'Aman' (which is where it comes from). Planted from its tiny pot in the shelter of the big walnut tree on the kitchen lawn, it has already reached two metres, with short branches held close to its trunk – an arborescent look that promises heaven knows what eventual height. It started to flower with the first helle-bores. They say you must be gentle with daphnes, and not cut them too enthusiastically; otherwise we would have a big vase of its ravishing pink flowers in a bower of its shiny green leaves perfuming the house.

S R BADMIN

What is the difference between an artist and an illustrator? There must be one, because practitioners classify themselves in one category or the other. Of course there are artists who couldn't illustrate (a book, let's say) to save their lives, and illustrators whose work will never be called art. But in the middle ground there seem to me to be fine artists who are classified as 'mere' illustrators, suggesting that their calling is in some way inferior. So what is the difference, and which artist (or illustrator) am I thinking of?

I love the work of Stanley (S R) Badmin. He portrayed the English countryside in the 1930s, '40s and '50s with a precision and sympathy that made him, in the best sense, popular. In the days of their enlight-enment, Shell commissioned him to illustrate their marvellous county guides. Many of us learned to see the country through his eyes: par-ticularly the trees. Has anyone understood and recorded the tracery of winter trees, or placed them in context, with such skill?

Does this make him a great artist? The orthodoxy of today insists that an artist should trouble us, excite our consciousness about some-thing beyond mere appreciation of the physical world, or at least make us aware of that old standby, the human condition. Art, as now defined, must induce strong reactions. Any reaction will do, including disgust. Nor does the medium matter: light bulbs are fine; so are turds. Motive, in other words, outweighs competence – by such a margin that mere skill with materials is counted against the protagonist.

There must, therefore, be a new category for people who represent what they observe with skill, care, even inspiration – but don't have pretensions to deeper, or less coherent, meaning. Disturbing their viewers is not their intention. Perhaps illustrators is the term for them. And for great 'illustrators', whose work is beyond mere competence, who are excited or inspired to dare to go further and find or create new convergences of ideas? We used to say 'artists'.

Does this cover it? Illustration stops at a safe point, within our expectations and comprehension. Art finds another dimension expressible only in the meeting of the medium and the subject. When S R Badmin drew a tree, he gave his pencil his understanding of growth. What David Hockney does is not categorically different.

GERTRUDE JEKYLL ON HER ROCK GARDEN

'Nothing is a better lesson in the knowledge of plants than to sit down in front of them, and handle them and look them over just as carefully as possible; and in no way can such study be more pleasantly or conveniently carried on than by taking a light seat to the rock-wall and giving plenty of time to each kind of little plant, examining it closely and asking oneself, and it, why this and why that. Especially if the first glance shows two tufts, one with a better appearance than the other; not to stir from the place until one has found out why and how it is done, and all about it. Of course a friend who has already gone through it all can help on the lesson more quickly, but I doubt whether it is not best to do it all for oneself.'

Take a really good look. Has the case ever been more clearly put?

February

CURIOUS MINDS

How I'd like to be able to claim descent from Jan Johnston. He was a Scottish religious refugee, born in Poland, who became one of the great natural philosophers of his day – a day in which scholarship was a pan-European affair.

He was born of Calvinist parents, when Shakespeare was writing his tragedies; went to school in Poland (where he learned Polish, German,

Greek, Latin and Hebrew) and university in Scotland. At St Andrews, in 1623, he studied philosophy, theology and Hebrew, then went back to Poland to teach, before setting off again to Germany, England and the Netherlands to study the related subjects of botany and medicine.

When he went back to Poland he became a royal tutor, taking three of his students with him on another tour, this time to Denmark, Norway, England, France, Italy and back to Leyden in the Netherlands, where his treatise on fevers earned him the title of Doctor of Medicine. His next journey was to Cambridge and Oxford, then Flanders and Brabant, then Paris, Montpellier and Lyon, then Bologne and Padua.

At the age of 33 he had already visited most of the great universities of Europe. I try to imagine him lugging all his books onto lumbering coaches for another week on the road. He had made his reputation, though. Heidelberg, Leipzig and Leyden all invited him to head their medical faculties. He refused, and settled in Sladwicka in the south of Poland, where he spent the rest of his life writing a series of encyclo-paedias, all in Latin. I have one of them here, his *Dendrographias: Sive Historiae Naturalis de Arboribus et Fruticibus*, published by a famous publisher and engraver, Mathias Messian, at Frankfurt in 1662.

By chance that was the year that John Evelyn read his *Silva*, the first English treatise on trees, to The Royal Society in London – the first scientific paper in the Society's history. Modern tree literature starts here, with two quite different books (Johnston's a catalogue in Latin, Evelyn's essays in English) initiating the study of dendrology.

Why, I wonder, did great minds suddenly converge like this? The science has progressed, through generations of dendrographers adding layer upon layer of experience and knowledge. It has become rather a different business now, with DNA analysis to correct its errors. But still there is a sense in which I can claim descent from J J. We both love looking at and listing trees.

MOVING ON

Only six weeks to go before we move house. There's a lot of memories and emotion tied up in a garden of more than 40 years. I planted most of the now-mature trees; our children grew up here and our grandchildren (three of them at least) will have it registered in their early memories. But no violins, I insist. The trees will grow on, and our successor has already shared some good ideas with us. We can only feel positive, and look forward to our next billet.

There is a contrast. From 12 acres to something like 1,000 square feet is down-sizing (or 'free-upping') as one friend called it. We are moving to a Victorian house in Kensington with a garden which (for the moment at least) stresses the paving element, so competition for space is intense.

I've given up even trying to make a list of plants we simply must take with us. Too many painful decisions, for a start – but also the feeling that it's wrong to hang on. Do I really want to walk around one garden remembering another? If I have discovered that a plant is good, grows well for me, fills a useful role and provides moments of real excitement as it shoots, or buds, or flowers, or when the leaves turn, or even as a winter tuft of hope, I'd like to take it, or a cutting or a wodge in a pot. But not at any price. Nurseries are full of unexplored opportunities.

Thinking about moving, though, has made me remember quite humble commonplace things I rely on and would miss. I was thinking about my favourite campanula, the peach-leaved *C. persicifolia*: what an easy loyal friend it is, self-seeding generously and then, unlike plants that go to ground, hide for the winter and only remind you they're there in spring, outfacing the frosts with a neat evergreen rosette of leaves from which, suddenly and vigorously, its summer spire shoots up. Then what wild-flower beauty it achieves with its clear porcelain bells, either white or a pale bluebell-blue. Just imagining it, on a dire February day, gives me goose pimples of anticipation.

There are flowers I forget between seasons. The snowflake is one; you may think it just a snowdrop with pretensions, but when it rises among and above them with its leaves not grey-blue but bright summer-green, not bashful like the snowdrops but almost brazenly open for business, it feels more like a visiting stranger than the streamside native it is.

March

IN SUSPENSE

This little walnut pedestal desk between the windows has felt the scratching of something like 500 episodes of *Trad* and at least a dozen books. This is its last *Trad*; not mine, I hasten to say. The last furniture leaves the house tomorrow, either for the sale room, our children's houses or (what seems an exiguous amount) our new lodgings in London. A new desk is ready.

In these last few weeks at Saling the weather has conspired to minimize any pains of parting. There has been scarcely an hour when a walk round the garden has not involved boots and scarves, and usually an umbrella too.

It is primroses that prove the heroes of a recalcitrant winter. Since they first pricked up their green ears in late December they have slowly spread their clumps, bulked up and opened a few flowers regardless of what sort of day it is. On the corner of the moat they have formed a small pale pool under the low branches of a wild myrobalan plum, whose little white stars in a vase in the hall look almost shockingly Japanese.

Hellebores are not easily discouraged; rather the boot is on the other foot – I'm discouraged from going out to consult their bashful down-turned flowers. *Daphne bholua* keeps going in good heart, but the fact that I am still talking about it on the eve of the equinox proves how stuck we are.

Even that most unfailing and beautiful harbinger, the weeping willow, has yet to show its peeping pale-green leaves. We have forced a reluctant white *Ribes* to open its flowers in the house. *Spiraea thunbergii* is brightening with tiny points of green; look carefully at the Japanese maples and you can see their pairs of tiny buds are swelling hints of energy to come.

But frost visits every night, followed by fog every morning. No balm tempts us out even at midday. There seem mercifully few reasons to dally.

April

DEEP BOSCAGE

Our new house is entirely surrounded by trees. We haven't seen it in summer yet, but as spring arrives I am starting to realize that the delicate curtains of twigs and branches have only one meaning: leaves will blot out any sight of the London around us.

It certainly wasn't my intention, tree-crazy as I am. Most trees are best seen at a little distance, not in your face. Our front yard is completely filled and canopied by a pink *Magnolia × soulangeana*, just now in full flower and, between you and me, really rather flashy. The neighbour's is similarly full of a weeping tree, as yet unidentified. In the street outside stands one of a row of extremely vigorous native cherries (an odd choice, surely, for a street tree). The houses opposite will disappear for seven or eight months of the year.

At the back, one neighbour of our 18-foot-wide garden has a flourishing walnut, the other a tall bay tree, and we boast a magnificent specimen of that bane of London gardeners, a sycamore, reputedly a hundred years old and definitely a fixture. Its wonderfully scaly trunk is six or seven feet round and the branches, not improved in elegance by constant lopping, blot out the next houses and what's left of the sky.

So it's gardening in the shade. Margery Fish, here I come.

WHIZZ ... IT'S GONE

Recorded history divides naturally into eras that can be defined by how the recording happened. For millennia, memory was alone. Memory was made redundant (or at least optional) by writing, later supplemented by illustration. Illustration became cheaper and more available with engraving. Then, barely 200 years ago, along came photography. We have seen the participants in, for example, the Crimean War almost as they saw each other. By the end of the 19th century came the movie; we are fully acquainted with the (rather jerky) movements of our forebears. Then speed becomes the essence of communication: in increasingly rapid succession we have the Telex and its relatives, then move on to the fax machine.

If I/we thought the fax was a lasting record of our communications we were wrong. I have just been sorting and filing my correspondence of 50-odd years. I had to be drastic. I read or skimmed everything I had filed over the half-century, bent on keeping 20 percent at most. When I came to the fax years, though, there were no decisions to take: the pages were faded to blankness; nothing was left.

So many of us had abandoned pen and paper already when email arrived. With it the succeeding eras of communication reached a precipice. Most of what passes between us now whizzes off into the ether ... what is it? Where is it? Is there any permanent record at all, anywhere, of the thoughts and messages that link most of us today?

TREES W8

There are cars circulating in London at the moment, scattering petals as they go from the accumulation on their roofs. The odds are they come from Kensington. The royal borough is blossom-crazy, with sometimes spectacular, sometimes frankly garish results. I hadn't realized, I confess, before it became my borough, what an arboretum of street trees it contains, or what a show they make in April and May.

The theme tree in our street is our native double white cherry, *Prunus avium* 'Plena'. It was one of our favourite trees at Saling, a sumptuous white cloud in April and as prettily motley as cherries get in autumn. There must be 20 in the street here, ranging from craggy old veterans to novices planted only last year. The disadvantage of cherries in pavements is the way their roots emerge from the ground as writhing monsters – as gardeners know only too well. I wrote a while ago about the ludicrous planting of the Avenue de Champagne, that noble address in Epernay, as an arboretum. When local authorities hire enthusiasts, people who love trees too much, I fear this is the result.

When I first saw the bare weeping tree in our neighbour's garden I took it for another cherry. Now it is in leaf I am thrilled to see it is the exceedingly beautiful and rather rare weeping Katsura, *Cercidiphyllum japonicum* 'Pendulum' – so pendulous, indeed, that its branches would reach the ground without regular lopping. Passers-by walk under a beautiful green parasol over the pavement. Its little heart-shaped leaves are now a brilliant tender green. In autumn it will turn everything from cream to scarlet – and the street will have that warm sweet elusive scent of strawberry jam.

There are some almost-avenues in neighbouring streets, with the trees correctly uniform on both sides. Ours, though, is a bit of a muddle. There are two old planes, a couple of limes, two hornbeams, a scattering of the default street tree today, *Pyrus* 'Chanticleer', and (horror) what looks very like the dreadful *Prunus* 'Amanogawa', that pink scarecrow from Japan.

May

HIS VOICE IS SILENT

To Strawberry Hill to see the progress of the restoration of Horace Walpole's riverside summerhouse. Is any house more famous and so little known? The reverend fathers who took care of it for so long loved it dearly and defended it well, but they had no money to restore its glories. Now some inspired fund-raising, boosted by a handsome Heritage grant, has set the wheels in motion. The results, sticking as faithfully as possible to Walpole's plans, tell us almost as much about him as his irresistible letters do.

Riverside, alas, the garden is no more, although the river has not gone away. The 200 yards between Walpole's raised terrace walk and the Thames have inevitably been filled with houses. Of the 40-odd acres of garden and park, originally in open countryside, some four remain. We know enough about Walpole's planting to reproduce some of it: young lime trees in serried rows already begin to form the *patte d'oie* whose alleys lead to his favourite bay window. One oak survives from Walpole's time on the terrace walk. More trees serve to screen the college buildings that could easily be uncomfortably close neighbours.

Inside, he achieved a truly wonderful deep brilliant guardsman-red with a wall-covering of silk mixed with the wool of a particular Cumbrian breed of sheep. The wool is so springy that even in a weave there are no reflecting surfaces. The scarlet in unremitting purity has no highlights to help your eye to focus. Your gaze buries itself in pure colour.

All this red is set off by intricate gilding: a throne room could hardly be more dazzling – and there are more intimate rooms where gilding traces a sort of Medieval allegro above your head. There is not yet much furniture, nor very many books in Walpole's famous library. The greatest want, though, I felt, as we explored, was the voice of the man himself. Perhaps an actor with a suitably camp voice could pronounce Walpole's commentary as he opened each door to reveal his latest jeu d'esprit. 'Gloomth' was famously one of the effects he aimed to create. He loved to pass from gloomth to brilliance. Where you do, from the grey Gothic corridors to the long gallery upstairs, you blink – just as he intended.

REVISION

I was nervous about going back to Saling Hall. Our successor there is a man of action, and I knew he would waste no time before tackling his new project. But what I saw when I went back last week amazed me – and made me realize how long I had let things drift.

Judy and I had often talked about felling the long file of Lombardy poplars that flanked the front of the house, memorable trees (they were planted in the 1930s) that contained the front courtyard, separating it visually from the churchyard next door. Last week they had gone. A loader was shifting their immense logs onto a pile bigger than a bus. The sense of light and air around the pink brick façade of the house was extraordinary. The rather gloomy presence of the towering trees was replaced by the broad green dome of a wild service tree I planted in the churchyard in 1973, looking in perfect harmony with the grey flint and gothic windows of the church. It was our predecessor, Lady Carlyle, who wanted to hide the churchyard from the bedroom window (so we were told). Her poplars had gradually become the main feature – and to see them gone gave me a gush of relief, delight ... feelings I could have experienced years ago if I had been more resolute. 'The axe is my pencil', said Humphry Repton. Knowing when to fell trees is as vital as knowing which ones to plant.

Not only the poplars are gone. Boring Lawson cypresses I should have condemned 20 years ago (but didn't, on the pretext that they were shelter from the cold east wind) are there no more. Old pollard bat willows have gone from the moat (I'm not so convinced about these); a dozen old friends – or at least acquaintances – are piles of firewood. There is less muddle, and less mystery too. Over the years our gardens create their own untouchable auras. Nostalgia feeds on inertia and vice versa. Seeing radical change, and knowing it was necessary, is exciting, surprisingly emotional, but broadly positive.

June

ROTHSCHILDS IN THE WOODS

Exbury, a garden that shows off its astonishing collection of plants like a museum, was largely the creation of Lionel de Rothschild in the 1920s. The Rothschild style is full-on; what J C Loudon would have called gardenesque. If Nature never made sylvan glades with smooth straight hedges, still less did it fill woods to the brim with a kaleidoscope of flowers of different species and varieties in the full spectrum of colours.

Exbury gains its dignity from its high vault of towering trees – above all oaks – that moderate light and temperature in their shade. It revels in the excitable showmanship of the Victorians –the Rothschild style, in fact, indoors or out. You see it at Waddesdon Manor in the rich recipe of Gainsboroughs and Versailles furniture and the extravagant full-dress bedding of the parterres. In the New Forest it takes the form of a dazzling display of rhododendrons, azaleas, camellias and every flowering plant and tree that can be fitted into 220 acres of immaculate woodland – along with the smartest of miniature steam railways.

Perhaps its high point, for this romantic gardener, is where after a sustained passage of ravishing camellias the flower power moderates, the trees thin out, and glimpses of sparkling water allow you to see white sails gliding by. You are, after all, on the Beaulieu River, the Solent is round the corner, and there is that faint smell of salt in the air.

POTTED ON

You see the plant you've been looking for growing lustily in a big pot in a nursery sales bed. You pay the five-litre premium, you take it home, dig the hole, add the fertilizer, knock the plant out of the pot – and a meagre little root comes out in a cascade of fresh compost. It happened to me again yesterday. The guilty nursery was Wisley. There should be a decent delay after repotting for plants to fill their pots again before they are offered for sale.

SWEET HOME

Our new garden is precisely one-536th the size of the old one. It means a totally different relationship with your plants, a new regime, which could (strangely) become hectically intense, a change down into a very low gear indeed, needing frantic pedalling.

My night thoughts at Saling Hall wandered round the acres enjoying, or dissatisfied with, trees or groups of trees, concerned with blanket-weed in a pond or when to cut some long grass. Spring (specially this year) unfolded week by week over a good three months. You could go off for a week without missing anything vital.

Here, in contrast, I will start awake with a brainwave: the shoot heading up the wall could be tied in a foot to the left; I could remove a couple of leaves to make room for that flower; the pot of lavender would get more sun on a higher step. It's a hectic little microcosm, held artificially in some sort of equilibrium by constant adjustments and daily doling out of water, dowsing one plant and letting another go thirsty to toughen it up. I know the greenfly (there are currently three) by name and take a magnifying glass to a spot of mildew. If anything gets out of hand, in other words, I have only myself to blame.

What does our little domain contain? We are still finding out. It has three levels, descending to the kitchen and the shady little patio outside it. The levels are important – and intriguing; the far quarter of the garden (the part that gets most sun) is raised up five steps, fenced off by a stone balustrade, in some ways looking like the poop deck of (shall we say) a frigate. It stands several feet higher than the surrounding gardens beyond its grey-brick walls. How this happened it's hard to say, except that it was a long time ago; our massive sycamore grows at this level, and you can't alter the ground level round a tree.

In any case the poop gives a good view towards the back of the house, which in turn has a ground-floor balcony, so at each end there is a comprehensive view, as from a hill into a valley. (See, my delusions have started already.) A relatively broad path leads up the centre, edged with box. Its stone matches the grey London brick of the walls. It widens in the centre to make room for a table, pots, a Mr Spit-Face splashing into a tiny basin. Whenever it was built (I suppose in the 1970s) it was done well, with good materials. The walls are trellised to nine feet or so and carry a green load of ivy, climbing hydrangeas, roses, honeysuckle and jasmine.

It is a well-furnished box, into which I plan to pack all sorts of joys. We have ordered the greenhouse. There won't be room to even tickle a cat.

July

A FRIEND, A BOOK AND A GARDEN ...

... that was the title Tom Stuart-Smith gave to a Literary Festival organized by the Garden Museum in the Stuart-Smith's garden last weekend. The timing was propitious: only the second weekend this year when a festival in a garden had no need for umbrellas. Saturday was warm and partly sunny, Sunday was a proper summer day. We needed the shade of the tent for the lectures that were the centrepiece; a tent you discovered within beech hedges in the heart of a garden as lovely, and in as beautifully timed perfection, as I could imagine. So beautifully timed, in fact, that groups of flowers that had been in promisingly imminent bud on the first day showed their colours to the sun on the second.

The garden crests a modest ridge in a corner of Hertfordshire miraculously preserved from new towns and motorways, sheltering among its high hedges, then suddenly bursting out into a long view over fields and woods. There are few gardens these days where perennials hold sway: here not in conventional borders but in great plats 30 feet or so across and deep. Their early summer costume is predominantly cream and white and a dozen shades of purply blue; in one room shading into pale pink, in another into stronger yellows – but in gentle transitions that only dawn on you as you rest your eyes on the whole panorama.

The Festival unfolded in the same seamless way, moving from the fundamentals of garden philosophy to depths of practical experience, represented by Piet Oudolf, the blunt authoritative Dutch designer who has made the whole world plant grasses. No grasses could be more beautiful, though, than the rippling filigree of the meadows round the garden we were in.

Christopher Woodward, the museum's hyper-energized director, pursued the vision of Arcadia with Adam Nicholson – himself a practitioner of moving prose. Sue Stuart-Smith spoke with extraordinary insight on the therapeutic properties of gardening, Hugh Cavendish talked about Holker, his Cumbrian estate, Sarah Raven about Vita Sackville-West. Anna Pavord talked to John Sales, Penelope Hobhouse to Tom Stuart-Smith ... the cast was exceptional and there wasn't time to hear them all.

There was music, there were oysters; when night fell, the colours of the garden deepened and glowed and a slow river of pale smoke rose vertically from the barbecue fire. It was an ambitious event that succeeded to perfection. How lucky we were to be there. The museum that does this deserves massive support.

SUN vs SHADE

The question becomes acute in summer: which would you rather have, a sunny garden or a shady one? The majority view is understandably for sun. 'South-facing garden' is a selling point. In town gardens you may have no choice. Our house is on the north side of an east–west street, the right house but the wrong garden? We had our doubts, but not any more – at least in summer, when it matters most. The summer sun starts the day peering over the eastern wall and finishes it beaming over the western one. The garden side of the house stays cool and the garden gets plenty of light. We are also blessed to have a tall tree in our neighbour's plot to the west. We have dappled light on a sunny day in the centre of ours. Unfortunately the tree is a walnut, a beautiful dome of leaves on a smart grey trunk, but a hailstorm of green nuts in early summer and a constant rain of half-chewed, half-ripe ones when the squirrels move in (they're never far away).

As to plants in the shade, our predecessors took the view that box was the only thing. We are trying everything my favourite advisor, dear old Brigadier Lucas Phillips, advises. His *Modern Flower Garden* is never far from the top of my book heap despite being 45 years old.

The hydrangeas are just coming on, the blue ones from Saling that I christened Len Ratcliff after our benefactor have pride of place: four big pots around the central (to use a grand term) piazza where we sit. The Brig says all campanulas tolerate shade. My favourite, *C. persicifolia* certainly does. The pelargoniums in pots need promoting to the sunniest part at the far end. The roses on the walls (I don't know all their names yet, but I know I don't like 'Fragrant Cloud') are doing fine – high up above the wall. The scarlet *Fuchsia boliviana*, a standard in a pot, has been brilliant. Runner beans have been a disaster; being late I bought plants and failed to read the word dwarf (in dwarf type) on the label. So my poles are bare, with a few ludicrous plants at the bottom. What, I ask, is the point of a dwarf runner bean when the whole point is their climbing?

We're experimenting with agapanthus. The plants we ordered at Chelsea have just arrived, with one flower bud each, seriously pot-bound. They've gone into deep gravel and old manure, watered every night until they get going. Not everything is perfect. We don't like a couple of the established roses; but how do you change them? Could one cut them down and bud onto the base? A *Fuchsia magellanica* has some lurgy that eats away its lower leaves, turning them brown – so presumably not a slug. There are lots of snails, but also the friendliest blackbirds and robin. Yes, on balance the shady life is a sweet one.

SUR MER

We're just back from a seaside holiday, this year perfectly timed for two weeks of perfect summer, when simmering in London is not the connoisseur's choice. The temperature on the Solent, with a steady westerly breeze over Christchurch Bay, was 5° C lower than on the commons of the New Forest five miles inland. I am discovering the pleasures of a seaside garden – not, I'm glad to say, one totally exposed to wind and spray on a beach, but walled and sheltered by the little house, with the sea over the salt marshes at high tide only 60 yards away. The air is heady with the scents of seaweed and saltgrass and tidal mud, and luminous with ocean light.

There is such a rewarding template for seaside gardening that there seems no point in being original. What's wrong with hydrangeas and montbretia and fuchsias and thrift? But drought can be a serious worry; the soil is basically sand and gravel and shingle, and rain often seems to skip the beach to fall inland.

When we arrived I had the deep joy of watering a parched garden. I turned the rusty tap on the water butt and heard the jangling of stored life and energy that had only been breeding mosquitos. As I watered I was cutting down the top hamper of everything that had flowered and withered. Water and fertilizer would bring a second flowering – or at least a fresh covering of leaves.

The garden is about 40 feet square, two-thirds paved, dedicated more to sunbathing and guzzling seafood than to horticulture. It has a campsis-choked pergola but otherwise no shade; apart from one raised bed the planting has almost all been low-growing. The house wall supports a climbing hydrangea; there are capabilities here.

At first I thought of a tree, maybe a pine, in the central brick-edged bed. Then I remembered a plant I was given by Cedric Morris in Suffolk many years ago; almost the only woody plant, as I remember, in his great open iris beds, a shrub growing perhaps two metres high with a propensity to sucker – could this be why he gave it away so freely? It is *Elaeagnus commutata* or silverberry, a North American native used for its nitrogen-fixing abilities in dreadful soil.

In the narrow garden facing the sea I have planted agapanthus and *Hydrangea quercifolia* – a favourite in my daughter's Riviera garden where it grows huge, flowers wonderfully and colours like a furnace in autumn. I don't expect such a performance in Hampshire. It drank the water from the butt like a desert traveller, though.

August

HOW TO CHOOSE YOUR HOUSE

It was the nursery that clinched it. We were house-hunting in London in March, in the dreary grey weeks when the East wind blew unrelenting day after day. One house had ticked the boxes only to be taken off the market; others were laughably unsuitable in various ways. One icy day we visited a house in a street we didn't know at all, to be welcomed into warm, well-lit, totally comfortable surroundings, decorated (said my wife) rather like an old-fashioned luxury hotel. Yes, I said, we could live here without even talking to a builder – though a chat with a decorator would be good. 'It's not really us', said Judy.

Next day she went back on her own to case the unfamiliar neighbourhood. Yes, there were cafés, cleaners, a Waitrose, delis – and just across the main road, only 100 metres from the front door of the house under discussion, a flower shop occupying the ground floor of a rambling old house. Inside, the scent of flowers was intoxicating. It was instant spring – and led, through the back door, into an Aladdin's garden, wintry though it was, of potted plants, potted trees, potted shrubs … an entire nursery. Narrow paths under tall planes lead the length of a film-set Georgian square – all nursery. She had found Rassells. We bought the house.

Rassells nursery, in Earls Court Road, goes back to the days when the road was a country lane leading to Holland House through Lord Kensington's farmland. His lordship, apparently, started to lease his fields to developers to pay his gambling debts (this was the early 19th century). His old lodge house on Earls' Court Lane he leased to a nurseryman, and in 1870 Henry Rassell from Sussex came on the scene. In 1897 he acquired the freehold of Pembroke Square (everyone else had to make do with a lease), opened his florist's shop, and started the business which is still there. I pop in for something almost every day – if only for the sight and smell of hundreds of happy plants.

IN MERIONETH

However much I look forward to a visit to our Welsh woods I am still amazed by the way they lift my spirits. What can I compare it to? A moment in music when you can't contain your urge to sing. Finding a fresh breeze on the beam that fills your sails and starts the water running noisily past. A first sip of champagne, indeed.

Entering the woods, feeling the powerful presence of the trees, breathing their unnameable smell, tracing in the seeming chaos of leaves the unalterable patterns of each tree's growth, the cool of their shade, the brilliance of their green, I am lifted onto another level of living and forget everything else. I become a forest creature.

Each time I visit a plot we have planted in the past 15 years or so I am shocked by the extent of new growth. We were here in June, when new shoots were just sketches of the picture to come. Three months later, two dimensions have become three, every tree has added maybe five percent to its height, but ten percent to its volume. The same space is even more overflowing with life.

A forest without paths is like a room without doors. Opening tracks and keeping them open is a forester's first concern. Brambles, bracken, gorse and birch saplings block your way it seems almost overnight. One of the great joys is carving a clearing to let yourself in. It's wonderful what a neighbour's big tractor will do.

And an excursion from this demi-paradise? To a true fantasy just up the road, the 'Italian' seaside village of Portmeirion, a Celtic Portofino with an impish sense of humour. Clough Williams-Ellis turned his romantic imaginings into reality here in this heavenly setting in the 50 years between the 1920s and '70s. Walt Disney must be mad with envy. Around his crazily eclectic all-sorts of campaniles and Cornish cottages, memories of Portugal and Wales and heaven knows where, C W-E planted every plant that loves mild seaside air, a whole wood full of wonders, and hydrangeas in thousands.

I come home to our workaday woods with my head full of plans that will come to nothing. Of a little New Zealand or a Sintra, a Santa Barbara indeed of exotic shrubs and flowers. Sheer folly. Nothing could be lovelier than the forest around me.

September

THREE-QUARTERS OF A SPAN

Autumn never announced its arrival more clearly than by today's damp chill after two days of almost unprecedented late summer sun. We have had our little garden sprinklers on every night for weeks; without them I'm sure there would have been no growth in the garden at all. The climbers thick on the walls (and the roses thrusting six feet above them) suck all the water from the ground. I don't grudge it, but I must replace it.

Meanwhile preparations are afoot for our new greenhouse. They started in May when we cleared the biggest bed in the garden (be under no delusion; it's tiny), digging out that bilious-yellow-leaved spirea, a red-leaved maple, a clapped-out pittosporum and a tall hibiscus. The hibiscus is doing well on intensive care in another spot. A neighbour accepted the maple; the rest went on a skip. We had to remove 80 bags of soil (through the house, of course) to lower the ground level for the future greenhouse. The plot has been filled with potatoes, runner beans, courgettes and salads for the summer. Now comes the prospect of building the base for the house, due to arrive in November.

It is a little gem of an aluminium greenhouse from Alitex; three-quarters of a span, the third quarter resting on the western garden wall. With its finials and its little spiky ridge it will look (we hope) as Victorian as if it came with the house, but need minimum upkeep. There are quite a few plants in pots waiting impatiently for its arrival before winter sets in.

———— October ————

OH DEER

The deer are nibbling the grass just outside the window as I write. Two does and a faun that can't be more than a few days old. Four more, with one buck, are showing their white backsides as they graze the meadow 100 yards off. They don't know it, but they've just won an argument. The broad meadow below the house, 18 acres dipping down to the Lymington River, will be theirs. Their private park. My foolish idea of a landscaped arboretum goes in the bin.

Young trees and deer don't mix. I learned the lesson the hard way in France years ago, when my landscaping ambitions were foiled again and again by game of various kinds. Red deer are more formidable than roe deer, and boar worse than either to a tree-planter and dabbler in streams and ponds. At Saling Hall we had a few visitors and – far worse – muntjac, but managed to handle them on our 12 acres. Here in the New Forest there seems no point. Indeed the deer *are* the point – originally of the whole forest.

And would a meadow dotted with new trees, however interesting or rare or fiery in autumn, really be more beautiful than a little green park with deer and the few scattered old oaks we have here? Certainly not so appropriate. We (that is our daughter's family) have a splendid piece of old oak woodland above the meadow. Gentle thinning of the big trees (and clearing of ponticum) will give us forest fringes to adorn with a few new trees I will have to choose with maximum deliberation and protect with scrupulous care. And I shall have much more time to enjoy the wildlife.

I LIKE FLOWERS

Now that the squirrels have almost finished chewing the walnuts on our neighbour's tree and dropping the remains on our garden, they are starting on our pots of bulbs. I have been planting pots in anticipation of the greenhouse we are excitedly expecting in a week or two, using what is left of our collection of wonky old handmade ones. (I scan old garden sheds, greenhouses and shops selling bric-à-brac wherever I go, hoping to find these increasingly rare veterans.)

Narcissus seem to be the squirrels' first choice, with *Iris reticulata* also popular and snowdrops an acceptable snack. Do tulip bulbs have less scent, or is it because I plant them deeper that they have (so far) been relatively unscathed?

The brick base of the greenhouse is all ready, a (very) minor masterpiece in reclaimed London stocks in their characteristic medley of soft colours: yellow, pink and grey. It is already hard to distinguish from the surrounding garden walls. The bricklayer who built it is from Croatia; a gentle smiling man with not much English. When I told him how I intended to fill it with flowers, he said 'I like this job. I like flowers very much. At home I have flowers everywhere; in the hall, in the kitchen, on the walls. People say I am like a woman.'

FUTURE BAGS

How carelessly, casually, unthinkingly did I once chuck armfuls, wheelbarrow loads, whole branches on the bonfire. How slowly, thoughtfully, with what infinite pains did I spend this afternoon dissecting, dividing, dismembering my prunings with secateurs to cram them into the council's black plastic bags.

It is the difference between the country garden and the urban one. There are no big gestures in a garden shorter than a cricket pitch and no wider than a front parlour. Nor in a garden whose only outlet is the exiguous all-purpose corridor between the back stairs and the front door.

There are compensations, though. Town gardening, I've decided, is like putting on reading glasses. The foreground is enlarged, the distance blurred. But the object of your attention appears in such clarity of detail that it can occupy your mind like a whole landscape. Is this what William Blake meant when he saw 'a world in a grain of sand'?

Today's job was reducing a climbing hydrangea that was blocking the eastern light from the new verandah, the library and the kitchen. They are powerful climbers, equipped for tall trees and long branches, their brown wood stout and flexible, their foliage dense and their flower heads many, copious and intricate. Structurally they are composed of multiple right angles or near-right angles, each ready to snag a plastic film. The only way to fill a bag with them is to chop them into little bits. By the end of three bags I know their anatomy intimately. *Hydrangea petiolaris* is more than a mere acquaintance now.

I look round the garden, the falling leaves, the growing climbers, the old growth to be cleared away – not to mention the tree to be pollarded – and see a future of black plastic bags stretching away to the distance like crows on a telephone wire.

November

PLUS ÇA CHANGE

There is endless sustenance and comfort to be found in old gardening magazines. Sustenance, because the ideas and answers flow seamlessly down the generations. Comfort, for the same reason. My resource on a gloomy November afternoon for many years has been *The Gardener's Magazine*, 'conducted' from 1826 to 1848 by the apparently unwearying J C Loudon in the intervals between writing his majestic encyclopaedias.

I picked up the volume for 1838 this afternoon. Gardeners' concerns 175 years ago were very similar to ours, but their candour and freedom of expression very different. In the September issue is an illustrated (with engravings) article on the Duke of Bedford's garden, just up the road from here on Camden Hill. One year into Queen Victoria's reign it is already the epitome of Victoriana: a restless mass of geometrical planting in the brightest colours, intensely gardenesque (to use Loudon's coinage) except for an orchard of 50 trees on the south slope. Every plant is enumerated in the engravings and its name and colour listed. It is in every sense a dazzling list.

In November, though, comes the critique, something no modern magazine would ever publish. Poor Duke, and poor Mr Craie, his gardener. Mr Glendinning of Bicton, having avowed that his 'few observations are by no means intended to detract from the praise that is so justly his due', lambasts both the design and the cultivation. 'The shrub with the spherical lumpy head', he writes, 'appears like an enormous hedgehog.' The beds are too close together, the paths are wrongly designed, and he 'strongly objects' to placing pots with plants in them on walls. He 'cannot see what business they have there.'

In the same spirit of candour the Conductor reviews front gardens, or 'street gardens' as he calls them. He strolls through Brighton commenting on the residents' efforts. No 15 Marlborough Place gets the thumbs up for 'no more than two square yards' containing 'dark- and light-flowered nasturtiums, Convolvulus major and mignonettes.' Nos 16 and 17 York Place seem to win his gold medal for their 'very select planting' in which *Lobelia gracilis*, *Anagallis coccinea grandiflora* and verbenas 'make a conspicuous appearance'. 'The pyramids of heartseases were remarkably fine.' Loudon even tasted one gardener's potatoes and thoroughly approved of their 'flavour and mealiness'. If a front garden was not up to scratch Loudon was not unkind; he moved on, but a ducal garden was apparently fair game. Today? The rule seems to be *De hortuis nil nisi bonum*.

Mr Craie, that same duke's gardener, had some ingenious tricks. Does this one make sense? To preserve a tender rose bush, in this case *R*. 'Lamarque', he budded a hardy rose near the tips of its branches. The yellow Lamarque survived the dreadful winter of 1837/38 thanks to *R*. 'Brennus', a crimson rose, being budded on the year before. 'Brennus flowered first, luxuriantly, and was followed by Lamarque, which also flowered well, though the latter, in all cases where the shoots were not budded, was killed back by the frost. It thus appears that the vigorous growth of the scion had thrown the Lamarque stock into a state of vigorous growth at a time when the Lamarque would otherwise have been quite dormant.' Does this make sense? Was it hardier because it was in growth? Does anyone do this today? I plunge back into my dusty old leather volume, eager for more horticultural history.

December

PRECIOUS STONE

It is typical of our national taste in gardening that a rockery is a place to grow plants we categorize as suitable and appropriate – rather than a place to admire rocks. Rock-worship is something bizarre and eccentric indulged in by the Chinese (craggy rocks, usually on end) and the Japanese (smooth rocks, often lying down), while we pursue our obsession with flowers and leaves.

Tell English gardeners that a warlord of 1,000 years ago took the garden rocks of his defeated rival as trophies, transporting them to his own garden miles away, and they will roll their eyes. 'And pine trees', you add, and faint comprehension dawns. Trees are plants. Excessive, perhaps, and impractical, but moving plants, even as booty, is something we understand. When we incorporate stone in our gardens, and not as a support for 'alpine' plants, we cut and dress it into architectural forms.

We do recognize menhirs. A fine standing stone has a place in our culture. One of the finest (I claim, with no modesty at all) is the rock I carried from North Wales to our old garden at Saling Hall. In its height (nearly nine feet), its texture (grey granite patterned with lichens that vary from light green to dull orange with the seasons), the frozen flow of its formation and the cragginess of its top, like a distant summit, it draws visitors like a splendid sculpture – and stays indelibly in my mind.

ST LUCY'S DAY

There were reputedly nine hours of daylight today, the shortest day of the year. It didn't feel like it. We opened the curtains on a pale-looking night lit by street lamps, and closed them again a good hour before tea. I was out, or at my desk, for the admittedly bright and breezy middle of the day; not, in other words, able or in the frame of mind to contemplate the garden. I did spend a happy half-hour absorbed in the greenhouse, swept leaves and tied up a climbing rose. The thrill of the day was finding a remarkably precocious camellia, just one pale-pink, complex and rose-like flower, on the old bush we inherited with the garden. A *sasanqua*, I wondered, flowering before Christmas? No, I think, just an impatient *japonica* – rewarded for its haste by pride of place on the kitchen table.

But I love contemplating; spending quiet quarter-hours with only my eyes engaged. Last thing at night (especially after good wine) I can gaze into the fire for an hour – even at the repetitive flames of our faux-coal gas fire. In our country garden it was a family joke how father dawdled away the dusk until on a dark night he had to grope his way indoors.

The garden is a different place at night, and with nights as long as they are in mid-winter, it is a place to explore. There are certainly lights to be seen: the yellow rectangles of neighbours' windows, the bright pricking of a plane (or is it a satellite?), the moon intermittent through gauzy clouds, the reflection of a street light off a wall, the red light on the tip of a towering crane three streets away in Holland

Park. They make a picture of sorts, eye-catchers in the black landscape of bare branches and gables against the sky, the backdrop to the dark foreground of plants and structures I know so well but can't see.

I switch on the garden lights and the deliberate theatricality comes as a shock. We inherited the lights, too, from our American predecessors in the house. They shine down from higher or lower on the walls, a dozen of them, throwing little pools of light, some half-obscured by evergreens, on the paths and steps. I have moved one to spotlight the monumental (or so it appears at night) trunk of our centenarian sycamore. They could be better planned, be changed to LED, and no doubt in expert hands make the garden look almost glamorous. But I think I'd rather have something more mysterious to contemplate.

2014

January

ENGAGEMENT OF ANOTHER KIND

What is a dilettante? Someone to be admired, scorned or pitied? Would you admit to, or maybe claim, the title? We had a lively debate about it the other night, one friend taking the fashionable view that it means uncommitted, non-serious, even amateur (and is therefore to be condemned). My view is pretty much the opposite: that it implies commitment of another sort, passionate interest rather than professional duty.

It depends on the context, of course: in medical matters we hope for certainty and rely on the apparatus of peer-reviewing. An amateur surgeon would not find many customers. In a different field (planning matters concerning historic buildings are on my mind at present) the common sense and taste that an experienced dilettante can bring can be far more valuable than the callow judgements of a professional planner.

It is not uncommon for the long-brewed plans of an owner and his architect, arrived at after years of study of a site, its surroundings, its history and natural conditions, to be rejected – or certainly (almost inevitably) modified – by an individual who has no background knowledge of the matter. 'I would prefer the door to be here', or the window to be a casement, or a wall to be lower or higher, is a common, and completely outrageous, statement.

Outrageous because this individual's opinion automatically acquires the authority of law. But I don't recommend questioning the qualifications, the judgement or even the bona fides of a planning officer. Seduction is more likely to produce the required result.

So yes, I am happy to call myself a dilettante – a word that means simply one who delights. A set of young aristocrats who made the Grand Tour in the mid-18th century (and were probably all at Eton together) met as a club under the name of the Dilettantes. Their inaugural meeting was painted by one of their members, Sir Joshua Reynolds. There are clubs and groups with similar leanings today, but only one claims the delightful name.

And there's another calling that has lost its meaning nowadays: that of the flâneur. A flâneur is one who strolls without intent – except to observe the world. Cornelia Otis Skinner, the author of *Our Hearts Were Young and Gay*, defined a flâneur as a 'deliberately aimless pedestrian, without obligations or sense of urgency, who being French and therefore frugal, wastes nothing, including his time, which he spends with the leisurely discrimination of a gourmet.' The critic Charles Sainte-Beuve called flânerie 'the very opposite of doing nothing'; Baudelaire called him 'the botanist of the sidewalk'.

Need flânerie be limited to sidewalks, though – let alone to the French? How else to describe what I do in someone else's garden?

AFTER MOTHS?

Woke in the night with the scent of a pot of *Iris danfordiae* filling the bedroom. I have never grown this tiny Turk before and was unprepared for its perfume. What insects are such flowers of the winter trying to attract? There are not many, and their scents, it seems to me, have something in common: a trace of honey and a musky facet which can become a little too strong at close quarters. Winter heliotrope and

Viburnum bodnantense are both better at a little distance. There are wines that do this to me; Müller-Thurgau, for instance.

When flowers use their energy to broadcast scent at night can it be moths they are after? Certainly they look eager for visitors; the little yellow irises stand bolt upright like nestlings with their beaks stretched open, beseeching food.

SHARE OF LIGHT

There's a limit to what the council will let you do to your trees in a leafy borough like this one. It has absolute power over the woody leafage. Not the power to plant a tree in your garden, of course, but the power to stop you disposing of it as you see fit. I am stuck, then, with a disproportionate amount of sycamore. I have reservations? A lack of proper respect? My problem: I bought the tree with the house.

In this privileged area, though, even the tree surgeons are a cut above the norms. I googled 'Tree surgeons, Kensington' and stopped at the second name. Not a name to forget easily: Fergus Kinmonth – and one I recognized as a member of the International Dendrology Society and a visitor to our Essex garden. How many dendrologists climb trees with chainsaws? Probably not enough.

Fergus came round and we talked about the two trees which, last summer, kept the sun from touching our garden: the sycamore and the neighbour's walnut. I know they get more than their share of publicity in this diary. But then they take more than their share of a diarist's light.

Tooth-sucking from both of us. 'They'll let you take off the same as last time', said Fergus. 'That's just the tips', said I.

'Precisely. This is a conservation area.'

'So what is it they're conserving?'

'People don't like it when the greenery they see from their windows is removed.'

I'm not keen, either, I admit. But here we have the politician's dilemma: 'If we want things to stay as they are, things will have to change' is not a message that public servants want to hear. So no radical tree surgery; just a snip here and there while the problem grows. Fergus and his team came and snipped – very handsomely and tidily, I must say. Not a twig is left: just a massive black tree-skeleton in the sky, ready to do the same again, plus a little bit – and need painful surgery again in a year or two.

DISPLACED

It has rained every day so far this year in North Wales – a state of affairs more unusual than you might think. The waterfalls are in splendid spate; just now we saw a group of daredevils canoeing down a fearsome sheer drop, free-falling through the spray. Our little river is in that sinister mood when it runs swift and silent, no ripples breaking its swirling surface. And the ground is saturated. I made the mistake of stepping off a hard track to skirt a fallen tree and went in to the top of one welly. Luckily not over the top, or I would have had to abandon it and limp back barefoot, the light quickly fading, half a mile downhill to the car – not a prospect to relish.

Worse, I was effectively lost. We have just clear-felled the spruce and larch on a wide stretch of hillside, and with the trees has gone all my sense of place. I was negotiating what had been a favourite bit of track, where tall trunks framed the first silver glimpses of the sea. Ferns were thick along the path, giving way to deep-green moss and gleaming threads of water under the dark rows of trees. The track turned left here by a flat grey rock to skirt the steepest slope. There was no rock, and no track; just stumps and ruts and snaggy branches higgledy-piggledy everywhere. Getting back down in the dusk was tricky.

Forestry is a messy business: for long years calm, verdant, woken only by the flitting of birds; then suddenly The Somme. The place you knew and loved has ceased to exist. At least I am responsible, or obediently following the cycle of planting and harvesting. Foresters are to blame for the biggest changes anyone can perpetrate on the landscape, eliminating beautiful familiar places at a stroke.

So what is a 'place'? How is it different from a map reference? A place has intelligence; it depends on understanding – of its purpose, its history, of the forces that flow through it. A landscape or garden designer's job, or one of them, is to show you where to cast your eyes, and where to put your feet. There are forces at play in a design: sight-lines and pathways and the interplay between them. They are different in different seasons; winter transparency and summer solidity; the sun lower or higher in the sky; pale shadows and black obliterating ones. Colours, of course, and textures, eye-catchers and passages of restful green or grey.

All these contribute to a sense of place. They give you confidence, explain, perhaps subconsciously, where you are and why, what the gardener wants you to observe and enjoy, where you should go next to be excited or to be soothed into a reverie.

A resourceful gardener controls your mood; invites you to share his own, then changes it. This is the reason for the overwhelming success of garden rooms, of Hidcote and Sissinghurst and their many imitators. Great gardeners do it by suggestion, by modulating scale and colour, enclosing you or letting your eyes roam free, splashing water about or letting it reflect the sky: there are a thousand ways.

The forest will grow again – but it will be a different place.

February

ENTER THE BOX MOTH

One person says La Mortola is on the way up; the next visitor says it's worse than ever. It's been like this since the 1980s, when a posse of busybodies, largely from the RHS (I was one, but the one that counted was the much-admired Director of Wisley, Chris Brickell), took action. The staff at this famous garden, the creation of the same Hanbury family that gave the RHS the land for Wisley, had gone on strike. The Hanburys had sold the property to the Italian state, little thinking what a mess Italian bureaucracy can make. What had been one of the world's best subtropical gardens, a superb botanical collection on the borders of Italy and France, at the very point where the Alps collapse into the sea, so steep and sea-surrounded that frost never comes, was a weedy chaos under soaring palms and cypresses and far rarer trees.

On my first visit, the striking gardeners were camping in a cave-mouth near the monumental entrance. Negotiations followed, with British botanists setting new standards for organization and mainte-nance. Eventually the University of Genoa took responsibility. The question is, how are they doing?

The other day I was pleasantly surprised. The garden covers 44 acres. You can't expect perfection. But the most exceptional parts, collections of succulents and cycads in particular, are well weeded, cultivated and surprisingly well labelled. The whole garden looks in good health – even the lower reaches towards the sea where the citrus orchard is criss-crossed with pergolas. There are areas of long grass and weeds, but no dereliction.

There was one black moment, though: the discovery of a new (to me) and horrific predator on the box plants. It is a moth (*Cydalima perspectalis*) and its yellow, black-spotted caterpillar which gobbles box leaves and shoots until the plant is bare. 'Piralide' is its vernacular name. It arrived in Europe three or four years ago, in Italy last year, and has (as you have guessed) no authorized treatment. One French gardener I know has gone on a spraying course to be ready for action, but the red flag is hoisted. What will it make of our island's weather, and miles and miles of box hedges, I wonder?

CACTUS COUTURE

The Riviera experiments with succulents; Morocco glories in them. In Marrakech, 1,000 miles further south, the world of cacti and agaves, euphorbias and all the swollen desert-dwellers is a play-ground for gardeners' wildest imaginings. It seems they like fat living after all, these prickly things that look so ferocious on the edge of survival in wind-blown wastes. In the gardens of French couturi-ers and Italian tycoons, a cactus can be voluptuous and its spines fashion statements.

The Jardin Majorelle in the heart of Marrakech was the work of the painter Jacques Majorelle more than 70 years ago. Its survival, and its present state as an attraction drawing 700,000 visitors a year, is due to the late Yves St Laurent. Nurture at this level of precision is something I associate with Japan rather than Africa. The very soil, its immaculate beige grains carved into ridges, into perfectly smooth terraces and gentle basins for irrigation, is a work of art. From it arise the sturdy pillars or the graceful curving stems of palms, and in their delicate tracery of shade, shapes of succulents so strange that they might have been invented in Disney's studios. Smooth blue leaves, waxy, warty, wrinkled, knobby, fasciated, absurd contorted shapes, or rosettes so regular and refined they seem still to be on a designer's drawing board. Planes of water like glass or gently stirring. A tinkling jet here in the sun, there a generous gush in the dark of a bamboo grove. And startling colours that need the brilliant sun to make them bearable: orange and searing ultramarine, lemon-yellow and deep Moroccan red.

The International Dendrology Society has the entrée to some very private gardens. We visited half a dozen, including the sumptuous villa of Yves St Laurent's partner Pierre Bergé. This was a super-privileged tour of a world that pushes the possibilities of plants as far as skill and artistry and money extend. What is even more striking about Marrakech, though, is the size and splendour of the public gardens being created along boulevards and in parks around the edges of the cramped and bustling town. There seems to be hardly a road that is not an incipient avenue of palms. King Mohammed loves gardens, too.

April

LIVERY HONOURS

Courson is celebrating its 34th year. It started, I well remember, as a gardeners' gathering on a domestic scale in the park of Patrice and Hélène Fustier's 17th-century château, 25 miles south of Paris down the autoroute that leads to Orléans. Simple stands went up on the grass, village-fête style. Nurseries crowded pots of plants on the cobbles in the stable yard, many of them plants no one knew were available in France. In one corner of the stables a dealer displayed priceless old botany books in their rich leather bindings. Roy Lancaster was a guest to judge a competition.

It seemed like a spontaneous celebration of the gardening passion we all thought France had lost. And since that time, sure enough, the green wellies and Range Rovers that became routine at Courson have carried the message all over the Hexagon (as France calls its mainland mass).

In the '80s, the British were smug enough to think gardening ended at the Channel. The explosion of interest and skill that is so evident since must be credited, to a high degree, to the Fustiers, to Courson – and indeed to its friendly neighbour the Château de St Jean de Beauregard, which now puts on a glorious harvest festival of a show each autumn.

Chelsea has a challenger in May, and both the October shows far outshine the RHS's dwindling autumn effort.

PROSPECT/REFUGE

I shall bungle the quote, I know, but Sir Kenneth Clark once wrote that there were two things all humanity is keen on. One is love; the other is a good view. He could easily have expanded his list, with pizza, a soft pillow, a crafty goal, a foot-tapping beat; but only love and a view made the cut. He was saying there is something pretty Pavlovian about views.

I agree. On family car journeys we used to laugh as the children chorused 'Look at that view!' every time we came to the top of a hill. Little Kitty would have none of it and hid her eyes.

Panoramas are views commanding broad sweeps of lower ground; Kent from the top of Wrotham Hill for example, or the Isle of Dogs from Greenwich Observatory (the view K Clark used as the coda to his documentary series *Civilization*; he was distressed by the first towers of Canary Wharf). View-classification is clear on this point; the narrow focused view, along, for instance, an avenue or a forest ride, is a vista. They both, it seems, give pretty universal pleasure – except to Kitty. But why?

I stumbled on an exhibition just now at The Royal Geographical Society which makes it all clear. Image, Instinct and Imagination: Landscape as Sign Language is the work of the nonagenarian geographer Jay Appleton and the photographer Simon Warner. They propound the theory of Prospect/Refuge, a system of thinking Appleton first proposed in his book *The Experience of Landscape* – and has since expanded in poems that are a cross between Hilaire Belloc and Milton's *L'Allegro*.

A Prospect is a primitive need: to survey the surroundings to look for threats and opportunities. A Refuge is its counterpoint; a place to hide or shelter from dangers or bad weather. Our pleasure in landscapes can be traced back to these two instincts or urges – to which Appleton adds hazards: water and fire, for example, from which we naturally recoil.

The exhibition analyses a series of striking landscape photographs, explaining their appeal on an instinctive level – which transposes, with no wrench at all, to our appreciation of gardens. Now I understand why I have dreams of looking down from a wooded height onto a coastal scene – a bay stretching away in the sunlight. Branches frame the view. When I found myself in that precise situation, looking out over Cardigan Bay from the woods we now own above Caci Deuii, out came my cheque book. Can there be stronger proof that Appleton hits the nail on the head?

LAND AND SEA

The drone of a lawnmower blends with the burbling of a diesel on the harbour. The smell of mown grass mingles with the marine smell of mud and seaweed. I have temporary charge of a different kind of garden: a walled yard only 50 metres from the sea, where frost is unlikely but wind is a constant presence. The walls give it more shelter than its neighbours have, but the air is rarely as still as it is today. Indeed the pines and macrocarpas and holm oaks planted to shelter the seaside houses are in a sorry state: last winter's gales burnt them a depressing brown. Some of the macrocarpas should be put out of their misery.

Most of the garden is paved, with slight changes of level giving raised beds. The planting is mostly low-growing, and today, with masses of aubrieta, pink and pale mauve, with iberis and a clump of lithospermum (lithodora if you prefer) starting its sharp sapphire stars, with forget-me-nots and a tiny pale-pink geranium, it is almost convincing as a natural seaside happening.

In a wall corner a choisya is entirely covered with its white flowers. Bluebells and borage have invaded a taller side border yet to flower. I have trained the long shoots of a rose, 'Madame Alfred Carrière', along the whole length of one side. A little wooden pergola will be nearly crushed by the end of summer under campsis, clematis, honeysuckle and a pink everlasting pea.

Last summer, with a meddlesome itch to add what the trade calls 'accents', I added a few plants of *Verbena bonariensis* and the silveriest of elaeagnus, a little multi-stemmed tree from the gardener/artist Cedric Morris's Suffolk garden. I remember how his walled garden had few vertical features. Irises of course – and this one little tree. Benton End was a much-travelled garden: Morris was always giving his plants away. His legacy lives on in glory at Beth Chatto's. And much more modestly down here on the Solent.

May

SHOW REVIEW

'A younger look', we were promised in the show gardens at Chelsea this year. How we would recognize it I'm not sure.

The look that struck me was a distinct taste for (indeed a heavy dependence on) the lightweight charmers of spring. Perhaps less (though not much less) use of white foxgloves, but complete abandonment, in some cases, to such wildlings as sweet rocket, buttercups, ferns, campion, *Alchemilla mollis*, vetch, verbascums, various feathery umbelliferae and almost universally *Iris sibirica*. The flowers were lightweight, but the supporting trees, it seemed to me, heavier and more numerous than ever. There was no questioning the charm of such stylized meadows, but where have the mainstream garden plants, the long-term stalwarts of the border, bred over centuries to be as unlike wildlings as possible, disappeared to?

The answer in some cases is the marquee, where the specialists display their thoroughbreds. It was worth braving the throng for Hillier's stand alone. Never was the Monument more monumental than in this bravura performance of tall trees, exceptional shrubs and witty variations on a dozen different colour schemes; Hillier's 69th Gold Medal in a row. Trad's own coveted Annual Medal ended up, after much debate, with Rickard's bosky display of ferns, from trees down to microscopic beauties. The idea dawned, then and there, of turning the always-shady end of our garden into a fernery.

------------ *June* ------------

JEWELS OF SPRING

Why is there no one in the Alps in June? It's the time when the cattle make their lumbering way up to the high pastures, their heavy bells clanking. The snow is lying in disjointed drifts where the sun is slow to touch it. Everywhere else is a tapestry of the most jewel-like of flowers, embroidering the lush new verdure of the middle slopes or piercing the brown grass above the tree line, where mats of rhododendron and juniper are stirring in their winter sleep.

First come tiny ivory crocuses and the fretted furry leaves of the pulsatillas, *Anemone sulphurea*, soon followed by its wide, candid, creamy flowers. Gentians are already flowering: the deep violet trumpets of *G. clusii* and the brilliant sapphire stars of *G. verna*. There are violets with big flat faces, a little pink *Thlaspi* in the middle of a stream, small purple orchids, soldanellas with pale violet fringes, lavender-coloured centaurea, primulas very like cowslips, shiny yellow globes of trollius, starry arabis, harebells, pale thrift, miniature alchemillas, many spurges and the rich-blue heads of a rampion, *Phytheuma orbiculare*, which I took for a very special clover in the long grass – and which I now learn is an emblem of Sussex.

All these on a single ramble in the Val d'Anniviers in search of what is said to be the most splendid old larch in the Alps. Alpines are not my natural territory. I expect all my plant names have been superseded long ago; my authority is Correvon's beautiful *Alpine Flora* of 1911 and its art-deco botanical paintings by Philippe Robert.

We found the larches, cohabiting with equally tall and craggy Arolla pines, perhaps 12 feet round and 60 or 70 high, punished by blizzards but waking fresh in the chilly sunshine. The tender first larch leaves springing from old fissured brown wood are as touching and inspirational as the most exquisite of the emerging flowers.

Not a soul about, apart from some mountain bikers on terrifying trails. The hotels are nearly all shut, the skiing is over, the summer holidays still to come. Yet in the weeks between the flowers appearing and the cows eating them (or have the cows the perspicuity to steer around their favourites to leave them to seed?) the sun is bright, the air still cool enough for long walks, the Alps are at their best.

July

BALM

To Kew yesterday for a linden-bath. That was the sensation as I walked in through the Victoria Gate. Straight ahead stands a big common lime, taller than a church and as wide as two, covered with its pale drooping flowers – and pumping out essence of mid-summer.

Turn left past the little temple and a huge weeping silver lime, *Tilia petiolaris*, is spreading its skirts in front of you, embalming the air. Then they come thick and fast, one species after another, a whole wood of limes, from a squatly spreading small-leaved one, *Tilia cordata*, like a green and yellow cushion, to soaring *T. petiolaris*, surely some of Kew's tallest trees. It is a curious fact about this splendid species (or is it a cultivar?) that it habitually divides into two, or often three, major trunks about 15 feet from the ground. They grow vertically with mighty vigour to make a majestic tower, their leaf-stalks (the petioles of *petiolaris*) twisting to show the silver-white undersides of the leaves. At this moment its cascading flowers are just opening and beginning to shower down their scent. More limes stand ready for their later flowering, with the fringe-leafed *T. henryana* from China coming last.

I headed towards the river from this honey-scented zone, skirting the sickly smell of the sweet chestnuts, to visit the Mediterranean area with its perfectly authentic-looking olive grove in a patch of rock-strewn garrigue and the cork-oak forest next to it. A huge specimen lies prone amid citrus and seedling pines next to a signboard exhorting us to protect this threatened habitat. Threatened, among other things, by the spread of screw-capped wine bottles and consequent decline in demand for cork.

I'm not sure about this. The demand for wine corks has grown exponentially in the past 30 or 40 years, since wine became the popular drink it is today. In the past, a relatively small proportion was given the dignity of a cork and capsule. Cork had many other uses, from buoyancy aids to insulation to high heels, but any decrease in oak-acreage due to wine must be pretty recent. It's not screw caps we should blame, but substitutes for its other uses. Let's have more cork-tiled floors – and thank goodness we're seeing the decline of the corkscrew.

AIRY MOUNTAIN, RUSHY GLEN

Forestry is inherently an untidy business. Each summer we come to North Wales to enjoy our woods, the mountains round and sea below, and each year another patch is a (temporary) eyesore. This year is a bad one: the February gales made a shambles of half a hillside, and fishing the trees out from the mess transferred a good deal of it onto the forest track. Ditches had to be scoured, surfaces scraped and loads of new stone spread and rolled in. Luckily we have a good roadstone quarry in the heart of the forest, but I have to admit there is a certain rawness about parts of the place just now.

It is easy to escape them. The bosom of the broadleaves is where I go, where a stream tumbles down white among the black rocks. There is a line of Milton's that rings in my head here: 'bosom'd high in tufted trees'. The distinct tufts of well-spaced oaks and beeches, ashes, some sycamores and innumerable birches pattern the hillside opposite like a gallery of portraits, now glowing gold in the evening sun. I have been surprised to learn how often a wood of originally close-planted trees needs thinning to make strong (as opposed to spindly) trunks: perhaps once every 15 years. I wonder where Milton's trees were?

A SENSE OF *PLAS*

I don't suppose the name Plas yn Rhiw comes up very often at meetings of the National Trust Gardens Committee. If there was a period when a sense of horticultural correctness pervaded the Trust's gardens, you wouldn't know it here, around this remote little manor house on the Llyn Peninsula, stuck out in the Irish Sea. A sense of place certainly: it would be bizarre not to plant the sort of half-hardy things the benign sea-air allows. Of fashion, inevitably: bright gardeners are always alert to new plants coming through the system. But, most agreeably, a sense of freedom to be as relaxed as befits minor provincial gentry happily hidden from the world.

The 'Plas', a word which in Welsh seems to cover anything from a mansion to a very minor manor, was restored by three spinster sisters from Nottingham in the 1940s, encouraged by their friend Clough Williams-Ellis of Portmeirion. Everything from the books in the bookshelves to the box-hedged enclosures of the garden, bursting with exotic shrubs, breathes an austere gentility in speaking contrast to tremendous views of sea and mountains.

August

PHOENIX AT CRÛG FARM

Tea on the lawn on a baking day with the hospitable Bleddyn and Sue Wynn-Jones of Crûg Farm Plants, the foreground a field of cows, the background the Llanberis Pass deep into Snowdonia. Every visit to Crûg Farm is a revelation of plants I've never seen before. Sometimes I can spot the genus, very rarely the species: Sue and Bleddyn still don't have names for half the plants they grow: just accession numbers. And the numbers grow lustily each time they do a trawl in Southeast Asia or Central America, two of their main collecting grounds.

They list over 60 trips on their website, starting in 1992. They collect friends, too: that day a Belgian nurseryman and his wife, every day a plantsman from near or far, agog to see what new things they are offering in their little sales yard, or growing in their propagating tunnels, or displaying in their romantically intricate little gardens between the house and the old farm buildings.

Last year they saw an accidental fire as a chance to add yet another garden. An old cow barn went up in flames; leaving its walls and the remains of its roof as a sheltering spot for more new plants whose hardiness needs testing. It is a completely eclectic mix, from maples to lilies – all with a new twist – via 50 things I've never heard of. Scheffleras seem to be a Crûg signature plant (they list 31 in their astonishing catalogue). Their elegant almost palm-like clumps and fingered leaves caught my eye several times, some with discreet yellow flowers, some with black berries. But it is absurd to pick on any plant, or even genus, in this garden of wonders. We left feeling as though the Creator had had another go with a new designer.

LONDON'S BUILDING

I'll spare you all the noisy and dusty details, but our nextdoor neighbour's house is being demolished, or most of it. Its Victorian elegance (if that's not too strong a word for the plasterwork and joinery of the 1840s) is going on the skip, to be replaced by the stark spaces of today's fashion. Only the front and side walls are staying – and while they've got the roof off, why not dig a basement as well?

Noise and dust we can live with; worse is the worry that we'll all fall into the hole, or if not actually fall, see scary cracks in our wall. Just over the road another end-of-terrace house like our neighbour's moved enough to split its neighbour down the middle. Admittedly they had dug a two-storey basement to fit in a 14-metre swimming pool. (Will the whole house smell of chlorine?)

All this is, of course, 'permitted development'. The government's Party Wall Act doesn't take account of the flimsiness of 19th-century-spec building. Builders used the cheapest materials they could get away with. Our previous London house, in Islington, was dated to October or November 1838; the evidence being that Baltic deal was used for the internal walls, then plastered over. Apparently there was a glut of deal in London docks that autumn.

If it weren't for the walnut tree that shades our back garden, there might be a basement under the nextdoor garden as well. The law, though, is more protective of trees than of neighbours' sensibilities. Wisteria is not a tree, says the law, so the massive one on the back wall – about to be demolished – has already gone on the skip.

Developers have some mad ideas. Having rebuilt a house opposite (my goodness, what a Media Room they built!), they hired a crane to lift five eight-metre cypresses over the roof into the back garden. Unfortunately the crane hit three parked cars, and they forgot to water the cypresses. Another crane, maybe, to lift the brown carcasses out again? And what will the council say about removing big trees?

September

PAUSE BEFORE FALL

Curiosity is a curse in a gardener. You can never be tidy if you are curious. I always want to know what will happen next. Will a faded flower set seed? Can I grow the seed? How tall will this climber grow?

What is that seedling in the paving? (I'll have to leave it till I see its flowers.) If your whole garden is a mass of mini-experiments, it will never merit a photograph.

Successes and failures? At the end of a long summer there must be conclusions to be drawn. Almost everything could do with more light. Hydrangeas have done well; geraniums, phlox, Japanese anemones, campanulas, *Thalictrum delavayii*, the inevitable *Verbena bonariensis* all earn their keep. The best performer, though, by far, is the redoubtable *Fuchsia boliviana*. We brought it as a standard in a mere 20-cm pot from Saling Hall. It has grown to four times the size, flowering vividly with its scarlet tassels of narrow bells all summer. Its fruit ripens, too, red berries turning black and (tolerably) edible. It propagates easily by either seed or cuttings. I shall have to chop off whole branches to squeeze it into the greenhouse for the winter – although I wonder if a plant this lusty wouldn't survive if I just stuck it under the verandah.

NUTAT HOMERUS

I must have been dozing to have missed my own 40th birthday – or rather Trad's. It happened in June: 40 years since the first number of the *Journal of the RHS*, reborn as *The Garden*.

I was in charge of the mag then, and looking for an editorial leader column. I decided to write it myself, but quasi-anonymously. I used the nom de plume Tradescant because it seemed to be a name uniquely associated with gardening, without any current claimants. I couldn't find a soul answering to it in England or anywhere else.

I'm still at it. It grew into a habit I was (and am) loathe to shake off. There is an odd comfort in slipping into a persona which is oneself, but not quite. I put on Trad's old tweed jacket, cuffs fraying and elbows patched, and record his current thoughts or preoccupations. Often they coincide with my own.

For many years we worked together in an ambitious garden of 12 country acres. We have gardened together in France, in Hampshire and Wales, and now have 1,000 square feet of Kensington as our headquarters. We have the constant stimulus of visiting gardens and nurseries, of conversations and the library; there is never a lack of matter for gossip and reflection. Will Trad make it to 50? Will he make it to 41? We shall see.

—————————   *October*   —————————

STILL NO JOKE

Fifteen or 20 years ago I offered readers a prize for the funniest roundabout in France – or rather a photo of it. I had lots of entries. It was the time when the *rond point* was a fairly new way of dealing with a crossroads, and local authorities seized on it as a means of self-expression or advertising. Most involved gardening of some kind, some in a flower-show sort of spirit, some so garish that no lights could compete, some ambitiously advertising local industry – a vineyard or a jet fighter – and many intentionally or unintentionally very funny.

Now it's gone beyond a joke. The old pleasures of motoring in France are threatened by such aggressive road-building that you can only approach most towns along miles of by-passes, through thickets of road signs, along narrow lanes of tarmac between overbearing kerbs and bollards, over speed humps steep enough to shake your head off. 'Toutes Directions' is the unhelpful universal signpost. If you can find 'Centre Ville' in the forest of instructions, it leads you into a maze from which you despair of escaping. If you ever come across the historic marketplace, its buildings are obliterated by more bossy signs and chaotically parked cars. There is no escape.

Worst of all, smaller and smaller towns are boosting their self-importance by aping big ones, installing *rond point*s and hiding their 'Ville Fleurie' boards with signs to their 'Zones d'Activités' (while activité ebbs from their ancient hearts). Hamlets aspiring to be villages are joining the game. My current prizewinner is a one-horse village in the Médoc we now call Arcins-Les-Quatre-Ralentisseurs. There is one speed hump to greet you at each end of the short street and two outside the tiny *mairie*. You laugh so that you may not cry.

HALLOWE'EN

It has been the longest growing season in living memory. My diary records a 'spring walk' on January 25th, and practically no overcoat weather since. The gardening press is full of advice about wrapping tender plants for the winter, even pruning clematis, when everything is still in full cry. What advice should it give for balmy days in November?

Fergus Garnett in *The Garden* enumerates the tulips that, he says, live to flower another year. Tulip blight apart, I have found that many do, if not with the vigour of their first go round. My favourite 'White Triumphator' has played its part as a ghostly fringe for maybe ten years, thinning a bit but still striking. It was more challenged by bluebells in a mixed planting around the lovely golden *Acer shirasawanum*, dwindling by degrees as the bluebells thickened. But it was still flowering five years after planting. Perhaps lily-flowered tulips are good repeaters: Fergus praises the slim orange 'Ballerina'; yellow 'West Point' has also gone on here for years and years. And the pale-pink (with yellow inside) stoloniferous *Tulipa saxatilis* that my college dean, John Raven, collected in Crete 40 years ago, comes up every April in a gradually widening patch. John's daughter Sarah must have caught the bug from her father.

The problem Fergus doesn't mention is that bulbs in borders end up speared on your fork. He advises replenishing scatters or clumps with fresh bulbs; but how do you find the present incumbents? I remember that the 'China Pink' is among the euphorbias that make one of spring's freshest exclamations. But each exploratory prod with the fork provokes a squeal from another skewered tulip. 'Tis a puzzlement.

November

KEW, THE PALACE

Kew Gardens was only lightly populated early one morning last summer when I set off on a habitual circuit: turn right after the

Victoria Gate, past the Palm House, through the rock garden, then left to follow the perimeter path to the rhododendron dell and on through the oak collection. The route takes you past the front of Kew Palace (a big name, I always think, for a fairly modest brick house, painted a powerful red, with rather awkward Dutch gables). A 'palace' only in being a former royal residence.

That morning there were two young women in long skirts and straw hats standing by the front door. 'Won't you walk in, sir?' said one of them, to my surprise. I turned. Their clothes were a little more than quaint – but their welcome was warm. Walk in I did, to find the house newly decorated and furnished to evoke its most royal era, when it was home to King George III, Queen Charlotte and their 15 children. The poor king, though, was in seclusion, suffering from porphyria. His physicians had forbidden him his knife and fork, fearing violence. It was an unhappy household.

Light has returned, though, in the house as it has been restored. The palace is celebrating the King's recovery. The royal knife and fork are back on the table and the original kitchen, marvellously surviving in its original state in the next building, is preparing his favourite dinner: partridge with celery in a cream sauce.

It is a brilliant restoration, masterminded, I understand, by Dr Lucy Worsley, the TV history presenter who is now curator of five of the Historic Royal Palaces. The Queen has lent back to Kew the furniture that was there in Queen Charlotte's day; the decorations, carpets and curtains are exactly reproduced. The royal silver teapot is beside her chair. The cramped conditions of a big family in a small house are very evident: two unmarried princesses had attic bedrooms like maids. And ghostly voices recall moments in the house's history; very poignantly the Prince of Wales comforting his mother, dying in her bedroom.

It is a giant step beyond Son et Lumière, this intimate evocation of history. It adds a quite unexpected dimension to a visit to Kew. Perhaps one day we shall be able to follow the great directors, William Aiton and the Hookers, directing the planting of their trees.

December

LOOK UP A TREE

Bean went live yesterday. Or to put it more precisely the online version of Bean's *Trees and Shrubs Hardy in the British Isles* became available on your computer. Botanists, and especially dendrologists, have been saying simply 'Bean' for exactly 100 years; since William Jackson Bean (was he 'Bill' to his friends?) brought out his book with its eight-word title.

As Head of the Arboretum at Kew (and hence one of Tony Kirkham's predecessors), he was well placed to list and describe his subjects in a judicious blend of botany and sylvicultural experience. By the 1970s his work was in its eighth edition, expanded from two volumes to five as new trees were discovered or invented, botanists wrangled, cultural knowledge piled up and noteworthy specimens multiplied. It became clear that in the digital age no one was going to revise such an encyclopaedia in the time-honoured way involving mountains of paper in correspondence and proofs. If the work was to survive and be revisable, it must be online.

The original publisher was John Murray (whose other authors included Austen, Byron, Conan Doyle, Charles Darwin and Sir Walter Scott). Sadly the Murray family sold the firm (still at its original home, 50 Albemarle Street) to Hodder Headline, which is now a subsidiary of Hachette – though still run by its founder, Tim Hely-Hutchinson). Tim H-H is also my publisher. I asked him if he saw any prospect of reviving Bean, and got the answer I expected.

Would he then, I asked, consider giving the rights to the International Dendrology Society as a charitable body which could and would put the work online pro bono publico, and hopefully in due course keep it revised and up to date?

The answer was yes. Two years of concentrated work later, the result is on your desk. I'm not going to roll the credits here, but two of the stars are John Grimshaw (whose guiding hand is visible in the lack of blunders in my own *Trees*) and Bill Hemsley, whose ingenious digits enable me to revise my *Pocket Wine Book* every year with no paper at all. *Trees*, by the way, to give it a shameless plug, is reprinted and back in the shops for Christmas. Please don't compare it with Bean.

UNCLUTTER

The last of the fallen leaves have gone in the bin. I spent this morning cutting down, raking and brushing up, tying in, shifting pots into winter quarters and generally battening down for winter. By lunchtime I could hardly recognize the place: plain surfaces where clutter had been accumulating all autumn.

Who said 'A plain place near the eye gives it a kind of liberty it loves?' Repton, I was going to say – only this time it was the less-quoted William Shenstone. In any case it's true: the foreground of a view, or the part of the garden you first step into, should be open, tidy, free from obstructions. But what does 'should' mean? Says Shenstone? Are there really any first principles of garden design – or for that matter any design – that determine its success or failure from the start?

I suspect most people would put tidiness high on the list. Or 'order', to give it a loftier name. Palpable regularity is, after all, the basis of French, Italian, Dutch ... anything but English (or oriental) garden design. Order for its own sake, though, can be less than satisfying: trite, even. Your mind (or mine, at least) looks for something more: an agenda. The easiest gardens to design are those with a clear function in mind. An orchard, a potager, an arboretum or a herb garden ... anything with a recognizable label gives the design a starting point, a raison d'être beyond the mere decorating of space.

And here, in a little London yard? Perhaps I'm lucky not to have too much space to decorate. I might define this as an outdoor room for growing plants. Whatever I call it, it certainly looks better when it's tidy.

2015

January

TIME TRAVEL

It's what I do on dark January afternoons: retreat a century and a half to the world of frock-coats and crinolines, the world of J C Loudon, John Lindley, Joseph Paxton and William Jackson Hooker, the years when gardening was just finding its scientific feet.

My time-machine is *The Gardener's Magazine*. I am deep in the issues of 175 years ago. John Lindley, secretary of the Horticultural Society, has just published his *Theory of Horticulture*, described by its reviewer as 'as useful and indispensable to the gardener as the compass is to the mariner.' Lindley began by explaining in plain terms how plants work, in a short guide to the horticultural application of vegetable physiology.' Such a thing, it seems, did not exist; gardening was learnt only by tradition and experience. The reviewer went on: 'If I had met with such a book as this 20 years ago, I would not have so many grey hairs in my head now.'

Paxton had just built the Great Stove at Chatsworth, the prototype for the Crystal Palace. Loudon enthuses about what the new Penny Post would contribute to gardening, making the distribution of seeds and cuttings possible as it had never been before. The nobility, and even commonplace millionaires, were investing in more and more ambitious gardens, nurserymen were flourishing and plant hunters ranging further than ever. And yet, in January 1840, the government announced it was closing down the royal gardens at Kew. All the plants were offered to the Horticultural Society – at a price. The Society declined; they were offered gratis to anyone who would take them away. And the greenhouses were to be demolished.

Strange, I think, that Paxton's boss, the sixth Duke of Devonshire, with his house at Chiswick, just between Kew and the Horticultural Society's Chiswick garden, didn't put two and two together. The job of saving Kew was achieved largely by John Lindley and his friends lobbying the Prime Minister, Lord Melbourne. His friend William Jackson Hooker became the first director of the new establishment.

I close my magazine and pick up the newspaper. What do I read? Kew's budget has been cut again. The world's most important botanical garden is to be cut down to size. They have already laid off 50 scientists. They may have to be closed to the public out of season. And London is to have a new public garden – on a windswept bridge, of all places, crossing the Thames from the Temple to the South Bank. At a cost of £175 million. Putting two and two together still seems to be too difficult.

February

OLD LIONS

Perhaps not everyone knows that the grand iron gates in Piccadilly are the entrance not only to the Royal Academy (Sir J Reynolds in bronze, brush poised, makes this pretty clear), but also to the botanists' Valhalla, The Linnean Society. Valhalla seems appropriate for an institution with a Swedish patron saint.

I was there this week for meetings of the International Dendrology Society (IDS) in the august council chamber. On the walls and the staircase hang portraits of every canonized botanist, some venerable trees and many plant collectors, from Linnaeus on – with a particularly colourful one of the late Professor Willy Stearn cheering up the council chamber. From the windows on one side you look down on the Royal Academy, from the other you survey Whitehall down to Westminster Abbey. It could go to a mere gardener's head.

The IDS holds its annual Winter Lecture here. This year it was Tony Kirkham's turn. His subject: 250 years of Kew Gardens and gardeners, from Princess Augusta and poor Fred, Prince of Wales, down the long avenue of celebrated names: Bute, Banks, Hookers Sr and Jr, Thistleton-Dyer (Tony's favourite, though a martinet. He wore a dashing uniform), Dallimore, W J Bean ... and Kirkham. Tony has been *capo* of the arboretum since 2002, totally immersed and most eloquent about his charges. The progress of Kew from a minor royal garden with a mere five acres of arboretum to its 300-acre splendour today makes a good story – especially since half a dozen of the original trees planted in the 1760s are still there, fêted as the 'Old Lions' and propped and botoxed-up as necessary.

The most wonky, now lying on its side, is the original Pagoda Tree, recently re-labelled *Styphnolobium japonicum*, but *Sophora japonica* to you and me. What an indignity, handing it a five-syllable genus at its time of life. What tin ears botanists sometimes have – or in this case the Viennese publication that got in first with a name in 1830. Surely the label should at least acknowledge the name it bore for most of its existence here. There could be an acronym, FKA (formerly known as) or even TYAM (to you and me). The other Lions, far less mangy than the first, are the oriental plane, the original ginkgo, the huge *Zelkova* from the Caucasus and the *Robinia*, named for Jean Robin, director of the Jardin des Plantes in Paris (who presumably got in first).

Princess Augusta might be nonplussed to find some of her old trees growing where they do. Shifting them around has long been a practice at Kew. When the Duke of Argyll, another acquisitive dendrologist, died, his nephew Lord Bute took a gigantic horse-drawn wagon and helped himself (or rather Kew) to the best trees on Argyll's Richmond estate – including the robinia.

GALANTHOPHYSIC

To the Chelsea Physic Garden on the first of its two Snowdrop Weekends. Nippy at 4° C with a north wind. A marvellous *coup de théâtre* on the way in: snowdrops as mobiles hanging from trees in little balls of moss; snowdrops as a rug round the cold feet of Sir John Soane in marble, and snowdrops in drifts along a newly created path winding through the trees down by the Embankment.

The CPG keeps getting better – and even apparently bigger, as more little gardens and gardens-within-gardens and different horticultural incidents enliven its space. It's hard to believe that so much can happen within its four acres, including a considerable arboretum of seriously senior trees. Somehow there always seems to be another unexplored or undeveloped patch to be transformed.

Nothing could be more inspirational for an urban gardener – or any gardener with very limited space. Here is the evidence that you can pack it all in, divide your space again and again, shift the focus from one style or environment to another. Rockery, economic plantery, perfumery, pond, bog garden, woodland garden, order beds, fernery, Antipodean collection ... they merge or contrast (more of the former in winter; the latter in summer) to make a magical garden walk, absorbing hours – even on a nippy January afternoon, when galanthophiles have their moment of glory.

I love snowdrops – but that doesn't make me a galanthophile. In the sales tent (same temperature as the garden, minus the wind-chill) patient volunteers with frozen feet were guiding us through the differences between the precious named cultivars. Most people ask about the big ones, largely selections of *Galanthus elwesii* with taller or shorter flower stalks, bluer or greener or broader leaves, and heaven-knows-what variations of exquisite detail in their flowers – at £25 a plant. I'm afraid I asked the obvious question: what about the unnamed varieties? 'Yes, we had quite a few, but a French woman took the lot this morning.' They have their heads screwed on, the French.

For all the winter chill, the most eye-catching plant in the garden was, of all things, a rose; a handsome mound, two metres high and three wide, of fresh green with reddish emerging shoots and tender leaves. It carried 40 or 50 pale-scarlet flowers looking none (or only slightly) the worse for the frost. *Rosa mutabilis*? I wondered. Then I thought of ours, hunkered down and almost bare. Surely a relation? '*Rosa odorata*', said a cold-footed volunteer. 'We used to say *Rosa chinensis* 'Bengal Crimson', but we're not allowed to any more.'

March

DOGS BY NAME; STARS BY NATURE

There are some plant families the Creator evidently worked on with gardeners specifically in mind. The dogwoods were one; Eden must have been full of them. Lighting up shady places and the downtime of the gardening year (not that one pictures Eden having much downtime) is their great family gift. Winter gardens rely on them as much as they rely on hellebores and heathers.

The most glamorous dogwood in fact takes things a bit too far – at least for any garden of mine. The Catwalk Tree would be a good name for *Cornus controversa* 'Variegata': if it could speak it would say 'Ta dah!' Where do you put such an eye-catcher: a creamy wedding cake that says 'Clear the room for my pirouette' and needs at least six square metres to perform in? The one I planted at Saling Hall, after years of hesitation, was kept in bounds by the muntjac, rather to my relief. They chewed off its extremities until I had to give quietus to the poor bedraggled thing.

Far more elegant and better mannered is its cousin, *C. alternifolia* 'Argentea'. It is a smaller plant, and less deliberate in its branching pattern. The tier-potential is there but you have to tease it out, year after year, with your secateurs. The leaves are smaller, on red stalks, mottled with white instead of cream, and charmingly twisted. Given the space it can hold the stage, but it doesn't bawl for attention. *Cornus mas*, our Cornelian cherry, and its Japanese equivalent, *C. officinalis*, are discreetly charming, too; claiming the limelight only for their precocious yellow flowers and autumn leaves. The star of this division is 'Elegantissima', the white-variegated version of *C. mas*. It's slow: it took 15 years to become considerable at Saling Hall, admittedly in deep shade, but then its October show of brilliant-red fruit among the delicate pale leaves was worth the wait.

I came to the 'flowering' dogwoods rather late in life, wrongly believing they only really worked in America. It was the Chinese dogwood, *C. kousa chinensis*, that opened my eyes; a pair of small trees flanking a woodland path in our garden at Saling. Neighbours came round in early June to discuss the relative merits of the one whose creamy sepals opened flat and the one whose sepals stood to attention. Their leaves turned different colours in autumn too, yet as far as I know they were both *C. kousa chinensis*. Many dogwoods, American ones especially, outgun them in size and colour of flowers. Those of *Cornus* 'Venus', a cross between *C. kousa* and *C. nuttallii* from California, are startling enough to shatter the peace of any woodland glade.

For our London garden, there is no playing with such grandiose ideas. The all-purpose *Cornus* we have here is the modest no-flowers-to-speak-of *C. alba* 'Elegantissima'. In winter its stems glow a warm red in the light of a lamp I focus on it. In summer its white variegation is perfect in a sunless corner. There are brighter-coloured stems: 'Sibirica' is an eye-catcher, 'Midwinter Fire' is another and I've always liked the yellow 'Flaviramea'. But the leaves are the clincher. In a tight dark corner a true dual-purpose plant as pretty as this beats all the aristos of the family.

THE PROFIT FROM PIANOS

James Lick never saw his conservatory. He ordered it at the age of 75; when he died, aged 80, it was still packed in crates, waiting for a site in what is now called Silicon Valley, at the southern end of San Francisco Bay.

Lick was a Gold-Rush millionaire – not from digging gold, but from building pianos and investing his profits in land. He learnt carpentry from his father in Pennsylvania, took his piano business to

Argentina, then Chile, then Peru, then Mexico, and in 1848 finally
arrived in San Francisco (carrying 275 kilos of chocolate) on the very
eve of the Gold Rush. Chocolate sold well, pianos were called for
(every bar needed one), and Lick's land went up in value. He built
houses in San Francisco, planted orchards in San Jose, bought ranches
in Los Angeles and the Sierras; he owned the biggest flour mill west of
the Mississippi and soon the grandest hotel in San Francisco. He built
the biggest refracting telescope of its time for the new University of
California – and commissioned the conservatory that now stands in
Golden Gate Park, a masterpiece of carpentry in redwood inspired by
the Palm House at Kew.

Golden Gate Park stretches from the heart of the city westwards
to the ocean on what was originally sand dunes. Its inspiration was
New York's Central Park, with winding drives among 1,000 acres of
woodland and meadows. Belts of Monterey cypress and pine protect
it from the wind with remarkable success. At its heart is the Botanical
Garden, initiated by the inevitable Scotsman, John McLaren from the
Edinburgh Botanics. Planting grasses to stabilize the sand, he said,
reminded him of the Firth of Forth.

Lick's conservatory found a home in the park. The crates were
auctioned, bought by the railroad tycoon Leland Stanford and given
to the city. If only Lick could see it now, a gleaming white presence,
arrestingly elegant, filled with flourishing plants. High-altitude
orchids are its principal collection: 700 species out of 1,000 known,
displayed among palms, tropical crop plants, aquatics and carnivorous
nasties around glinting ponds under the glistening white roof. There
is a lightness of touch here, a vegetative cheerfulness perfectly apt for
the most beautiful city in America.

SPIRITUAL HOME

Home from a preview of spring in California: hillsides blue with
lupins, orange with poppies – and, unusually, green with grass. They
won't be green for long. The West Coast is three years into drought.
Almost no rain so far this year, and precious little in the snowpack

in the mountains. Spring is too early, too warm – and wonderful. Magnolias are going over already, but against the rich green of redwoods the dogwoods are lighting up, daily more dashing and elegant in their balletic poses, branch-tips up.

California has been my second spiritual home since I was a mere 17. I came in a gap year, and twice I have come close to moving in, dazzled by the brilliance of light, the fecundity of nature, the sense of space and freedom. But each time I felt the pull of Europe. I realize the privilege of living so close to France, Italy, Germany ... the world's most sophisticated capitals, the sources of our vast and complex culture. It would feel like living at the far end of a long corridor; much too long. I go crazy with delight in a redwood forest with a whale-watching beach at the foot of the hill. I love the quirky beauty of San Francisco, the windy Bay, the flying fog, the pastiche Victorian architecture – and the stories. But then it's time to come home.

June

YOU HAVE BEEN WARNED

To Kew on a perfect June day for a serious all-day session on, of all things, tree safety. The International Dendrology Society organized the seminar with Tony Kirkham, the head of the arboretum, as a consequence of his horrific week in court last year after a branch fell off a cedar and killed a girl.

Accidents and Acts of God are old-fashioned concepts with little, if any, place in current law; blame culture has to pin every misadventure on a cause, and the cause on an individual. The Royal Botanical Gardens owned the tree (a cedar of Lebanon); Tony Kirkham is responsible for all the 14,000 trees in the collection. If a tree is unsafe (the presumption if it sheds a branch), it should have been made safe. Under Health & Safety laws Tony might have had to go to jail.

His audience yesterday were people who either own or manage trees in arboreta or parks all over the country. I think they were shocked, all of them, at the risks they are running in letting anyone near their trees. Their duty of care extends to every tree and every branch, and the only way to satisfy a court is to show that you have inspected the tree in question, satisfied yourself that it is not about to break up, and kept records of your inspection. It is only the fact that Kew does have a long-term, fairly elaborate and fully documented inspection regime that saved Tony from clink.

True, the family of the unfortunate girl were on the attack, hired a QC and an expert (who turned out to be not extremely so in court). We were full of questions. Does the duty to inspect apply to trees in ordinary gardens? (Yes.) Does it apply to trees in woodlands or forests? (Yes.) What about the notorious and mysterious phenomenon of 'Summer Branch Drop', when a major branch parts company with its tree without warning, for no perceptible cause? For some (or no) reason this happens most often in June, July or August. There is even a superstition that the time to stay away from trees is on July 22nd and 23rd. Tree professionals prefer to let SBD stand for Sudden, rather than Summer, Branch Drop – not having a clue how it relates to a particular season.

We spent the afternoon on a practical tree-inspection tour of the arboretum, following Kew's three-stage system: first walk (or even drive) by at three miles an hour with your eyes skinned, looking for broken or split branches, splits in trunks, signs of weeping or surface fungi. This you should do as often as possible, within reason. The second stage is to come back and examine what you spotted. Carry a mallet to tap the trunk for hollow resonance, and an iron rod to prod the base for soft wood. Take action as needed: cut unsafe branches straight away.

Stage three is for when you can't tell, or decide, because the problem is hidden inside. This is when the expensive toys come out: an electronic device called a Picus Sonic Tomograph that reads the speed of sound-waves through the trunk to build up a picture of the interior. You hit a nail at intervals round the tree; the sound travels fast through sound wood, slowly through rotten wood and not at all through hollow cavities. The rule of thumb is that if one-third of the trunk is solid, the tree can stand. Less than that means the chop.

Of course other factors come into it. A hazard (the possibility of something going wrong) is not the same as a risk (the chances of it doing damage). There is obviously more risk where more people congregate, by a path or a road, than in the middle of a wood. Your action can be proportional to the risk, so when a grand old specimen by a path begins to look a bit wonky, Tony Kirkham's first step is to move the path. More people walk on short grass than long, so he lets the grass grow or creates a wide circle of mulch around the trunk (which is also, of course, good for the tree). There is a degree of proportionality in the precautions you must take – but the fact remains: the buck stops with you.

And you must contemplate the possibility of extreme bad luck: the Kew cedar branch not only brought down two others, but a huge chunk of wood bounced. The poor girl was six metres outside the radius of the tree.

It was a landmark case. Not long afterwards the National Trust was able to use the same defence of regular inspection and records. But it sent a shudder through the gathering. We all went home to brush up our logbooks.

IN MEMORIAM

A warm weekend's visit to the battlefields of Ypres; apposite, one hundred years to the day after my father was wounded there by a round from a German Maxim machine-gun. He carried the bullet in his wallet for the rest of his life in an envelope marked 'German bullet that wounded G F J in June 1915 at Ypres, taken out at Guy's Hospital by Sir W Arbuthnot Lane.'

He was secretly rather proud that he had been operated on by this famous surgeon (the model, it was said, for Sir Cutler Walpole in *The Doctor's Dilemma*), very soon after having been wounded. Trains were shuttling injured men from the Front to Calais and London. 'I woke up', he wrote to his mother, 'in a London Hospital.' He was lucky. But six months later he was back with his battery (he was in the artillery) in the same spot.

The cemeteries tell the story of some of the worst battles. The bodies were buried near where they died, at the beginning of the war in nearby churchyards, soon in plots appropriated as cemeteries. One of the biggest, with 12,000 graves, is beside the principal 'dressing station' by the railway.

The cemeteries are gardened by the Commonwealth War Graves Commission, to a standard the royal parks would be proud of. There are miles of straight edges and immaculate hedges with white headstones in parade order. Some have pavilions or cloisters whose walls carry the endless lists of the dead, recorded by regiment. Tens of thousands are anonymous, but those who were identified carry the name, rank and regiment of the soldier, and most of them his age, very often between 19 and 25. In June, scarlet roses and bright-purple lavender form our tricolour with the white Hopton Wood stone that was generally used. Their trees form an arboretum, well chosen and perfectly kept. There is much to learn in these battlefields – even about gardening.

July

GOOBRA FEATHERS

Louis XVIII is a monarch you don't hear much about, France's last and perhaps fattest. He lived for a while at Hartwell House, was too overweight to walk, and had a *prédégustateur* who doubled as librarian of his 11,000 books. This chap's job was, among other things, to pass fruit as acceptable for his majesty.

My authority, Edward Bunyard (died 1939, pomologist and epicure) relates how everything stopped when Christophe, the gardener, knocked at the library door with a new variety of peach. Petit-Radel, the *prédégustateur*, waited while Christophe, with his ivory knife, cut the fruit in four. The first quarter he judged for its juice, the second for its flesh, the third for its aroma and the last for its harmony.

Bunyard, in his *Anatomy of Dessert*, came down in favour of the nectarine over the peach, on grounds of both its flavour and its smooth skin, though with some reservations about texture: less buttery, more fibrous than the peach. He cites 14 varieties, and 20 of peaches (La Quintinie, Louis XIV's gardener at Versailles, listed 33). Since then breeders have selected and bred scores more. Rivers of Sawbridgeworth, for example, offered a whole aviary of peaches with bird-names: 'Kestrel', 'Goshawk', 'Sea Eagle', 'Peregrine' .... Apples and pears have been bred in hundreds. Where are they all?

The RHS has given an Award of Garden Merit to a mere five (the nectarines are 'Lord Napier' and 'Early Rivers', the peaches 'Duke of York', 'Peregrine' and 'Rochester'). Look for the name of the variety in a supermarket: the country of origin is usually all we're told. The truth is we don't have librarians who *prédégust* or gardeners knocking at their doors. The supermarket buyer *prédégusts*, or certainly should, but is more concerned with price and shelf-life.

What you do find these days is flat peaches – a happy sport of the ancient fruit that suits both shops and customer (and even waiters: they don't roll off the plate). Flat peaches grow on the branch face to face, like headphones – another of Chinese nature's endless repertory of brainwaves. Their flesh is as sweet and juicy as any peach (so juicy there is apparently one variety you can drink with a straw; Louis XVIII would be in raptures). They pack perfectly, tighter than round fruit, to please the carrier. There is even, so I read, a nectarine or fuzz-free kind, though not yet at Waitrose in Kensington. Its name is 'Mésembrine'. My father used to call peach-fuzz 'goobra feathers'. He wasn't in favour: definitely a nectarine man. What advance can we hope for next, since we're doing so well?

The hardest peach to find in a shop is the *pêche des vignes*, the profusely juicy red-fleshed kind that ripens as late as the grapes in the vineyards where you usually find it planted. It gives the vigneron, they say, an early warning of mildew in the air. You need a bath after eating them, but if by some miracle a flat and fuzz-free sport appeared, I'd certainly have a word with Waitrose.

TO COIN A FRAISE

While mugging up on fruit history I've come across a curious strawberry fact. Our big juicy ones superseded the little European native wood (French *fraises des bois*) or alpine strawberries (some debate here: are they the same or different?) when the American *Fragaria virginiana* met and married the Chilean *F. chiloensis*. This latter had been introduced (here's the curious fact) by a chap called Frézier (fraisier: geddit?) – or in Scots, come to that, Fraser. Our strawberry's botanical name is *F. × ananassa*, ananas being French for pineapple. One of our best and tastiest varieties is 'Cambridge Late Pine'.

Note to supermarkets: please label our strawberries (and indeed all our fruit) with the name of the variety as well as where it's grown. And don't harvest strawberries by cutting off their stalks and leaving just the green ring of bracts. You need the stalk to pull out the central plug when you put the strawberry, crunchy with sugar, in your mouth.

Who said, incidentally, 'the raspberry is the thinking man's strawberry'? Discuss.

DOG DAYS

The visitors' book proves it: I was last here 50 years ago – and nothing has changed. The broad white verandah still looks out over orange trees to the steep terraces of vines going down to the river. The house, verandahed all round, sleeps like a planter's bungalow on any tropical station, lawns shaded by thick trees (in this case limes), screens closed against mosquitos, the rooms complete capsules of times long past. Deep beige armchairs, faded prints, dusty books, the polished dining table, have not changed since the 1960s. Probably not since the 1920s, when the Gilbey family bought the estate, 150 acres of vines and the stone barns where Croft's port has been trodden time out of mind.

The upper reaches of the Douro, 100 miles from the sea through range after range of steep hills, are dry, hot and fertile. When we arrived the other day there had been four days over 40° C: conditions that make great vintage port. It's a long time since we slept as past generations have, bare under a sheet, hoping for a draught from windows open on both sides of the house, resenting the mosquito screens that block the free passage of air. The thermometer drops to 30° at dawn: I get up and open all the doors to let the cool air in, and doze off just as the sun shoots its first shrivelling rays into the house.

The early morning is when the vines can get to work, photosynthesize and swell their grapes. In this exceptional summer *veraison*, when the grapes turn from green to red, is already under way. By mid-morning, vines that stood trim and gleaming have started to droop, their stomata closed; evaporation exceeds the power of their roots to find water in the parched soil. They look hangdog until evening, metabolizing nothing, losing time in the journey to ripeness. Fig trees show signs of the same stress, their big leaves limp. Olives, on the other hand, with their small grey leaves, seem immune to the heat. The agapanthus are unbothered, too, baking under the dry stone walls. And orange trees gleam on regardless.

I'm afraid I react like the vines, with the advantage that I can hide in the shade and dip my feet in the fountain. Our hosts' Labrador, on the other hand, has found a niche in a flowerbed and lies between hydrangeas and agapanthus with a lime in her mouth for refreshment.

August

CHANCE ENCOUNTERS

I should know the Cotswolds better. My two lifelong favourite gardens, Rousham and Hidcote, are there, or at least en route. But I am always confused by the tourist-board names. This on the Wold, That on the Water, One on the Hill and Another in the Marsh. High-hedged lanes wander dementedly between clusters of cottages, all buff stone, many thatched, all painted in Farrow & Ball colours. One gets lost.

This excursion started at our favourite pub, the King's Head at Bledington, with few clear objects, turning aside when a church tower, an intriguing signpost or a Garden Open sign hove into view.

Sezincote and its Indian gardens were shut, as we learnt at the gate, but at Bourton the Hill we found Bourton House garden open. I had missed its election as the Historic Houses Association/Christie's Garden of the Year in 2007 and was caught unawares by its quality, its mastery of palettes and idioms, from some of the coolest to quite the hottest borders I have seen, from severity in topiary to a box parterre like a nest of serpents, from placid pastoral to hothouse exotic. Does a bird of such bright plumage in the calm of the Cotswolds conform to the rule that gardens should reflect and interpret their surroundings?

Another chance encounter was Minster Lovell. The name on the signpost was somehow familiar, but at first the sign seemed a wrong steer; the lane led only to an isolated church – if a fine one. Behind the church, though, was a revelation: the pale ruined towers of a medieval mansion on the green riverbank of the Windrush. How rare it is to find an important monument these days uncluttered by signs and gift shops, not a teapot in sight. This is the mansion the Coke family left behind to establish themselves in Norfolk at Holkham. It is not a violated abbey, just a great house left without a roof. Why?

English Heritage deserves a prize for its sign, a brief history of the house with opening times: 'Any Reasonable Time'. Nowadays such a non-prescriptive notice is a rare sight.

PILGRIMAGE TO THE LANCASTERS

It was déjà vu all over again when I turned into Roy and Sue's drive in Chandler's Ford, a leafy suburb just south of Winchester. I've seen so many pictures and heard so many stories. What feels familiar, though, on looking closer turns out to be almost subversively alternative. You know the genus but you never saw this species before. It happens again and again.

Roy is genial, passionate (we all know that from television) and loquacious. 'Isn't that a ...?' you start. 'Yes, I collected it with (half a dozen well-known collectors may feature here; very often Mikinori Ogisu, his Japanese chum) on Emei-shan.' (I've learnt that China's holy mountains are honorifically labelled 'Shan'. Mount Fuji, come to that, is called Fuji-san; are they related? Gongga-shan, alias Minya Konka, seems to be Roy's favourite peak.) '... It was growing with *Abies delavayii*, and a daphne, and a lily I'd never seen before, before breakfast one day outside a village in Sichuan. I'm not mad on rice at breakfast. We'd just seen an extraordinary mahonia with coppery leaves ...' Perhaps I parody, but Roy's reminiscences are worth as long as you've got.

His selective eye has been focused on woody plants (and not only woody ones) since he worked at Hillier's Nurseries nearly 50 years ago. He has a thing about mahonias – and things, for that matter, about 100 other genera as well. I came away from his garden with 'Roy's Choice', a selection of the cross made in the Savill Gardens in John Bond's days between two Lancaster collections, *M. gracillipes* and *M. confusa*. The first has dangling flowers with red sepals and hard, armoured, almost scary leaves, the second an altogether softer look, far more and narrower leaflets and more conventional flowers. The 2013 Chelsea Plant of the Year, *Mahonia* 'Soft Caress' seems to be a variant of a subspecies.

I would never dare plant things as close together as Roy does. He packs a whole botanical garden into a typical suburban one. It looks busy, of course, but still in the way Loudon called gardenesque. One trick is persuading shrubs to climb the house walls, encouraging them with supports, then clothing them with a climber or two – underplanted with two or three other rarities. The monster honeysuckle, *Lonicera hildebrandiana*, has shot up and needs hacking back from a bedroom window.

September

LA RENTRÉE

La rentrée is the French term for it: the back-to-school end of summer when French roads are jammed with cars leaving the beaches and mountains. There is no notion of dawdling, of spinning out the last few days, even if only to avoid the nose-to-tail roads. The sense of a sudden descent from holiday nirvana to dull routine, with a year to wait before the next escape, is deep in the French psyche. And funnily enough the last Saturday in August often sees the weather change in sympathy.

Suddenly you are aware that the sun is too low in the sky. Driving west at teatime is irksome. The dark closes in before you are ready for it. The cry goes up: *'J'ai froid, chéri. Mon châle.'* And leaves detach themselves one by one from the plane trees and rattle to the ground.

This year the grape harvest is early, healthy and plentiful, a smiling vintage promising lots of good ripe wine from coast to coast. Winter was mild, spring early, the summer hot and dry with enough rain in August to swell the berries. Picking grapes is always hard work, but there has been a party atmosphere in the upmarket vineyards where they still pick by hand; in the rest the towering yellow picking machines have been roaring all day long.

We are in La Provence Verte, the Provence north of the A8, of high ridges and deep limestone clefts where vines occupy enclaves of flat land hemmed in by forest. The dominant tree, and the one that gives the woods their startling greenness even at the end of a hot summer, is the Aleppo pine, its name taken from the now-tragic Syrian city (although it is a native all round the western Mediterranean). Drought doesn't bother this surprisingly delicate-looking tree with long slender needles, two to a bunch, of something between apple- and lime-green. They are graceful and soft to the touch and form an airy canopy on trunks that are often sinuous. Around habitations they are joined by the dark verticals of cypress and a few evergreen oaks.

I'm never sure whether the ground flora is properly called *garrigue* or *maquis*; I think it depends on whether the soil is acid or alkaline. This is limestone, and relatively fertile to judge by the thickness of the scrub, the height of some of the trees and the number of seedlings. Where it thins out and bare patches appear I'm told we can put it down to allelopathy (related, perhaps, to allergy); the effect plants can have of inhibiting their rivals for space or nutrients through their roots, their volatile components (there are plenty here, with resinous leaves in hot sun) or by what happens when their leaves decompose on the ground. I'd heard of juglone, the unfriendly substance produced by black walnuts; and eucalyptus often seems to poison the soil around, but didn't know the same was true of so many components of *maquis* (or *garrigue*). The effect, in any case, is the scratchy scattering of scented plants that includes the prickly little kermes oak, juniper, cistus, mastic (aka *Pistacia lentiscus*), thyme, lavender and masses of rosemary.

October

DAMN BRACES

Relaxed. It's the one thing that everyone wants to, and thinks they should, be; a zero-sum positive: your face, your clothes, your body-language, your vocabulary, your house, garden and writing style must be, or aim to be, or appear to be, relaxed. Every magazine and paper says so, and reports admiringly on anyone who carries it off. Why is it the thing to be? Is it because modern life leaves so little time and space for relaxation?

'Relaxed' seems to have the field to itself. What is an admirable, acceptable, fashionable, alternative? No one is admired for being tense, or formal, or uptight. Correct? It sounds as though you're trying too hard. Of clothes, 'chic' perhaps gets away from it, with 'shabby' as a positive qualifier.

The subtext of 'relaxed' is that you're in charge – if only of yourself. You have mastered the situation. You know the rules well enough to ignore them. Rules? Sports have them, but does the rest of life? There are laws, and being relaxed about them can get you three points on your licence. But for most of us, white wine before red is as far as etiquette goes. Cheese before pud? We should be relaxed about that; though oddly it is one thing that gets serious society, dining-out society, uptight.

All this is prelude to a gardening question. What is the admiring epithet to use about a gardener whose garden is, shall we say, relaxed? Perhaps in his day Capability Brown was considered relaxed. Surely doing away with straight lines, 'jumping the fence' and so forth, was relaxing. 'Damn braces, bless relaxes', wrote William Blake. Did he never edge his lawn?

WHAT IS A GARDEN FOR?

And when you've finished your garden, what then? We tend to dodge this question, saying that a garden is never finished, is a process rather than a place ... there's always something to do. True if you are a collector, a plantsman, a naturalist or just a passionate observer. Most gardeners, I suppose, start with some sort of plan, or concept, or start to adapt whatever garden they buy or inherit to their idea of what is beautiful or useful. They go on fiddling. It never quite fits their notion, or their notion changes over time. They see something that inspires them or piques their interest, on television, in a magazine or at a flower show. They see a 'gap' and make the mistake of filling it: does it call for an urn, or a shrub with strident variegation? In the process, they lose track of their original concept, realize that football takes precedence over potatoes, or netball over roses. They eventually grow stiff with age, give up digging and read up on alpines.

The answer to the question 'What is your garden for?' eventually emerges. It is to fill part of your life not covered by work, or satisfied by news – or even by family. Does it have a spiritual dimension? Poetic or artistic might be a fitter word. What it does is make you pay attention to the routines of nature – which is surely an excellent purpose in itself.

November

RUS IN HOUNSLOW

Here am I, a Londoner born and bred, a resident for half my life, a committed gardener who fancies he knows something about architecture, a life member of the National Trust – and I had never been to Osterley Park until last Sunday. I had supposed it was just a sad remnant of a great house stranded near Heathrow and bisected by the M4. We arrived to find pure England, left-behind England, unsullied parkland with magnificent trees around a house on a near-ducal scale. Yes, the motorway rules out rural silence, but if you can stomach the aircraft at Kew or Syon, they are no worse here.

Osterley is a friendly park, open to the neighbours (and there are plenty) all year round. It is a farm with a herd of cows grazing meadows apparently never ploughed, and a real farm shop selling its own produce. And it has a garden becoming a fascinating recreation of 18th-century taste in the borough of Hounslow, 20 minutes from Kensington. We arrived through an autumn mist that veiled the surroundings. As we walked up the drive, skirting a lake noisy with water birds, the sun pierced the mist, low in the afternoon sky, to outline half a dozen serious cedars of Lebanon, trees that must be contemporary with the massive red-brick house. It was a memorable moment of discovery.

The National Trust can do things so well. You could believe the owners were still in charge – though they left at the end of World War II. The 350 acres they gave the Trust is more than the extent of Kew Gardens; enough to feel like real countryside. The Tudor stable block is where you feed and buy your souvenirs, happily free of advertising and bossy notices. The house (with much of its Adam interior intact) shelters you on wet days, and the garden has the unmistakable sense of renewal by imaginative hands. There is a plantsman and a researcher at work here.

You can see it in the ordering of the flowerbeds, awkward perhaps to our post-Jekyll eyes, but precisely what Georgian gardeners appreciated; each plant a solo performance. It is clear from the labelling of the beds. The American garden reflects the excitement of newly imported exotics from the American colonies. The walled kitchen garden is a cheerfully productive playground for vegetables and flowers and fruit jumbled together. All of it is organic. New tree-planting around the park is original and unexpected, and the mile-long promenade around the lake and through the woods must be wonderful in spring with its meadow flowers and bluebells.

The head gardener is Andy Eddy, originally trained at Kew, then at Sissinghurst, and now with a ducal domain of a garden where he can play duke – and duchess. I shall soon be back.

WINTER UNDIES

We amateurs are not obliged to keep our gardens looking spruce and jolly in the winter. Some of us cut down our borders for tidiness' sake, some hang on to withered plants and rhapsodize about seedheads and hoar frost, some think bare soil has a beauty of its own. Public gardeners don't have those options; beds in parks need a winter suit as much as a summer one.

I admit I have seldom thought about the pressure on a public gardener to come up with new schemes to entertain his regular visitors winter after winter – nor the technical know how required. From seed catalogue to bedding-out and from bedding-out to digging up and chucking out is a whole year's programme.

A GARDENER'S EYE

It can be a curse, having a gardener's eye. It means a critical view of almost anywhere plants grow. Appreciative, too, of course – but sadly that happens less often. A practised gardener's glance takes in every weed, every sickly plant, colour crime and misplaced tree. It makes no concessions to wayward taste. At best a too-loud scheme could be labelled in a forgiving way as 'ironic'. A too-quiet one? The kindly explanation is ignorance; the poor things don't know what possibilities they've missed.

We gardeners pounce on every moat, blithely unaware of our own beams. We have different levels of tolerance, of course. ''Er indoors cannot abide a weed. It can block her entire view – until she spots another.' I go the other way, muttering 'A sweet disorder in the dress ...'. A gardener can never be bored – at least not in daylight. The top of a bus provides endless fodder for critical analysis, from park maintenance to street furniture (surely legitimate; we are experts on outdoor spaces) and above all front gardens – though side streets, admittedly, offer richer variety than bus routes.

'Critical' is the key word. The one scenario that could lead to boredom is the improbable one of perfection. How frustrating it would be to contemplate a perfect garden. It is the feeling I get when I look at those 17th-century prints of great estates, their endless alleys and waterworks impeccably aligned, one half precisely echoing the other in witless symmetry. Happily we know that a close-up view would show us gappy hedges, wobbly edges and bedding past its best.

I remember only one garden where criticism could find no chink in a seamless performance. It was at Castel Gandolfo, the papal summer residence in the Alban Hills. The clipped cypresses were finished with nail scissors and I counted, I swear it, nine gardeners sweeping a path with brooms. In unison.

One could always, I suppose, question the economics ....

December

SPRUCE OR FIR?

The tennis court in the square is covered with Christmas trees, some with nylon jackets, ready to deliver, others being appraised for height and spread, colour and smell. Rassells, our favourite nursery, just across Earl's Court Road, owns most of Pembroke Square and its tennis court and turns it into a Christmas-tree bazaar each year. In this shirtsleeves winter, it's a busy spot.

When was it that Santa took a closer look at the forest and realized he could improve on the standard Christmas tree? Until a few years ago, your British Christmas tree was the Norway spruce, *Picea abies* – presumably because the British forest was full of them. The even commoner alternative, the Sitka spruce, *Picea sitchensis*, is drawing-room unfriendly, and its needles would penetrate a tank.

We were spoilt for choice: Douglas fir, Noble fir, Scots pine or Nordmann fir. The last, *Abies nordmanniana*, wins – although I gather American connoisseurs will pay a premium for *Abies fraseri*. The poor Norway spruce lost out after a century of service because its needles fall off, as we all know, once the Christmas hearth has got going. Indeed, loosely attached needles are a problem with almost all spruces. Fir trees are apparently better made.

There are other considerations, though: we all want a slender spire, but some are more densely branched, more or less droopy, softer, shinier or more fragrant. My choice for smell would be Douglas fir, but it looks a tad too relaxed. Pines, with their spaced-out bundles of needles, simply look wrong hung with shiny balls and candles and little angels. Noble fir, *Abies nobilis*, a noble tree indeed in a forest, is very stiff and blue and tends to have long bare shoots between the whorls of branches. So *A. nordmanniana*, sleek and dark shiny green, with short, soft needles all round each shoot, if not amazingly scented, is the one that's coming home.

HITTING A CULTURAL BUFFER

Hermione Quihampton is not the name of a fantasy duchess trailing fags-ends and empties as she devastates the garden. La Q is the former wife of an Anglo-French farmer who became very much part of our life at our old house on the fringes of the Auvergne. Picture her tall enough to be called stately, immensely red-haired, loquacious, brusque and funny, upholding the English way of Open Gardens at her billet in very profonde France. Not every French village has a 'Best Garden Seen From the Road' competition. I suspect Hermione is behind it; at any rate she is up there among the laureates.

She initially took over from the often-absentee gardener (me) at our old place, planting the parterre with every blue flower she could find, the taller the better. By autumn, the box hedges were submerged in a breaking surf of toppling herbs. She baked cakes, made hedgerow jam and, bit by bit, took over vineyard duties from our less-motivated vigneron. The grapes glowed, their leaves perked up and signs of mildew faded when she bore down on them. A year later she had read the wine-making books and started edging me out of the cellar. I think she loved the saccharometer, the tall glass jar with its bobbing float; the fermenting froth was pretty exciting too – and the wine not bad at all.

Her Open Garden attracts the idle and curious, of course, as they do everywhere. In France, though, the second element, the charitable contribution, is sometimes less well received. Hermione tells me of a group of seven who pitched up full of horticultural anticipation, and then read the sign about the children's charity. 'I think they hit the cultural buffer', she said when they turned back to their car.

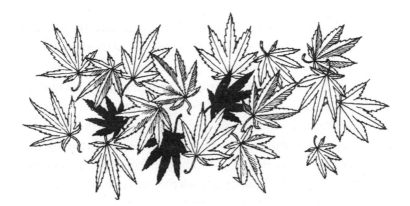

2016

January

CONTRE JOUR

It's the moment that makes a good photo   far more than the aperture.
Does anyone say that Capa's shot of a Spanish soldier dying needs
more focal depth, or the lovers kissing on a Paris street could do with
more light?

Which suggests that our camera-phones, or phone-cameras, have
a better chance of taking good photos than more sophisticated kit,
proper cameras that need adjustment. Their margin of error is astonishing: if you know even the rudiments of photography, you have the
ideal weapon to hand.

And what does the perfect moment consist of? A soldier just cut
down, a moment of passion in the street are messages about death and
love; nothing could be more elemental. In both these famous photos
there are no distractions, no other people, no fussy backdrops; chance
has isolated the protagonists and made them monumental.

A plant, a garden or a landscape can seem elemental, too – but
what makes it so? Of course, the light. A shaft or beam picking out an
object, whether from the front, the side or from behind, is the most
obvious way of making a point – a picture with, as it were, its caption

built in. Conversely, a bright general light with only one object caught unlit could make a different point. Shooting into the source of light, *contre jour*, can be the best way of characterizing certain plants: pale flowers, for example, with their petals glowing, their veins minutely delineated. The sun setting behind flowering grasses ....

The artist with his brushes has always had the advantage over the photographer. He doesn't have to wait for the light to strike. He can store moments in his memory to reproduce, work on, elaborate and combine at leisure. Did Monet grab his palette and rush out into the garden when the sun broke through? Maybe. He was an artist-showman (dare I mention Damien Hirst?) building up a body of garden impressions to create a market primed for his output. Wouldn't he have loved an iPhone?

The show at the Royal Academy now (I believe there are a dozen Monets) is called Painting the Garden. Is there any room for quieter, smaller, but just as loving garden paintings by British artists? Or even for David Hockney's all-encompassing woodlands – surely the modern equivalent of Giverny? Sadly, no.

WEATHER REPORT

Years ago Trad used to do periodical weather reports – partly because no one else seemed to; they just grumbled. In Essex in the 1970s I spotted a warming trend. In the '80s it was the coming Ice Age everyone was talking about. I kept painstaking records of rainfall and temperature in a book in the greenhouse for 41 years without learning very much, let alone being able to plot a pattern.

Rainfall at its meanest was something like 40 cm, in the whole of 1976; I think one year we were blessed with 100. Our coldest winter was 1982/3. A lot of favourite plants were killed; I have fondest memories of an *Abelia triflora* 12 feet high, graceful as a fountain, its pink flowers divinely perfumed in June.

Like an idiot (and lots of other gardeners) I took this as a sort of divine command, or at least a pretty strong hint, not to try growing them again – and so missed their company unnecessarily for the next

30 years. You find out that a plant is tender when it dies; meanwhile you should enjoy it. It may be a gardener's pleasure, but it is certainly not a duty, to keep everything alive year after year.

Then we came to London, and now take for granted that cafés have tables on the pavement all year round and most pub drinking is outdoors – things unheard of a generation ago. So yes, it's got much warmer. Is it global? Is it our fault? Is there anything we can do about it? However sketchy the evidence, vox pop says yes. What would it have said if the chilly predictions of the '80s had looked likely to come true?

February

HAYWIRE

This must be the strangest winter London has ever seen. March may blast it all away, of course, but I am more worried about the spring. There won't be one if it's all happened already.

Anticipation is so important. Excitement as each bud opens and flowers gradually make their appearance. But what if you are looking forward to a concert and you keep hearing the soloists, with no warning, loosing off in the street, under your window, out of context? In the end, there is no concert; they have all sung their hearts out and have nothing left to give. That's what I fear. Last year Bonfire Night dragged on for weeks as people let off their fireworks whenever they felt like it. I don't want to see spring dissipated, limping along week after week with no crescendo, no climax.

CALIFORNIA CONKERS

Days are warm and nights cold in February in the Napa Valley. Wine-growers prefer cold, fearing budbreak too early and tender new shoots in the frosts of March and April. Hence the surprising sight of vineyards unpruned, still with their tangled top-hamper, when much of Europe gets pruning with the new year.

After four years of drought the valley is celebrating a week of heavy rain. Brilliant-green grass is a rare sight here; all summer the fields are buff or brown, but now the hills are emerald under the ghost-grey oaks festooned with Spanish moss. The vineyard cover-crop of mustard is celebratory yellow, the almond trees in every yard pale pink (two colours to keep apart if you can). Explosions of mimosa are over; magnolias are well away, and in the hillside grass blue borage, the first orange poppies, blue lupins and the tiny magenta dodecatheons or shooting stars, primulaceous plants with swept-back petals rather like cyclamen, are jewels in the ditches.

But my favourites are the buckeyes, *Aesculus californica*. They form the lower layer of the forest, under oak, redwood and fir, with the gleaming madrones, the Western version of our strawberry trees. Buckeyes break into leaf before almost any tree, salad-green in the bare undergrowth. Cold doesn't seem to bother them. In early summer their long candles are as elaborately detailed as orchids. By late summer their leaves yellow and fall, leaving their grey tracery, wider than high, dripping with shining teardrop-shaped conkers.

For several years I collected them on Napa hillsides at vintage time and took them home. I planted them but they never germinated. Then one year I scooped some up on my way to the airport. They were in pots the same day and came up as eagerly as horse chestnuts. In 15 years we were on the third generation.

There is one tree here I would love to plant at home; the luscious pale-green and very faintly blushing camphor tree, *Cinnamomum camphora*, that spreads its long branches over many Japanese shrines. It catches your eye in any group of trees, looking edibly tender – which in England, sadly, it is.

TOO GOOD TO BE TRUE

Do you have a pale-flowered orchid hovering nearby, in your bathroom, in your office, in the lobby? If it needs occasional watering, it's a plant. If it doesn't, it's a pseudo-plant. You can also tell the difference by touching it.

The story of phalaenopsis, and its metamorphosis from rarity to banality, was told to me in a California greenhouse where rows of identical plants stretched to the horizon in colour batches from white to fire-alarm magenta, green, cream, ginger ... anything but blue. There were monsters and miniatures, dressed by the right so that their identically curved stems formed tunnels along the benches. At one end a team of Mexicans were potting up hundreds more. They were needed for a party in Beverley Hills.

The secret is, of course, micropropagation of stem cells of hybrids with lots of ploids. (My attention wandered during this part of the tour.) There are dozens of species, from the Himalayas to Australia; between them, it seems, almost anything is possible, and since the '80s orchid nurseries have been on a roll. But so have whatever you call the nurseries that do fake flowers: the distinction is becoming blurred.

The purist in me sees the multiplication of varieties, and the endless novelties with their twee names, as a sort of betrayal. This is not what gardening is about. I would rather struggle to cultivate a creation of nature in all its simplicity than choose between the latest colourways of something man-made. Am I just being po-faced? Or has it nothing to do with gardening?

———— *March* ————

JASMINE ATTACK

It comes as something of a shock to see a cosseted houseplant making a nuisance of itself, rampaging away, smothering other plants, and generally calling for a dose of weedkiller. The sweet little winter-flowering jasmine, *J. polyanthum*, wears an air of nursery innocence with its Mabel Lucy Attwell little-girl complexion. No one would suspect what a thug it can become – until they see how it has behaved over the past winter in a London garden.

It has mounted and straddled our neighbour's wall, climbed the unpruned roses waving a metre above it, smothered the ivy and launched shoots long enough to reach the ground and root on our side. A seedling has appeared on the other side of our garden too. The smell is divine, but the threat is manifest. Flowering began in December and is just past its climax. Admittedly there have only been a few nights of frost, but the idea that this is a tender hothouse thing has become absurd.

On our recent visit to California we saw it seeding prolifically, smothering rose bushes and climbing trees; the prettiest picture, but rather alarming. We read plenty of scary things about climate change, but a jasmine attack is something new.

April

ROOT MAP

'Surely there can't be any space in here' I think as I stand with my trowel and a plant pot, intent on infiltrating yet another favourite into one of our diminutive beds.

I have a mental root map of the garden. A few are all too obvious; the sycamore's, for example – and it's no good trying to plant the clematis there, where the trellis needs help to hide the goings-on next door. The *Viburnum × burkwoodii* has had the wall to itself for 20 years and has its roots akimbo; thick forearms right on the surface. No room to plant a pot, so perhaps I'll try a climber from seed. *Eccremocarpus scaber* would help, with its plentiful lacy leaves and little red (or, if I can find the seed, yellow) flowers.

In another spot where you'd think the rose, the chaenomeles and the hydrangea, never mind the sarcococca and the hellebores and ferns next to them, have completely filled the soil with roots, my trowel meets hardly any resistance. How come the residents haven't taken up all the parking space? (They certainly have on the road outside.)

So the new columbines (white), trollius ('Alabaster'), brunnera (blue), and rose ('Iceberg') I brought home are safely installed. It suddenly dawned on me as I cleaned my tools that I was wearing rubber gloves to plant them. I've never done that before. Am I growing lily-fingered in my old age?

EN ROUTE

Hergest Croft must be the only garden I have known virtually all my garden-conscious life. Originally it was a Rugby School connection: the Banks family (all Rugbeians) have been gardening here on the Welsh border for five generations; we have been friends with three. The gene for botany (or horticultural botany, which is not quite the same thing) is so powerful chez Banks that each generation has enlarged, focused and documented what is one of the best collections, of woody plants especially, on this island. The rarest plants grow among the biggest, and many of the trees are both.

Herefordshire lies on our route to North Wales. Hergest Croft is bang on the border in the little town of Kington. I know my way round the garden now, across the lawn where a dozen magnolias compete with a vast view, through a belt of huge beeches to the domestic garden, or so I think of it, a sort of walled garden without walls. Long borders of (just now) spring flowers, brilliant with tulips, lead on to beds busy with produce, to greenhouses and fruit trees, all workmanlike and all the more effective because effect is not the aim.

In fact that is the secret of the whole garden, as you walk on across an orchard to the ornamental garden around the family's former, deeply last-decade-of-Victorian, red-tiled house. If there was a plan to the garden, besides enjoying the views, the old trees in the surrounding parkland, the croquet lawn and tennis court, conservatory and rockery, and the company you can still feel lingering in long frocks and blazers, it has long gone in the indulgence of a passion for plants.

Magnolias and camellias may be most prominent just now (the Bankses, by the way, grow trees, magnolias in particular, from seed in the congenial spirit of enquiry that leads to many happy results). But your eyes swivel from carpets of long-established narcissi, still betraying eyes adept at blending colours, to a rare *Lindera* sketching spring in a burst of pale yellow, to the biggest *Cercidiphyllum* in Britain filling the sky with tiny purplish leaves beside the British champion red fir towering up 45 metres. Hergest Croft is at once spectacular and comfortable, a botanical garden in content, and Eden in spirit.

May

SICILIAN EDEN

The garden of Eden, being we suppose somewhere in the Middle East (Noah, after all, grounded on Mount Ararat) and with a subtropical climate (the apple being, let's say, an orange), made a big thing of water. My imaginary Eden certainly does. No doubt the Creator opened the heavens whenever the gardener thought a nice shower would bring on the beans or the aubergines, but I see the water supply being organized into pools and conduits, with here and there a bubbling spring or a sparkling cascade. The dappled shade is provided by fruit trees, the best authorities say palms, and an arboretum of perpetually flowering trees of convenient stature.

What's more, I've been there. Last week, in fact. It is in Sicily. We went with an International Dendrology Society tour to see the rarest trees of the island and were guided to this paradise between Siracusa and Catania, where the fertile land sloping directly to the Ionian Sea has been tragically trashed by heavy industry: the land of the Cyclops is now an oil refinery. But a little inland and a little uphill, with the cone of Mount Etna on the northern horizon, the orange groves that give us blood oranges still spread for miles. Among them lies my Eden, San Giuliano, its guardian angel Rachel Lamb, trained at the Cambridge Botanics and now director of this heavenly place.

The symbolism of the garden is clear – at least to me. The gates open on to a nightmare of ferocious spiny succulents, a cactus confrontation to deter the doubtful. Then comes reassurance: a calm passage of trees in lawns. Then the gate to the *gabinetto*, the garden of sensual delight, where plots of every desirable plant, for scent, for use, for colour or consumption, are interspersed and nourished by a grid of brightly running rills. At the entrance water gushes in an arc from heaven (or at least an elevated spout), overflowing a big stone basin to feed radiating streams. These, some tiny, shining ribbons three inches wide, rush or glide like veins and arteries among the lush-growing plants. From time to time a shower of volcanic dust descends to fertilize the soil.

Intimacy is the essence of a *gabinetto* (the word can mean cupboard, closet, loo, laboratory; almost anywhere private and privileged). This is a series of small rooms within an orchard on the edge of an orange grove. A high stone lookout seat gives you the long Etna view; look the other way and the orchard envelops you. There are little clearings for vegetables and herbs, here a garden of salvias, there an alley of pink grapefruit trees festooned with roses, a snatch of English lawn or a brimming stone water tank. Shade and soothing sound shut out the harsh Mediterranean world. It is easy to understand how Adam forgot that one of the trees was forbidden.

SEEING RED

Why is red such a tricky colour in the garden? Use it accidentally (out of a mixed-seed packet perhaps) and you throw a random emphasis onto the spot where it lands. It grabs the attention. It is intended to. Red is the colour of danger, of domination – and of painted lips. Use it deliberately and you can dictate where people look, influence their whole reaction to the picture you are painting.

The huntsman's red coat is one of the oldest tricks in landscape painting. Turner famously infuriated Constable by painting a red buoy in the foreground of his sea painting to upstage his rival's elaborate and highly contrived *The Opening of Waterloo Bridge* hanging next to it. What's more, he did it as an afterthought, on varnishing day, as an act of provocation. That's the power of red.

Why does red do this to your eye? Chromatically speaking, it is so close to green that dogs (they tell me) can't tell the difference. And yet it appears to us as green's diametrical opposite. It lies at one end (the longest-wave end) of the spectrum we can see, with the quiet violet at the other end. Are 'quiet' and 'noisy' valid descriptions of colours?

In a garden, red indicates your policy, if not your philosophy. Christopher Lloyd at Great Dixter changed tack completely when he abolished a rose garden with its colours in gentle harmony and brought in cannas and dahlias and everything strident. It amounted to a career move; out of middle-aged respectability and convention and onto the cutting edge. The daredevil.

Myself, I'm leery of it. I've never painted a door red – almost always the clean but bashful colour we call 'château grey'. Light has a lot to do with it: hard Mediterranean light takes strong colour in its stride; bougainvillea is an example. Plant it in our island's softer light and it looks like an accident in a paint factory. On the other hand, they can't have too much of that scarlet pelargonium 'Roi des Balcons' in the window boxes of the Black Forest or the Tyrol.

In my timid garden, on a ground of as much green as I can manage on walls of yellow-grey London brick, white is a pretty daring colour. Cream to blue, and pink so long as it's pale, are as emphatic as my delicate sensibilities can entertain. Sometimes I remind myself of Lizzy Bennett's father, who said something like 'A small pullet's egg, lightly boiled, is not unwholesome.' Rather daring, though.

WHAT'S LEFT

It's taken me a long time (all my life in fact) to pin down a trait that steers my way of looking at my surroundings – gardens, views, streets – above all, buildings. My eyes fly to the oldest. In a park it is the oldest and grandest trees, avenues, fountains, gazebos – the evidence of past intentions. I am a prisoner of history (as indeed we all are) and my sentence demands that I look for its traces wherever I go.

It is most demanding in London, as the city dons and sheds its never-resting coats of scaffolding. The crane-count in the past few years must be the highest it has ever been. It's true that every great city throughout most of its history has been a building site; it's only later generations that see the finished (for the time being) scheme. The Roman forum was never a pristine panorama of pillars and pediments; there was always scaffolding in the picture as another temple or monument went up or had a facelift. Athens the same; Paris (imagine the mess when Haussmann was bulldozing his boulevards) and now London. Exhibitionist towers are the mark of our times and we have lost control of where they go or how tacky they look. And a new threat goes beyond tacky: the threat of a 'garden' bridge to block London's most majestic view, the Thames between Westminster and the City. Who in his right mind would try to grow plants on the most exposed possible site?

So I wander the town with my eyes skinned for relics of its past; easy to find in the quiet residential areas of terraces and squares, harder and harder in commercial streets where old buildings, if they have survived thus far, have their ground floors hacked out to make shops and their façades hidden by the banal fascias proclaiming Boots or Tesco.

The Victorian pub on the corner, the calmly handsome Georgian house front hiding a solicitor's office, the pompous Edwardian stone front of the old Town Hall (now a dance hall), a quirky bit of timbered building or even a war memorial are precious clues about the past. These are the things that give you a sense of place. And they make me sad that all this history happened and I was not there to see it.

EMERALD ISLE

Back from a week in Ireland. 'The magnolias are over', everyone said. Ah, but the rhododendrons are in full cry, every leaf is fresh in the sun, and two of the most audacious gardens I have ever met were gleaming in the sunshine between the showers. Nor were the magnolias over; not by any means.

Mount Congreve is a legend – in the sense that few people used to see it. I tried to visit in the days of its creator, Ambrose Congreve, and failed. He had reached 104 before he died, still gardening, in spirit at least, in 2011. For the moment, his 80 acres of intelligent, intricate and supremely picturesque planting lives on. For how long is a delicate matter, between his trustees and the Irish government. For the moment, what the garden needs, and richly deserves, is more visitors.

Congreve was apparently inspired by Lionel de Rothschild at
Exbury to create a woodland garden for the vast variety of rhododendrons, azaleas and magnolias. Exbury Gardens are spread over
200 acres, gently sloping to the Beaulieu River. Mount Congreve has
a mere 70, tumbling down (almost diving off a cliff at one point) to
one of Ireland's biggest rivers, the broad, reed-fringed Suir a few miles
above Waterford.

We are used to magnolias as single specimens, sometimes groups,
but rarely a forest. The Congreve way was different. He planted hundreds of seedlings of one particular *M. campbellii* that now form a
wood of pale-barked trunks perhaps 60 feet high. His style was decisive: a wall of pieris, a long ramp of one Japanese maple, another wall
of an orange azalea, facing one of purple. The colours are calculated:
this is picture-making with plants on a heroic scale, and with breath-
catching results. A gardener told me how Ambrose, as he called him
(though possibly not to his face), rode his horse around the garden
every morning, often before breakfast, then re-emerged mid-morning,
fork in hand, and worked with his gardeners all day. He was, I am told,
weatherproof. No bothy for him in a shower; he gardened on.

Thomas Pakenham of Tullynally comes from the same hardy race,
with as little restraint in planting. *Meetings with Remarkable Trees*
was the first display of his splendid – indeed unique – tree portraits,
20 years ago. In his company, it must be said, every tree becomes
remarkable, intrinsically, scientifically, whimsically, pathologically,
and as a source of human stories.

Four hours of walk and talk only skimmed his collection, scattered through parkland, woods and gardens. Tullynally is a great grey
Regency Gothic battleship of a house surrounded by beeches and oaks
of the biggest size. Among them, then on and out into the countryside,
the new collections go, many of them from Pakenham-collected seeds
from China or the Himalayas. Reaching 80 seems only to have invigorated him. Half a mile from the house, magnolias form a glade, then
camellias, dogwoods, tiny rhododendrons just planted out – without
guards. Have rabbits gone the way of snakes in Ireland?

UNBEATEN TRACKS

Who was Isabella Bird? Her name kept cropping up when I asked a Japanese friend questions about history; it seemed that Mrs B was a prime source. Then I learned she was a Victorian traveller – and what a traveller. She went, alone, to the limits of the visitable world – and beyond, particularly in Japan.

This was in 1878, when the country had been open to foreigners for only 25 years, and was very far from being modernized. In the north, which she explored with patient thoroughness, there were essentially no roads. She searched for rideable horses (even the best were broken-down nags) and hacked with her native manservant/interpreter from village to village, recording every detail. Lodgings were local inns, devoid of any privacy or comfort. She was mobbed as the first foreigner (let alone foreign woman) ever sighted. Fleas and mosquitos were everywhere. Often there was only beans and rice, sometimes an egg, to eat. Tracks were often streambeds – it rained incessantly – and she was constantly coming off her stumbling mount. But her prose never falters, and at times becomes poetry. She spends a week examining the great Shogun shrines at Nikko, detailing every carving in its overwhelming decoration. She identifies plants with a keen botanical eye, she describes the Shinto rites: a whole expedition could not have done more.

In Hokkaido, when she reaches the land of the 'hairy' Ainus, the indigenous tribe conquered by the Japanese, she shows total fascination with the 'savages', as she calls them. She finds them physically far more attractive than the 'puny' Japanese, and I suspect falls half in love with a young warrior. She spends weeks recording their language, moving from coast to mountains, to compare dialects. And it is clear they fall for her.

This Edinburgh housewife (her married name was Bishop) was not often at home. Her accounts were written in letters to her sister (there were 44 from Japan, thousands of words in each). How she handled pens, ink and paper on horseback through floods is a wonder in itself. But Japan was just one trip. She explored the USA, by steamboat to Cincinnati and St Louis, then the Great Lakes to Canada. She reports on each emerging city in detail, recounts appalling voyages on the stormy lakes and the paddle-steamer passage down the St Lawrence, shooting rapids where one in eight ships came to grief.

Where else did she go? To Malaya (the 'Chersonese'), China, Korea, Persia, Tibet and Australia – each one a volume. Since I found Mrs Bishop on my Kindle, she takes every bus ride with me.

June

GROTTESQUE

Would you like a grotto? Do you warm to the idea of a cool, shell-lined cave, water dripping from stalactites, mysterious reflections in a dark pool? They're back in fashion. I just went to what must be the most beautiful grotto of modern times at the Ballymaloe Cooking School near Cork, a crustacean mosaic, a pristine masterpiece of a summer-house (no water, admittedly) that perfectly expressed the spirit – of what? Grotteity? Grottiness?

Last year's winner of the P J Redouté Prize for the best garden book* in French is a tombstone of a volume on grottoes, illustrating a score of magnificent creations, some glistening bright, some spooky, all cool retreats from the sunlit world. It classifies them as, for example, Primordial, Diluvian, Labyrinthine, Sacred, Tellurique, Profane, Underworldly – and the Introductory chapter is called *Ouvrir l'ombre* – opening the shade.

As it happens, we have a grotto of our own, deep in the Welsh woods; a rocky tunnel 100 metres long that set out to be a gold mine but drew a blank. Its mouth, protected by an iron gate, is a gloomy hole overhung by ferns and issuing a dark and gleaming stream. Penetrate the depths (take a torch) and you are in a world of black, dripping rock, with here and there a little cascade to cool your collar.

The grotto spirit, though, can be expressed in less ambitious ways. I have been looking round this tiny garden for a corner to transform into an alcove plastered with shells, with perhaps a pretty dribble into a basin. For now we just have a tank with a Mr Spit-Face like a Green Man and four goldfish: two tiddlers and two gorgeous 'comets' with wide waving tails called Halley and Haley (Bopp).

*The book is *L'imaginaire des grottes dans les jardins européens* by Hervé Brunon and Monique Mosser. Oh yes; moss. Another essential.

July

WARM ENOUGH YET?

I wish I had kept count of the number of plants that were considered exotic, or treated as tender, when I started gardening, and are now seen as mainstream. I remember, for example, planting my first agapanthus. It must have been about 1972. I waited until June, dug a hole in the sunniest and driest spot, buried crocs and gravel, and tenderly tucked them in. 'Headbourne Hybrids' were supposedly the only strain with a good chance. In October I covered them with slates on bricks to keep off the winter rains. They are still flowering, as far as I know, 45 years later.

Is it acclimatization, breeding, know-how or climate change? Possibly all these things. London, of course, has been practically subtropical for years now. Remember how we once marvelled at the old olive tree in the Chelsea Physic Garden? Now blue and white agapanthus ('Blue Storm' and 'White Storm') line a wall in this Kensington garden, shaded for most of the day, and flower well, if not lavishly. The trick, I find, is to be generous with water and a high-potash feed in spring and summer. Our best plant is 'Northern Star'; tight-filling the same large pot for five years; it has six tall stems on the point of flowering. I keep its saucer half-full all the time. This year's new treat is a variety called 'Queen Mum' I bought from Hoyland Nurseries from Yorkshire at the Chelsea Flower Show. The flowers on its long stems are white, but each petal starts off blue; more of a specimen for a pot, I think, than a border.

Trachelospermum jasminoides ('star jasmine') was thought doubt-fully hardy until quite recently. Now smart London is full of it. I was amused to learn that one name for it in the USA is 'confederate jasmine'. Why? It grows south of the Mason-Dixon Line.

HAPPY RETURN

Can there be a greater satisfaction in gardening – or in life itself, for that matter – than seeing your careful plans coming to fruition? It is ten years since we sold our place in La France Profonde. Veteran readers of Trad may remember my probably obsessive accounts of tree-planting, building and garden-making in the wide-open spaces of the Bourbonnais, the northernmost part of the Auvergne. Bocage (as in Normandy) is the term for the repetition of field and copse and wood and hedgerow that makes such soothing and satisfying prospects.

The vast green rug of the Forêt de Tronçais, over 25,000 acres of tall oaks, the best destined for wine barrels, dominates the region. Our little farm lay in its pastoral fringes. Charolais cattle, bulky and pale, are the main signs of life around the red-roofed farms.

We were delighted to find that our successors have kept everything going as we planned it – even our ancient Land Rover. We bumped around the familiar tracks, looking up at trees I remember as little saplings. Pines we planted in 1994 have had their first thinning and now look like grown-up forest. Oaks that seemed so reluctant to grow at first (and needed expensive protection from the deer) are now an impenetrable green wall, house-high.

Better still, our successors keep the network of rides open and mown for their horses; perspectives that were lines on the ground are now gloriously three-dimensional; the shape we gave the landscape in our imaginations is a reality of masses and spaces, shapes and textures, with a logic that reveals itself as you move.

In the only spot where the gritty acid soil is deep enough, with enough moisture, I planted half an acre of American oaks and maples to fire up in autumn. Sugar maple and swamp, scarlet and willow oak are trees I could only dream about at home. Here in acid soil and a continental climate (it was 35° C when we were there) they far out-grow the native species.

And the parterre we squeezed in an awkward sloping trapezoid space between house and barn has acquired authority; you can't imagine the enclosure filled in any other way than with its beds of box, its walls of hornbeam, troughs of hydrangeas and a froth of blue and white flowers. Only my vineyard has gone, to make a paddock. They were right: the wine was never going to be great. It needed a forgiving, or proprietorial, spirit to see its virtues.

August

SELFIES OF A SORT

It's the sound of God washing his world. Gently rinsing it, rather, with a night of unemphatic rain. I am out on the verandah at midnight, mingling the scents of orange blossom and Pauillac, my bedtime glass. The rain is a cocoon, soothing away all other sounds. Time to reflect on a month away on visits to gardens, houses, churches and the seaside. A dry month, at times too hot; hence the luxury of this healing rain.

My iPhone has become my chief remembrancer. Shameful to admit, but the snaps in its camera are my garden notebook; more than that – almost my diary. What's more it knows where and when I took them.

It tells me that in the past month I've been to the Loire, Burgundy, Arbois in the Jura, Champagne, Kew, Suffolk, Exbury, Dorset and Stourhead. The photographs recall people, plants, places ... but in that fatally selective way that (if you're not careful) screens out more complete memory. It's an obvious trap. We laugh at tourists and their selfies in front of iconic views: endless smiles; how many memories?

There are, of course, occasions when photography becomes the main object. Then I will circle round an object, or investigate a garden or a building, for hours in the hope of a telling angle and the right light. The camera fills up (only it never seems to) with alternative shots that are impossible to edit properly on its tiny screen, and are usually disappointing downloaded at home. Choosing the best shots of a sustained session takes longer than the shoot itself.

My favourites from July? A wonderful waterfall we found near Arbois on the river Planches, where a cascade crashes out of a forest to form a staircase of pools and line them with marble-like tufa. An octogenarian topiarist in Burgundy carving yew *pièces montées* in blazing sunshine, a cave of ancient wine bottles belonging to an avant-garde sculptor at Jasnières on the Loir. Then our old garden and woods in the Auvergne, a German military cemetery in Normandy with a thousand mophead maples in parade order in the rain, a girl in a restaurant in the Jura, the magnificently austere cathedral of Laon in Champagne, isolated on its hilltop, and back in England, sailing down the Beaulieu River past Exbury gardens, Christchurch Priory and Sherborne Abbey for glorious medieval vaults, Stourhead for its lake and its magnificent tulip trees. You can travel a long way and see no finer sight than Stourhead.

September

TRAVEL HOPEFULLY

Discuss: lower your aspirations and achieve a higher success rate. It's logical; baying for the moon has never had a success rate at all. Contentment is most easily found by starting with low expectations. It's a good excuse not to frequent three-star restaurants.

I am, I admit, that kind of gardener. Or at least part of me is. I can't quite bring myself to admire groundsel (except for its example as a profligate survivor) and I don't weed random seedlings until I'm sure of what they are or might be; I can accept half-hearted flowering in a plant I am fond of, delay deadheading and leave fading plants standing in the hope of some aesthetic justification for their remains.

You won't find me dropping everything to go and tidy up; you will, on the other hand, find me loitering with secateurs when there's a deadline at my desk.

Perhaps this is the moment to say that I am pleased (or not displeased) to be harvesting my total crop of eight tomatoes. Tiny ones at that (but red). They have endured a small pot, intermittent watering, a life lived in 80 percent shade, and an attack of whitefly. So I shall enjoy them as a minor triumph.

The process of gardening is more important than the result – until, that is, you open for the National Gardens Scheme. Who was it who said 'to travel hopefully is better than to arrive'? I had to look it up too: it sounds rather 'Confucius he say', so I was surprised to see that it is one of my favourite authors, Robert Louis Stevenson. As a young man he wrote sententious essays, collected together as *Virginibus Puerisque*. That's where you'll find it.

Is it, though? Better than to arrive, I mean. What is a gardening arrival? The moment when the shutter clicks and you have something for your album? The moment you pour yourself a drink and sink into a chair? What will you be thinking about as you take a sip? Whether you can get away without mowing before the weekend?

Even Japanese Zen gardens haven't arrived. Daily raking is existential for them. The Grand Condé's chef Vatel killed himself because the fish was late. Gardeners take heart; there is no gardening equivalent.

NIL BY HOSE

We are mourning a sudden and puzzling loss. One of our favourite plants at Saling Hall was the pale-purple-flowering *Abutilon vitifolium* 'Veronica Tennant', an almost instant little tree, growing five feet in a year to 15 feet or so, with grey-felted vine- or maple-leaves and wide-open papery flowers like the most innocent of hollyhocks. True, it's a short-lived plant, perhaps six or seven years, but in our narrow garden our plan was to grow it against a wall to help screen us from next door. I reasoned I could prune off any forward-facing growth and encourage the sideways branches to form a screen.

VT took some finding, and when she arrived, via Rassells, they warned me not to water it. Not even once. I argued that I had seen its parents growing in a Chilean rain forest; odd, I thought, for a plant with such fragile flowers. 'Not a drop', said Richard Hood. She, VT that is, started slowly in the dry ground below the wall, then after six weeks shot up in rude health to way above my head. Success, I thought, until one morning she was suddenly, obviously, dead. Had I broken the no-water rule? A couple of showers had, but also I fear a cavalier hand with the hose. This was no flood; the soil around seemed quite dry. But Richard was right. I can't find a specific warning in my reference books, except in Michael Howarth-Booth's still-useful *Effective Flowering Shrubs* of 1970. He calls *A. vitifolium* 'a miff'. What miffs her is evidently water.

——————— *October* ———————

THE BIG APPLE

October is the month to visit New York. The sun is bright; the air is clear and relatively cool – though this year I was too early for the firing-up of fall. My favourite room in that city looks down from the 19th floor onto Central Park. The lake glints just below, embosomed in trees. The towers of Manhattan stretch out beyond. The bookcases filling the walls contain a glorious library on the history of gardening and landscape. This is the office of Elizabeth Barlow Rogers, the person who revived the Park from its nadir in the 1970s and is now President of the Institute for Landscape Studies. This is where she edits *Sitelines*, its magazine.

We first met when I was touring radio studios to promote my wine atlas and she was on a parallel course, discussing her first book: *The Forests and Wetlands of New York*. It was as though she was the first person to notice that all the concrete lies in a spectacular landscape of woods and cliffs, marshes and islands. Look out of the window as your plane lands at JFK. Below you lies Jamaica Bay, a vast wildlife refuge that competes with Essex for its wandering muddy shoreline, home to (they say) 300 species of birds, not to mention horseshoe crabs, terrapin and mosquitos. In the distance are the Manhattan skyscrapers, beyond and around them the Hudson and the East River and Long Island Sound, Staten Island, the cliffs of the Palisades ... a dramatic natural context that city people easily forget.

Central Park is there to remind them. Forty years ago it was neglected, overgrown, filthy and dangerous. Then Betsy was appointed Administrator, the first in the role. She instilled order, found volunteers to clear up, plant up – and give money. She inaugurated the Central Park Conservancy, recruiting the great and good to support the park. Not long ago one Maecenas signed a cheque for $100,000.

So the park is looking good, perhaps as good as it ever looked since Mr Olmsted and Mr Vaux set it all in motion in the 1850s. We walked over from Central Park West to the Boathouse on the tree-fringed lake, through the Rambles, a supremely romantic piece of woodland landscaping where paths wind up and down among what seem to be wild woods, though suspiciously floriferous with flourishing native flowers. It was Michaelmas-daisy time; their delicate pale flowers scattered under the trees in pools of light. Great whaleback rocks are a leitmotif of Central Park; indeed the dark-grey schist, its surface often polished by schoolboys' trousers, is the necessary bedrock of all Manhattan's towers.

A gondola from Venice glided by; under the spreading, just-yellowing elms of the Mall a piper played by the monument to Sir Walter Scott; a faint whiff from the veldt wafts over from the zoo; fountains play among banks of chrysanthemums. It will soon be time for the sweetgums, the maples and the oaks to catch fire. Much as I love Kensington Gardens, there is nowhere on earth like Central Park.

NEVERLAND AND AFTER

In their time Haseley Court and Folly Farm have both been among England's most influential gardens. One is a classic of Lutyens and Jekyll's Edwardian years, the other a masterpiece 50 years younger. But 'in their time', it struck me, gives quite the wrong impression. Their time is now.

I visited them both in June with the patrons of the Garden Museum. Folly Farm in Berkshire has been restored with great pains and immense scholarship, seemingly regardless of cost, by Jonathon and Jennifer Oppenheimer. The house is famous in itself as one of Lutyens's typical excursions into the Neverland territory he shared with J M Barrie and Randolph Caldecott. I have always loved Lutyens, and believe the secret of his juggling with ideas as modern as his contemporary Frank Lloyd Wright and as old as English vernacular materials, is essentially his sense of humour.

He loved catslide roofs, fantastic chimney stacks, huge oriel windows and little dormers in improbable places – almost as though he were illustrating a book for children. In the garden his trademark – or one of them – is ingenious changes of level involving curving, sometimes almost circular steps, beautifully made of mixtures of brickwork and carved stone.

Folly Farm has all these things, originally planted by Gertrude Jekyll, no doubt in her intricate palette of colours. Now Dan Pearson has had a go – and the result is, to my mind, a marvellous match for Lutyens's whimsical grandeur: decisive, original and harmonious. Small ideas or fiddly colour arrangements would be wrong. Colour schemes are brave enough to embrace massive spaces, and often the plants themselves are supersize, too.

Haseley Court in Warwickshire belongs to a later era, the lean years after World War II. Nancy Lancaster, who made the garden, was the American socialite decorator who gave grand houses permission to be shabby, and shabby ones permission to strike grand attitudes.

Her ideas live on, at one end in the Mayfair showrooms of her firm, Colefax & Fowler, still the headquarters of chintz de luxe, at the other in such establishments as the Hotels du Vin, where gaps in the floorboards are justified by expensive soap in the bathroom. Shabby chic signalled aristo confidence; easier to do indoors, you'd think, than out. Somehow just not weeding doesn't cut it.

Haseley Court became a beacon of good taste not because it was neglected, but because the Lancaster eye used powerful signals of ancestral glories and gardened gaily around them with no apparent inhibitions. Ancient topiary was a good starting point. Nothing says long tradition like a whole chess set of crisply cut yews. Visiting Haseley with her successors, Desmond and Fiona Heywood, I realized how deep the Lancaster style has sunk into our psyche (or certainly mine). From the walled garden, brimful of what seems random planting around old apple trees, colours from Matisse, to the long canal with green banks under willows, I recognized my own efforts at Saling Hall – or rather what inspired them.

GOING QUIETLY

I've never really believed Marie Antoinette said 'Let them eat cake.' I prefer the story where she looks out of her window with a cry of delight and sends for the gardener to ask who had the pretty idea of scattering yellow leaves on the lawn. That must have been on the day the staff at Versailles had downed tools.

The last leaves are hanging in the sycamore as I write. Three weeks have seen countless thousands fall. We have filled ten bin bags for the council to take away. It's no way to run a sustainable garden, I know, but where do I make a compost heap in this tiny space, how much use is sycamore compost, and where would I use it?

Everyone agrees that the South has seen a glorious autumn, a slow glow in calm weather for weeks on end. We haven't seen frost or strong wind; few trees have excelled as brilliant individuals; instead they have all concurred in gradual transformation through fading green and yellows to a uniform dull gold. One of the most sustained performers, in buttery yellow, has been the humble field maple. Liquidambars, the usual motley stars, have gone quietly; *Pyrus* 'Chanticleer', the pavement pear, is the exception round here, turning brilliant pale orange with touches of red. The magnolia in our front garden, with huge leaves, A4-sized ovals some of them, provoked by a spring haircut, is the last to shed. The plain swept surfaces, when all the leaves are gone, have their own appeal – though Marie Antoinette might not agree.

DREAM COME TRUE

If the Honourable Charles Hamilton was rewarded for his eminent taste with a sojourn in heaven, yesterday he and I were looking at the same scene. Painshill, his Surrey Elysium, was looking more perfect than he can ever have imagined it: trees grown taller in more variety, lawns smooth-shaven, follies secure in gleaming perfection and only his Temple of Bacchus still a building (or rather re-building) site.

The low sunlight flooded each monument; Gothic eminence, craggy grotto, five-arch- and Chinese bridges, mausoleum, Turkish tent and the naked Sabine struggling in the bronze arms of her naked Roman captor. It glittered on the lake in crystal reflections, picking out every detail of proud swans and gilded autumn trees. It lit the black platforms of the tallest Lebanon cedar in Britain and the bare vines of his vineyard tipped towards the water like Johannisberg towards the Rhine.

When Hamilton last saw it, 250 years ago, the trees were young, the buildings they now shade and embower selfconsciously new. Now he must swell with pride, and search anxiously for each new American plant, shipped with such care from Mr Bartram in Philadelphia, to see how it is acclimatizing 3,000 miles from home.

His ingenious waterwheel, pumping water to the lake from the River Mole below, slowly turns like the hands of a clock marking the years, drops from its mossy paddles glinting in the sun. A team of gardeners rakes oak leaves into russet piles. Time is on holiday here – which is its habit in heaven.

November

CROESO Y CYMRU

I was surprised (and perhaps a little alarmed) that they'd noticed, when the *Lonely Planet* guide chose North Wales as number four in a list of the world's top ten regions to visit in 2017 – the only one in Britain, which is of course absurd.

Until then I had supposed we were alone in finding that our mountainous area ticks all the boxes. A large chunk of it is the Snowdonia National Park, stretching from Conway on the north coast to Aberdovey seventy miles to the south, and twenty or thirty miles inland. I'm sure what the *Lonely Planet* people like is the hiking and biking, the rock-climbing and the vast beaches, although they do describe it as 'a haunt of in-the-know foodies' – which will surprise most people. Incidentally, they're quite right.

I can't deny that our own little corner, our woods, suspended above the estuary of the River Mawddach, is beautiful. Over the too-silted-up estuary rises the granite wall of Cader Idris; to the left the peaks around the Dinas pass, to the right the sea, Cardigan Bay and from the top, on a very clear day, the Wicklow Hills. Behind lie the Rhinogs, not specially high but dauntingly wild; miles of bog and rocks with no tracks except the Old Harlech Road, scarcely visible on the ground but marked by an 18th-century milestone: XI Miles.

Our woods have won two gold medals at the Royal Welsh Show, in 2005 and 2016, perhaps for careful forestry, but as much, I suspect, for the pleasure they give the judges. They could hardly be more varied, in trees or topography: rushing streams, little lakes, remnants of old oak woodland in the valley bottoms, lots of beech, some red oak and higher up larch, Douglas fir, and of course the spiky Sitka spruce that will produce timber even on bogs and rocks. Everywhere birch, rowan and the pale-green larch seedlings. Gorse, too, of course. I forgive it its barbs when I breathe the honey scent of its flowers. From each of our high points, views to make you catch your breath.

I don't know how the *Lonely Planet* found out about it, though.

December

SHORT DARK DAYS

It's darkness, not lack of interest, that keeps me out of the garden in December. There is plenty to enjoy when you can see it. So how much precious garden space is it worth, I was asking myself, devoting to plants 'of winter interest'. If that means their one virtue is winter-flowering, with 11 nondescript months, probably not much. Besides, the roster of all-rounders is pretty limited: you can enjoy *Mahonia* 'Charity' and *Viburnum × bodnantense* in everyone else's garden. Camellias, too – at least in this neighbourhood. Not everyone, I know, relishes delayed gratification, but my most absorbed moments just now are spent looking for future promise. It's the swelling bud that hypnotizes me, more than the picturesque wreckage of last year's growth.

Having said that, I have just paid a visit to a garden where the ebb and flow of the seasons is on unselfconscious display. Waltham Place near Maidenhead has been an Oppenheim family home for almost a century, but also functions as a laboratory and school for ideas of sustainability and biodynamics that are rarely played out for all to see. Its Head of Education told me it is also used as therapy for people suffering from dementia, with encouraging results.

A morning of drizzle and mist dramatized its qualities. Winter here is as much a celebration as spring is – or if that's over-egging it, as much of a statement. It is a picture of plants in their plenitude – and past it. Tall grasses, sere and pale, play a large part in December (as they do at Wisley). The bright squirrel-brown of beech hedges seems to give off heat, and the red stems of Siberian dogwood blaze in the mist. Everywhere there was something that called me over for a closer look; many seedlings, of course, with their green look of promise, even if their fate is to be weeded out later.

Following the phases of the moon is routine here. I was shown two mature hedges of *Lonicera nitida*, one solid, chunky and full of leaf, the other half-bare, with dying branches and naked twigs. Both, I was told, were trimmed in autumn; the first at the proper phase of the moon for pruning, when the sap is in the roots, the second at the wrong moment, with the sap risen. Was the gardener reprimanded? I am an agnostic in such matters, but I shall look up at the moon nervously when I next get out my shears.

2017

January

PLANT OF THE YEAR

Trad used to do a Plant of the Month, when we had a big garden and many choices. This the first time I've done a Plant of the Year – but really it's a Plant of Many Years; ten at least.

I love orchids for living in slow motion. Writing about a genus so closely and intensely studied is like treading on eggshells, but this cymbidium (I believe its name is, or was when I bought it, 'Rum Jungle') has lived in the same modest plastic pot all this time. You couldn't get a toothpick in among its curling roots. It lives on water and neglect, most of the year in a shady spot behind the greenhouse, where I top up its saucer when I remember, sometimes with a drop of Growmore in the can. (Could I be drummed out of the RHS for offering such unscientific advice?)

I brought it into the greenhouse in October and into the warmth of the house, by a north-facing window, in late November and gave it a little orchid feed. The flowers have been erupting for four weeks now – and of course stay pristine for weeks. Each flower of this rather ghostlike cultivar has a double red line faintly picked out on its lower lip, presumably to guide insects straight to the action.

My sister sees rescuing near-death orchids as a sacred calling and would scoop a tiny pot with a shrivelled phalaenopsis off a skip in the street for intensive care in her kitchen. Actually there is nothing very intensive about it; only patience and a strict regime. No food, almost no water, domestic temperature and a refusal to give up. The joy when a tentative bud appears repays months of nurture.

PSEUD'S CORNER

How limited, stilted and inhibited our gardening vocabulary is compared with, say, the jargon of the art world.

I look in vain in our literature for the sort of punchy phrases I noted on the walls of the Royal Academy during its Abstract Expressionism show. I have never read of a garden, for example, 'dense with corpuscular motifs', or 'by turns visceral and cosmic'. Would I recognize them, I wonder, if I met them among the hedges and lawns?

I did find some expressions, though, I would love to attach to a garden. A 'spiritualized space' sounds more at home in a garden than on a canvas, and I challenge – who? Arabella Lennox-Boyd or Tom Stewart-Smith? to plant me a 'lush but fragile impasto'.

Perhaps the real difference is that art critics have to maintain an illusion of more significance than meets the eye. Language can easily become a veil concealing a void of meaning. Gardening is realism made physical, permanent and in full view, with no room for commentary or excuses. Once it could use references unmissable by people who had been to the right school, or done the Grand Tour, to express political or religious messages – to those who knew the code. Sadly, we have thrown away the code book; what would, say, a Brexit garden or a Momentum garden look like? Not free of weeds, the latter. I fear the furthest the current idiom will get you is a genuflection to a Dutch gardener who paints in grasses.

BRUTAL DINGE

Concrete has never had any appeal for me – and I could express it more strongly than that. It has noble and necessary uses: Norman

Foster's astonishing Millau Viaduct, for example, curving on its slender pillars 300 metres above the Tarn. But in its brutalist heyday in Britain in the 1960s and '70s, the cult of concrete usurped the place of brick and stone. I cannot wait to see some of its worst outrages demolished.

The Household Cavalry barracks in Knightsbridge is one of my pet hates: horses in a tower, indeed. The old barracks was a dashing brick range festooned with trophies and helmets, with a stone ball on each buttress. I bought one from the demolition people for the garden at Saling Hall, but I can't forgive the dingy grey intrusion on the views in Hyde Park. You could argue that the Hilton Hotel is worse – or at least taller, but the barracks is ours, built with our money, which makes it a self-inflicted wound. The street side is appalling, too; an immense length of grubby grey wall.

This is concrete's shame; its grubby grey, inevitable as rain-streaks and made far worse by rough-shuttering. Architects would probably say (indeed, have said) that it demonstrates their honesty to show the grain of the timber they use. All it does is collect even more dirt. The National Theatre on the South Bank is a dreadful example – in this case, of the grain of Douglas fir. Its architect, Sir Denys Lasdun, said 'there is something aphrodisiacal about the smell of wet concrete.' *The Economist*'s architectural correspondent described it as 'an aircraft carrier in collision with a Norman keep.' It's fine at night, when all you see are the lighted windows. By day it is the epitome of dinge.

Concrete in gardens, once it spreads from the paving up the walls, or into a brutalist pergola, brings drabness into what should be light, elegant and gay. Of course there are exceptions. Fallingwater, Frank Lloyd Wright's house astride the river at Bull Run, Pennsylvania, balances concrete slabs on a composition like a mobile, airy and graceful. Its concrete is smooth, clean and not remotely brutal. Even so, Wright once said he would prefer it covered in gold leaf.

Concrete is fundamentally a cheat. You can pour it into any shape (as Zaha Hadid did in the absurd white wave of a café, like something from *Moby Dick*, in Hyde Park). It never shows you how the building works, where the weight falls, or how the structure supports itself. Timber, bricks and stone do that; concrete is carving in blancmange.

February

OIL, NOT WATERCOLOUR

Back from Snowdonia after our customary mid-winter visit. By the beginning of February there were already tiny signs of spring in swelling buds, hazel catkins, a few snowdrops. There was snow dusting the hills over 180 metres; on one west-facing grassy bank the first wild Welsh daffodil had opened. In *The Winter's Tale* Perdita says

> *... Daffodils,*
> *That come before the swallow dares, and take*
> *The winds of March with beauty ...*

This is February; more evidence of climate change?

A sunny day in winter here is disconcertingly beautiful. The hills have a richer palate of colours even than their spring swatch of pale-to-dark greens or their yellow-to-khaki-to-ginger autumn coat. Winter colours come in fine brushstrokes and filigree detail. Oaks, trunk to twig, shine light grey in the sun, ashes silvery white, sometimes orange, birch twigs smoky purple; you can pick out their populations across a valley, distinct from the red of Japanese larch among the grey-blue of Sitka spruce. Hemlock and Douglas fir are coachwork green, the rocks among them various greys dotted with white quartz or stained yellow with lichen. Bracken smears the hills with brown. Gorse, even now, pricks bright-yellow stitches, and a stream flashes silver. There is nothing watercolour about this painting: it has the full tone of oils.

REVISION

The first sniff of spring today: aconites opening, snowdrops unsheathing, tree buds showing signs of life. There is a growth scent in the air, despite the frost, that makes my spirits surge. It also makes me think how deep my hibernation has been these last months, and how timely. The dormancy of the garden has given me a respite from the temptation of outdoors, time to sit and concentrate on the book I'm writing.

Or rather rewriting. I first wrote it half my lifetime ago, in 1973. How I had the nerve I don't know. I was mocked in *Private Eye*: 'Johnson admits that until he had signed the contract he had never seen a tree.' Miraculously, readers don't seem to have twigged that I was only one step ahead of them, if that, in my studies. What they could tell was that I was loving it. Not half as much, though, as I am loving revisiting my old state of innocent ignorance to bring myself up to date.

The solid elements I can add now are, first, experience. In 1973 I had planted a mere handful of trees and never cut one down. Thirty-seven years later I have planted thousands, some of them successfully, others no doubt ill-advisedly, and cut down almost as many. In other words I have turned forester as well as gardener. Decades of collecting, observing, calculating and just adoring trees have given me a lot, probably too much, to say.

Second new element: refreshed expertise from John Grimshaw, whose *New Trees*, introductions, that is, since 1970, was published by Kew last year. John is, unexpectedly for a tree expert and enthusiast, resident galanthologist at Colesbourne, the Gloucestershire estate of the Elwes family. Henry John Elwes was the (Edwardian) co-author, with Augustine Henry, of the monumental *Trees of Great Britain & Ireland*. There is a pleasing symmetry here.

I can handle the temptation while the ground stays hard and until we see touches of leaf. The counter-pull of books piled round me, the red fire and the cold hypnotic screen are holding their own for the moment. I must press on before my resolve thaws, too.

LAKE OR POND?

Is our New Forest water a pond or a lake? A reader has put me straight. It's not just a question of size. A lake has a water surface big enough to allow a swan to take off. It's an elegant solution, he suggests, because it involves the surroundings as well as the water. Quite a big pond in the middle of a wood would still be a pond; remove the trees and it would attract swans and become a lake. So it's up to swans to decide.

The swan measure rates the Round Pond in Kensington Gardens a lake (they love it) – but can a lake have a hard bottom and masonry margins? And things are different again in America. *On Golden Pond* was a movie about a lake, and Menemsha Pond, where I remember dropping anchor once in the fog between ghostly buoys, each with its cormorant, is an arm of the sea .... But then Martha's Vineyard is not a vineyard ....

A BETTER NAME

Crocuses are so sudden. There have only been three days of open weather, wide light skies with clouds you can count, a breeze without an edge, and they've come out of hiding. The weather, of course, is a February Feint. Next week, the blizzard. But it's a little trailer for spring just when you're starting to need it.

Crocuses are like snowdrops, interesting as individuals but sensational in whole armies. I wouldn't say that about roses. It's worth going a long way to see a woodful of snowdrops, and most certainly worth going to Kew to see the little tommies. *Crocus tommasinianus* is not (I imagine) a connoisseur's plant, but the impact of a tennis-court's-worth, its mauve suffused with a silvery sheen in the sun, is unique. Do they glow at night? Propagating them is not a problem; they may be the only weed with an AGM.

Their name is scarcely in their favour, but call them Crocus de Tommasi and they sound much better. The suggestion comes from a charming website I stumbled across, as one does, looking for more than the dull physiological details. The stories collected by besotted amateurs make far better reading. This website is called In Paghat's Garden and comes from Puget Sound in the state of Washington. Sadly Internet entries are rarely dated (surely something its masters could fix), so this may not be hot news.

Paghat tells me that *tommasinianus* is derived from the botanist Muzio de Tommasi. In the first half of the 19th century he explored Carinthia, Friuli and Dalmatia, in the southern part of the Austro-Hungarian Empire, with, among others, George Bentham (of Bentham and Hooker), and also found time to be Mayor of Trieste. I love to be told that Germans call it the 'elphin crocus', and I shan't struggle with *tommasinianus* again.

March

A THOUSAND MILES SOUTH

Home from a week in Andalusia and the Algarve, luckily in a warm spell after a cold winter – there, not here. It was 29° C in Seville and the plane trees were straining to leaf out. Orange trees are, of course, the Seville speciality, lining the streets and squares; at this time of year you have to pick your way among the windfalls. Soon the air will be tangily sweet with the white blossom among the sumptuous green leaves.

In the Algarve, the windswept meadows around Cape St Vincent, the bottom-left-hand corner of Europe, are painted yellow, sharp invigorating yellow, by the rampant Bermuda buttercup, *Oxalis pes-caprae*. How this South African native wood sorrel encircled the globe (or at least its temperate middle) is a cautionary tale. I remember admiring its shamrocky leaves and picking a vase-full of its long-stalked elegant flowers years ago on the Côte d'Azur, wondering what exotic jewel it was. Then I remembered sieving out the tiny bulbils that its pink cousin flung around in our kitchen garden. It has Dead or Alive posters up now from the Mediterranean to California.

We were in the brief season when grass covers the hills; greener, tenderer-looking grass than any northern lawn, every blade distinct on the tawny ground. On the downland towards the Spanish border, the wandering River Guadiana and the dams that cluster round in sudden little valleys, dots of brilliant white mean the cistus is coming into flower, its new shoots gleaming bright sticky green and each wide white petal stamped with a maroon blotch. Slim graceful asphodel grows head-high among the cistus; 'French' lavender is already bright-purple and green tufts mean tulips are on their way, their colours still unrevealed.

A thousand miles south of London, spring seems scarcely more advanced, but then no one plants precocious ornamentals there. The excitement is concentrated in the vegetable plots; a patch of succulent spinach is worth more than a camellia.

IN MEMORIAM

My thoughts keep turning, as each excitement of spring bursts on us, cherries chasing magnolias, the grass a blue haze of speedwell, to a dear friend who had just made the garden of his dreams when he died, unexpectedly and unnecessarily, last October.

Simon Relph inspired me to be a gardener. He was the first friend I had who used Latin names for plants – which I originally thought was an affectation, until I too started repeating those mellifluous syllables *Alchemilla mollis* in my head and the whole absurd complexity of gardening germinated in my brain.

He loved planning gardens for friends; usually ambitious plans calling for builders. His own gardens were ambitious, too – certainly in the range of plants he grew and the awkward spaces he managed to grow them in. Finally in retirement he bought a house in Somerset and spent a year absorbed in building a formal raised pond for his fish, with a series of radiating arches and raised beds, in which he crammed all his favourite plants. Just now they are identifying themselves, their buds opening and shoots lengthening, beginning to claim the spaces he gave them. More raised beds are all ready, damp brown well-manured earth, ready for him to sow his vegetables and plant his fruit. I grieve for him and the beauty he will never see.

PLANTS BEHAVING ODDLY

Has this been the best year ever for Kew's magnolias? It doesn't really matter; last Friday they were sublime, under an azure sky with the proper proportion of fluffy white clouds, and an improper one of big shiny aeroplanes. The air was balmy, the breeze just enough to dislodge a petal here and there to brush past you on its way to lie at your feet. You must hold one to your cheek; there is nothing softer or cooler.

In the woodland garden the breeze jostled the white erythroniums from Oregon. Some pointilliste had filled a meadow with purple and white fritillaries. In the alpine house *Tulipa sosnowskyi* from the Caucasus was in orange and yellow flame. By the lecture rooms the huge bones of *Eucalyptus dalrympleana* shone white in the sun. Congested green flowers burst out of maples, embryo catkins from wingnuts, and tiny green points of leaf everywhere. All too soon? When times are out of joint like this it is difficult not to feel a little surge of panic. Is this thrilling performance the swan song?

But then Kew induces the sense of a Grand Order of Being: each plant listed and assigned a place. At Kew God proposes, man disposes.

April

A TEARING HURRY

A diarist must beware of mentioning the weather too often. It was admittedly half the point of Gilbert White's diaries, and there are times and places where it simply grabs the limelight. I was probably pretty boring about the drought in Essex (and most parts) in 1976. Watching the sky became an obsession, and dragging hoses my principal exercise. The aftermath called for comment, too. The deluge killed plants that had survived the drought. Venerable beeches that had managed to make deeper roots to find moisture (their customary ones are near the surface) drowned when the floods came in October.

There was no ignoring the great gale of October 1987, either. But what about this spring? For the second year running winter has failed to show up. The first quarter of the year has been consistently mild. Phenologists (those whose bread and butter is recording dates of budding, leafing and flowering) say that one degree centigrade above average means one week earlier leafing.

The resulting coincidences of flowering are alternatively a) charming, b) bizarre, c) disturbing, or d) the writing on the wall. No scientific evidence is needed to know that, for example, London now has a pavement-café life that would have been unthinkable 20 years ago. Wine-growing in the South of England is no longer an optimistic eccentricity. It is making good money. Nor is it only England; growers in Champagne are nervous about losing the racy acidity in their grapes that gives champagne its edge in every sense.

Meanwhile Beaulieu Heath in the New Forest is an extraordinary sight. The gorse has gone mad, painting the whole landscape a brilliant searing yellow. It is all in flower at once (and the smell, of vanilla and coconut and honey, is intoxicating). The vast gorse mounds where cattle and ponies shelter their hindquarters in winter storms, turning their heads to the wind, are ramparts of a Buddhist colour I fancy artists call gamboge, relieved here and there with the white of blackthorn. Whatever happened to the traditional blackthorn winter?

May

FANCY DRESS BALL

An ambition achieved: for years I have wanted to visit the legendary island of Tresco, to see its garden of all the things we can't quite grow anywhere else in Britain. Somehow the journey to the Scilly Isles always felt like an insuperable obstacle. Resolve arrived this spring. The 'transfer', as a travel agent would call it, was an entertainment in its own right: 7.06 at Paddington, 9.45 at Exeter St David's: an hour to visit the startlingly beautiful cathedral (which by itself made the whole journey worthwhile), 11.45 take off from Exeter Airport in a Skybus Twin Otter, 12.20 land at St Mary's and 1.15 catch a launch to Bryher.

Bryher is the nearest of the Scillies to America, England's westernmost habitable point, a tiny island just west of Tresco. At night its rocky reefs and peaty downs are swept every half-minute by the beam from the lighthouse on Bishop Rock, the starting-line for liners challenging for the Blue Riband of the Atlantic. Bryher also boasts the Hell Bay Hotel; extreme comfort roguishly named after a sailor's death-trap, a reef-rimmed lee shore notorious for shipwrecks.

The islands were serene, the sea a glassy azure, the air cool and the sun bright when we took the five-minute boat ride to Tresco's tiny village. No sign of the famous garden except, peeping over a low hill, tell-tale tattered tops of tall windbreak trees. Only long-serving Monterey cypresses have that ragged silhouette. Twenty minutes' walk brought us to the garden gate – and another world.

We were in the horticultural equivalent of a fancy dress ball. The climate is subtropically benign, insulated by the Gulf Stream. It can very occasionally break down, as it did in 1987, when frost and snow destroyed all the tender plants, and in January 1990, when a hurricane felled most of the 130-year-old shelterbelt and almost all the biggest trees. The head gardener, Mike Nelhams, tells the epic story of recovery from these disasters in *Tresco Abbey Garden, a Personal and Pictorial History*.

I found myself floundering with many of the genera, let alone the species, of the plants in his lists. *Aeonium* with its varnished maroon leaves, *Banksia*, *Beschorneria* leaning lasciviously, *Bomarea*, *Carpobrotus*, *Coleonema*, *Doryanthes*, *Dryandra*, *Fascicularia*, *Furcraea*, *Kunzia* …. The impact of so many strangers at once is overwhelming. It was almost a relief, after an hour or two of wandering through such a brilliant palette, to emerge to the quiet beauty of gorse and campion and bluebells and wild garlic lining the island's narrow lanes.

Tresco Abbey Garden, we learned, was begun in 1834 by Augustus Smith from Hertfordshire, the heir to a fortune, who leased the island from the Duchy of Cornwall and became Lord Proprietor – as his great-great grandson Robert Dorrien-Smith is today. When the Smith family arrived they found the remains of a Benedictine abbey in the most sheltered spot on the island and built their house beside it. It remains a sequestered place, shaded by New Zealand tree ferns, while the dazzling profusion of the Mediterranean, South Africa, Australia,

Mexico and Chile spreads up the hillside above in a pattern of paths and steps and pools reminiscent, in places, of its Riviera contemporary, the Hanbury Garden at La Mortola.

The Dorrien-Smith family have persevered for nearly 200 years, living on the island they rule, loyal to a marvel of horticulture which is entirely their invention, and still bursting with innovation, new ornaments and new plants.

AKA VIPER'S BUGLOSS

The plant of the moment at Tresco, if I had to choose one, was the echium from Madeira, *Echium candicans*. When it was accompanied by the monster geranium from Madeira (*G. maderense* is happily naturalized on the islands) the sight was one of the most splendid in gardening.

I believe I've hinted, over the years, at my faiblesse for anything blue. Unconsciously I seek out blue flowers in gardens. In nurseries I head straight for the blue plants. It is a minority colour; there are ten pink/mauve/reds and maybe 20 yellows to each blue – and true blue, in the range you might call French, butcher's or sailor's, is rare. Ceanothus gives us some pretty punchy deep blues; hydrangeas tend to wobble between blue and pink. Borage is a clear lightish blue ... but its tall subtropical cousin, *Echium candicans*, is the real deal.

The Scillies are mild enough to make a shrub of it. It would struggle in most places on the mainland. Its cousin *E. pininana* can get close, as an almost ridiculous spire, for a year or two, though often wandering from blue towards red. Its other equally lofty cousin, *E. wildpretii* from Tenerife, lets the side down by being red, thus of scarcely more interest to my blue-besotted eyes than a red delphinium.

On a visit to Cambridge the other day, though, I had a 60-volt shock. One of England's most photographed walls is suddenly under siege. The splendid sandstone flank of Clare College, the left-hand part of the view of King's College that symbolizes King's, Cambridge, and sometimes even England on calendars, is a frenzy of flowering spires.

The enterprising head horticulturist at King's College, Stephen Coghill, spotted a perfect south-facing site for his seedlings of *E. wildpretii* and *E. pininana*, the soil essentially gritty hoggin, and seized the chance. Almost incredibly, 18 months later, the seedlings planted out in April last year tower over two metres high. Maybe one day *E.candicans*?

RIVER CHUCKLING BY

The garden has just been soaked, almost drowned, for the first time in many weeks. I was out before breakfast emptying saucers and discouraging snails. Relief was written on every flower's face.

The picture last week when we arrived in Wales was very different: the hills were an unaccustomed shade of khaki, the silver streams switched off. The next day we were at Bodnant when the heavens finally opened. Somehow the scene changed from beautiful to magical in the rain. We had not been there for four years (all wrong, since our woods are only 50 miles away). How could we have stayed away from Britain's/Europe's/the world's greatest gardening treat?

Large parts of Bodnant are seriously steep. I have never really fathomed how the area of a steep slope is measured: is it the surface as seen from the sky or from a point at right angles to the slope? As contour lines crowd together on a map I suppose it must be the latter. It makes a difference when you are planting – or indeed weeding. In any case it's a big 80 acres.

Furthermore the area of tended garden, accessible, nurtured and with all its plants labelled, is rapidly increasing. The hillside opposite the house, across the little river Hieraethlyn, had seemed a garden too far for many years. Now it is very much part of the tour, with generations-old specimens on show once again, and lavish planting in between.

The famous laburnum tunnel is apparently the feature that attracts most visitors. Its long yellow curve was just beginning to light up. What I had almost forgotten, though, was how grandly the wide terraces descend westwards from the house, embracing more and more of the sublime landscape, claiming and pulling in the Carneddy mountains across the Conwy Valley as part of a stately, unbelievably ambitious plan.

There is a phase of momentous tranquillity when you reach the vast canal terrace with the prim and pretty grey-and-white Pin Mill to the left, almost too pretty and party-dressed for such an elemental prospect. Then you are precipitated among soaring trees and dazzling flowers deep into the quiet dell, to hear the river chuckling by and follow it for a good half mile, in awe of forest giants and enraptured by the glow of flowers.

July

PLANTS AND THE MAN

If anyone deserves the title of the plantsman's plantsman it is Maurice Foster. We visited him at White House Farm in the green depths of Kent last month, after an interval of ten years. He hasn't changed: still the rather impish, beaming figure with an unparalleled flow of botanical fact and anecdote to keep you happy all day. Maurice can recall every moment in the finding, naming, provenance and propagation of every plant in his collection of – I can't remember how many thousands of taxa. His passion goes far beyond trees; he will be as eloquent on a rose, a grass or a lichen – well, maybe not quite as eloquent on a lichen.

The garden of White House Farm encompasses some four acres, a stretch of woodland a further three, and the arboretum beyond it, seven. On Monday mornings, Maurice told us, two helpers get a briefing for the week: the heavy work to be done. The rest he does himself; a dizzying prospect as you look around you.

In ten years the arboretum has grown from a field of sticks to a leafy heaven of prodigious variety. Certain recurring genera amount to comprehensive collections: hornbeams in a variety no one would have thought possible; tilia, quercus, magnolia the same, berberis and philadelphus .... But a list of genera can sound like a dull plantation, and this is a magic wood of surprises and questions – to which Maurice has the answers.

Ten years is nothing in the life of a garden, or a gardener. At Saling Hall I was still planting more trees after 40 years – closer and closer together. When I started I put them far too far apart, before I discovered that the thing trees (not perhaps all trees) like best is each other's company. Every perambulation raised the question of priorities: does the beauty of that tree take precedence over the rarity of its neighbour? One or the other has to go. There were occasional duels, but I tended to let the happier tree win. The context, though, was different. I was trying to paint a landscape; in a landscape it is the spaces, more than the details, that count.

In the end an arboretum is a wood of different trees. In a good arboretum they are congruous; themes emerge, comparisons are close enough to be useful. White House Farm has all the beauties of a wood, but one where your eyes are constantly drawn to details of design you never expected to see.

TURNING SAND INTO SOIL

We have just been three days by the sea where the pine forest of the Landes meets the Atlantic on a beach 100 miles long, dazzling sunshine giving way to a misty sea fret and the relief of a faint breeze.

The Landes, or rather their forest, is a feat of man versus the environment. Two-and-a-half million acres of shifting sand and swampy waste were tamed during the 19th century. It was a desert known only to the shepherds who crossed it – on stilts. The first experiment in stabilizing the sands was made in the 18th century, planting marram grass along the shore. Even now when you walk where nothing grows, the fine white sand shifts and squeaks under your feet.

But the grass fixed the sand enough to plant pines, the local pin maritime, *Pinus pinaster*, a rugged two-needled tree with copious resin (collecting it for turpentine became the local industry). In due course they were followed by holm and cork oak; by arbutus, phillyrea, sea buckthorn, gorse and broom, willows and of course brambles. All contributed to the sterile dunes in stability and fertility. Their humus turned sand to soil.

Some of the dunes along the coast are still shifting, and so steep that you slide one pace backward for each two that you climb. There is an unexpected smell of curry in the air; curry plant is one of the pioneer sand-fixers. Then comes 'la lette', a shallow valley protected from the sea-wind where pines, gorse, brambles and willows have a firmer hold. Then the forest, low at first, grows taller as you go inland and humus accumulates. The regular array of pines lets in enough light for what becomes quite a lush understorey. In places the arbutus, shining bright green, is the dominant plant, above acres of ferns.

It is hard to believe that only ten years ago, in 2007, very nearly a third of the 2,500,000 acres were devastated in a gale. It was a regional catastrophe. There was no means or manpower to tackle the chaos of fallen and broken trees. The price of timber fell with them. We expected to see devastation still – and there are places where land has been newly cleared and cultivated; the sand has become soil enough to raise crops. But the vast expanse of forest, one of the greatest feats anywhere of land reclaimed, still stretches to each horizon.

WITH BREN AND VASCULUM

'You'll just have to press "Go"', they said. 'He'll do the rest.' Interviewing a broadcaster as eloquent as Roy Lancaster could be a challenge. How do I press 'Stop'? I interviewed Roy on the Mound at Boughton House (a uniquely visible spot for an interview) about his latest book, *My Life with Plants*. The title I would have given it is *The Education of a Plantsman*, in reference to Russell Page's masterpiece, *The Education of a Gardener*. In a sense it's a plantsman's equivalent.

I read it (or most of it) at one long sitting. Roy recounts in his unmistakable voice, and in a degree of detail that once or twice reminded me of Patrick Leigh Fermor's total recall of events 40 years ago, how his schoolboy passion for ornithology was converted one day to botany (or at least plant-spotting) by seeing something strange growing in a potato field. His schoolmaster didn't recognize it, nor did the Bolton Museum curator, nor the Botany Department at Manchester University.

It was sent on to the Natural History Museum, where it was declared a Mexican species of tobacco plant by no means routine in Britain. Young Roy got a letter from London; 'Dear Mr Lancaster ...'. Roy had found his calling.

From the Bolton Parks Department he was decanted into the Malayan Jungle to do his National Service. The picture of a young man with Bren gun and vasculum studying natural history while confronting the commies sums up the quintessential Lancaster.

Perhaps the most fruitful part of his career was his years at Hillier's Nursery in the 1970s as amanuensis to Sir Harold Hillier, and its fruit: the almost incredible *Hillier Manual*, detailing some 7,000 woody plants, readably, learnedly, and all too temptingly. In those days you could actually buy the great majority from Hillier's. It was an opportunity some gardeners leapt at. Arboreta were born (including mine at Saling Hall). Then commercial reality broke in; happily in 1977 Hillier's Arboretum was accepted by the Hampshire County Council as a charitable trust and thrives to this day. Roy's story goes on with travels to (and books about) China, Japan, the Americas ... collecting (and converting the plant-blind). Television followed; Roy and Sue made a garden ... it is a lovely story, and a faithful portrait of a lovely man.

August

BUXUS NOT SO SEMPERVIRENS

It was the shock of my gardening life. A phone call from my sister, just back from a week away. 'Come and see my box.' The caterpillar had come, and in a mere week had destroyed the entire framework of her garden. Her box hedges are bare, brown, leafless. The only colour is hundreds of green caterpillars crawling and munching and leaving their tiny brown droppings. Not since Dutch Elm disease killed all our elms in the 1970s have we seen such devastation of such an essential and universal plant.

My sister lives in a terrace house near Ravenscourt Park. Her garden, leading out from her kitchen, is the centre of her life. Her tomatoes, figs and grapes and apples could supply the family. But the structure of the garden, the chunky parallel hedges culminating in balls of box, is dead, an eyesore to be cleared away – no mean task. And then what?

The RHS website recommends BugClear as a spray to kill the caterpillars: I've used it and it has no effect. Local advice here is that pyrethrum can be effective. You can buy it (until it runs out) under the brand name Py. It is too late, here, for pheromone traps, but I'm following up a new biological insecticide called Topbuxus XenTari that apparently poisons the caterpillars as they feed.

As replacements, substitutes for the box, there are plenty of ideas being mooted. *Ilex crenata*, teucrium, euonymus all field candidates. Even (and why not for a chunky hedge?) yew. For my sister's garden (and mine, when the dread moment comes) I'm contemplating myrtle. I'm not sure how it will react to a strict clipping regime; will it sprout new leaves as willingly as box? And where do I look for dozens of tiny myrtles? But myrtle, like box, has an aura, an ancient garden history, a presence that the other stand-ins can't claim.

A BATTY BALLOT

We don't expect to spend much time on the broad sandy beaches of Snowdonia in August. Nor did we. But days of solid rain had done magic for the streams that chatter and gurgle through our woods. There are springs where I've never seen them before: the expensively surfaced tracks are watercourses, their stones washed loose, and some of our streamside paths have become streambeds. But the new roof on our old mine building keeps us dry, and its new skylight lets in daylight we never had before.

There is a whole complex of ruined mine buildings where our gold mine used to be – or rather would have been if they had ever found gold. This was in the 1840s and '50s when gold fever seems to have broken out around the world: California, Australia, Canada, Colorado, New Zealand, and even Wales. (South Africa and the Klondike came later, in the 1880s.) For a short while the Mawddach Estuary was a baby Ballarat.

Our mine includes the remains of the grinding shed, where the power to grind the ore was provided by a 9-metre overshot water-wheel, a couple of other buildings now reduced to their grey stone gables, and what we take to be the canteen and the manager's office. The canteen has a huge hearth and the manager's office a little one to keep his back warm as he watched his workers (some of them seven years old) through a panoramic (by Welsh standards) window.

But the best part is the mine itself, a horizontal 'drive' hacked and blasted a hundred metres into the hillside – at which point they realized that copper was the best they were going to get. The mouth of the mine is our grotto, a jagged hole in the hill, dark-grey stone adorned with ferns, with a slow brown stream flowing out into the woods.

When we bought the property I was worried that someone might be tempted to explore, wander in and fall in the darkness, so I installed a gate of vertical iron bars. Years later I had a letter from the Welsh Bat Authority in Cardiff, telling me a colony of bats hibernated in the dripping blackness. Was I aware, it asked, that lesser horseshoe bats prefer horizontal bars? How do you answer such a batty question?

———————— *September* ————————

MOOD CHANGE

Now the cyclamen are declaring their unremembered or unexpected presence almost anywhere that seems unpropitious, but especially in the bottom of box hedges, and also in a pot of *Pelargonium ardens* (whose flowers, if it hadn't stopped flowering, would have made the most alarming Great-Dixter-type clash of knicker-pink and flame-red); the mood of the garden has changed.

Geraniums that dominated the summer have pretty much packed it in. *Anemone* 'Honorine Jobert', of course, is still the lamp in the leafy corner. The little white stars of *Aster divaricatus* in their modest floppy way are a reminder that Gertrude Jekyll had an eye for a good plant. The most modest of fuchsias, 'Hawkshead', has woken up and droops its miniature white bells among the muddle of plants planning their retirement.

Flop is the feeling in a border where *Sedum spectabilis* 'Brilliant' looks fagged out. Wonderfully enduring and upright and still flowering *Acidanthera murieliae* (I forgot to water their pot until midsummer) are the sweetest-smelling thing in the garden, as well as the most elegant. And there are leaves that are paying their rent despite a dearth of flowers: *Salvia vitifolia*, pale, soft and striking, and *Fuchsia boliviana* against the east wall. Why didn't you dangle your scarlet tubes this year? Not one.

Now our total tomato crop is in: 11 tiny ones and another ten teeny, the greenhouse star is the bizarre *Brillantaisia owariensis*. I begged a cutting when I saw a pot of something rather like a long-stalked hosta in a French friend's dark stairway. I had no idea it would respond to light and lots of water with long spikes of salvia-ish purple flowers. It is apparently an acanthus cousin from Madagascar and those parts.

In Kensington Gardens meanwhile only one tree has committed itself to autumn; the tall gleditsia outside the Cambridges' quarters is shining yellow. Sweet chestnuts all over the gardens have such a crop of nuts they look like green chrysanthemums. A cluster of hawthorns, *Crataegus prunifolia*, are firing up in deep shades of red and orange and gleaming round scarlet haws. No cold night has come along yet to change the whole leaf palette.

HOUSE & GARDEN

It was Lionel de Rothschild who said, talking to a City gardening club in the 1920s, 'No garden, however small, should be without its two acres of rough woodland.' I was reminded of him when the Duke of Devonshire, taking a party of Garden Museum patrons round

Chatsworth the other day, said 'We realized there is something like 15 acres of woodland between here [the arboretum] and the house doing nothing special, so we've asked Tom Stuart-Smith to do us a design for it.' I'm not sure whether the 15 acres are included in the 110 acres of the present garden, or will bring it up to 125, but the signs are that Steve Porter, Joseph Paxton's current successor as head gardener, and his team will take them in their stride.

To say that the Cavendish family is restless is an understatement. Renewals and new projects are the lifeblood of Chatsworth. The scaffolding is slowly coming off the house after ten years of constant building work.

We came up to see the beautifully staged exhibition called House Style, of fashion in the family over the centuries (they have been here for nearly five). The plants and the rocks that went to Chelsea two years ago, to make perhaps the best garden ever created at the Show, are being reintegrated into the garden around the trout stream that flows down from the moors above (and that flowed, or so it seemed, through the Royal Hospital grounds).

The rockery that Paxton built of massive gritstone blocks is one of the horticultural wonders of the world. It is in the middle of being restored to its original monumental stony state. But then so is the cascade, and the Emperor fountain – though perhaps not quite to the 276-foot (84-metre) plume it once reached. The sense of creative energy, and sheer all-encompassing competence, at Chatsworth is palpable. All the more winning, then, I thought, is the gentle, almost whimsical vegetable garden. There is no bare earth to be seen, few rigid ranks; just a tapestry of leaves and flowers that wouldn't frighten Helen Allingham.

AGAINST THE ODDS

Bluebell Arboretum and Nursery had been on my must-visit list for far too long. Its name comes up so often when I look up anything woody and unusual. I wasn't very clear where to find Ashby-de-la-Zouch, alluring though it sounds; the answer is between Leicester and Burton upon Trent, a part of the country I hardly know at all. Zouch, my screen tells me, derives from *souche*, a tree stump. Could there once have been such a whopper there that they put it on the map? Or might it have had a less corporeal significance, as in The Noble Stem of Jesse?

What stands out in a garden on a first visit is above all the plan; it should be clear, and it should make you want to explore. Then it is all a matter of timing – and late September is very much between seasons. Early autumn colour was largely yellow, brightest in *Cladrastris kentuckea* (or *lutea*), the so-called Kentucky Coffee tree. Its little fragrant flowers alone hardly make it worth growing, but it can be a glowing golden beacon in the fall. *Celastrus orbiculatus* was almost equally bright, but I'm not sure the tall tree it was strangling would have been very keen. Red was provided mainly by berries. Every time I see the American *Ilex verticillata* I make another resolution to plant it. A deciduous holly doesn't sound particularly tempting when we have so many evergreen kinds, but it carries masses of scarlet berries like few other shrubs.

Two generations of Robert Vernons have created first the garden and nursery, then an expanding arboretum. I asked 'young' Robert, why here? 'Needs must', he said. The site they were hoping to buy was sold for housing. Ideal this is not. Open soil and good drainage are, you would think, the first requirements. How encouraging it is to see how many things are thriving on stodgy clay with only shallow trenches for drainage. The secret, of course, is in sensitive and specific cultivation; the excellent labelling includes notes on their different mulches and when they are applied. There was a pungent smell of spent hops from a local brewery in the air.

The garden is mature, personal and intimate, a meandering journey through a deeply interesting collection of trees, shrubs and generous clumps of perennials. The eye-catchers, of course, in September were hydrangeas; even the fading panicles of *Hydrangea paniculata* are graceful and full of light. Anyone would be tempted. 'Do your customers know what they are looking for?' I asked Jason, the manager.

'A few', he answered. 'The trouble is they expect big plants, but we can't grow fields of rareties. They can be a bit crestfallen when they wait a year and then are given what looks like a stick in a pot.'

———————————— *October* ————————————

WORTH WAITING FOR

For a moment I thought it was a kingfisher. Then, as I looked up from my breakfast, I saw that the streak of piercing blue was the incredibly dilatory *Salvia vitifolia* opening its flowers, not exactly kingfisher colour, but sharing that startling brilliance, along with gentians, the windows at Chartres, one or two delphiniums perhaps, but little else.

Breakfast turned surreal when I saw, just beyond the salvias, of all things, a heron, right beside the diminutive tank that holds Halley and Haley, our two Comets. The heron hopped onto a table for a better look, then up to the greenhouse roof. I must have made a noise as I scrambled for my camera because he then shrugged his wings and flapped off over the garden wall. What extraordinary eyesight herons must have to catch the reflection on a tiny patch of water as they cruise by. Have they fished out the Round Pond and the Serpentine? I've put bamboos over the Comets in their tank, just in case.

But salvias. How long they can wait before flowering. At Kew this week the Great Borders have gone quiet, with *Anemone japonica* and *Aster* 'Mönch' performing almost alone among the bleached grasses. The star turn of the season is the long south wall above the Rock Garden, perhaps 100 metres long and three metres high, almost hidden in a tidal wave of salvias. Purple and pink and dusky red are dominant; labels are hard to find in the profusion of admittedly not very interesting foliage.

I recognize the now almost ubiquitous *S. guaranitica* 'Black and Blue', waving its terminal blobs of flowers even higher than the wall, *S. involucrata* halfway up, lingerie pink, *S. leucantha* purple and grey, *S. patens* the secret searing blue and *S. canaliculata*, a miniature of the same. Long thin scarlet spikes of what I suppose is *S. coccinea* (but these have rusty indumentum-backed leaves and stems) are the most eye-catching, but the whole generous jumble, in the low afternoon sun, is a spectacle worth waiting for.

November

BONFIRE NIGHT

Little brushstrokes of yellow, green-yellow and orange hang from bare branches over the gleaming pavement. Windows palely lit, street lamps warmer, headlights reflected in puddles, the handsome bulk of the pub, all windows blazing.

You only deduce shapes in this pointilliste night-scene. And only two are palpable: the full moon, brilliant among the black dominoes of chimneys, and a file of stuccoed porticos, dressed by the right in precise perspective. Random bangs and fiery glimpses in the sky emphasize the solid stillness of the street. This is London. And I am a Londoner. It moves me.

WILDFIRE

Back from a week in California, staying in one of America's most beautiful gardens. Two weeks earlier, the skyline around had been lurid with flames and the air tainted with smoke. In several towns everyone was evacuated. The Napa Valley, the Sonoma Valley and the surrounding hills were threatened by the worst forest fires in memory.

Molly Chappellet's garden on Pritchard Hill is so perfectly integrated with the landscape of forest and vineyard that the three elements flow together – and her house so much part of the garden, so shrouded in plants and overhung by trees, that fire is a hazard no one ignores. But a fire like this month's, driven by such a gale, has never been seen.

It broke out in the night, on October 8th, in so many different places that the local fire brigades didn't know where to start. Ten days later fire-fighters from all over the West, even volunteers from Australia, were involved. Eventually it consumed almost a quarter of a million acres. It threw flaming embers so far and wide that the countryside is full of random blackened scars. In some it was a mere grassfire that left tall trees singed but unburnt; in others tree tops torched each other for mile upon mile.

California's summers (and torrid summers all over the States) make the shade of trees indispensable: they are integrated into every farm, village, housing estate and city centre. We drove to Napa over the hills from Sacramento to the east, and to our consternation began to see cinders ten miles from the valley and its vines. The blackened patches were often spaced hundreds of metres apart. The wind had been so strong that sparks, or embers, flew that far, landing on tinder-dry grass. Spring rain had raised unusually tall grass; summer had baked it golden.

Coming down into the Napa Valley from Atlas Peak we saw the scale of the disaster. Miles of mountain forest were in ashes, the buildings scattered among the trees either unaffected or completely destroyed. So hot were the fires that all that was left was a chimney, a charred washing machine and often a burnt-out car. Melted aluminium engine blocks were pale puddles on the road. Anyone without a car was at the mercy of the flames – yet miraculously only 42 people died, while nearly 9,000 buildings burned.

In this valley of vineyards the fires were largely frustrated. They leapt among the trees but paused at the edge of the vines. Green vines are not dry enough to burst into flames. There was scorching at the edges, and the smoke will have tainted the ten percent of the crop still unpicked. The vineyards in the main were effective firebreaks, but all the rest of the country is forest: oaks, redwoods, pines, buckeyes, madrone and mesquite. Fire is part of its life cycle. The forest has burned periodically throughout history. It's the houses in it that are the problem.

POINT OF CONTACT

I've written thousands of picture captions in my time for various books and magazines. They are the writer's, or editor's, first point of contact with the reader. Whose eyes don't flick first to an illustration, then to the little explanation contained in the caption, before committing to read the bulk of the text? The sort of illustrated books I've written are constructed round this formula. Punchy captions packed with a surprising amount of information are best. 'Three facts a line' is my motto. And yet I've seen captions as clueless as 'A church in France'.

Garden picture books can make lovely browsing, but captions determine the way we look at the photos. They can just tell you that the plant in the foreground is *Persicaria* 'Firedance', the rose 'Maigold' or the hills in the background the Brecon Beacons – or they can interpret the scene for you. Culturally (it's acid soil with high rainfall), historically (the terrace was built in 1900; the name of a designer), pictorially (the yew on the left balances the pergola on the right), ecologically, chromatically (colour contrast or harmony), hortatory (it's time to get mulching) or even gnomically – in the spirit of Little Sparta.

Whatever captions say, they direct your attention to this aspect or that. They prevent the garden from speaking for itself. I have often been tempted to label some garden incident, or corner, or vista with some form of notice, written on paper or carved in stone. If you have tried to create a mood, uplifting or contemplative, there is a temptation to say so. Avoid it. If you need to, you have failed.

2018

January

TREE TV

It was a joy to watch Dame Judi Dench on television telling us how much she loves trees. Walking round her garden – others might call it a young wood – with some well-informed guests, Tony Kirkham in particular, telling her (and all of us) things she undoubtedly already knew, as well as some she didn't. In either case her reactions were impeccable: surprise and delight registered as if it were a Shakespearean Act V.

She even had Shakespeare for company, weaving in his sonnets, from *Rough winds do shake the darling buds of May* to the inevitable elegiac

> *That time of year thou may'st in me behold*
> *When yellow leaves, or none, or few, do hang*
> *Upon those boughs that shake against the cold,*
> *Bare ruined choirs, where late the sweet birds sang.*

It had not dawned on me before that Shakespeare in his youth probably witnessed great abbey buildings being demolished and used as quarries. The Acts for dissolving the monasteries were passed only 25 years before he was born. It took many years to complete this looting, so he must have seen and wandered in 'bare ruined choirs' while their choristers, brutally dismissed, looked for work where they could find it. What television that would have made.

STUART SWAGGER

I am a sucker for those timeline charts that bring unrelated events together. What were the Chinese, or the Mughals, up to when Queen Elizabeth I was on the throne? Were the Aztecs building pyramids at the same time as the Egyptians? (No.)

The current exhibition of King Charles I's collection at the Royal Academy made me realize how my own patrons, John Tradescant *père et fils*, witnessed, and were part of, the most thrilling moment in the history of English taste, when the Renaissance arrived in England.

There was nothing colourless about the Tudors; they revelled in bright colours. In gardens painted figures, posts and fences must have produced a sort of fairground feel, where today even in winter we scrabble around for any plant in flower or with coloured leaves; paint would somehow be an admission of failure.

But the Stuarts, when they came to the throne, brought richer, more saturated colours, style, lustre, elegance, brilliance, confidence and swagger to the court. Shakespeare wrote his greatest plays. Inigo Jones, designer of royal masques, went to Florence to see how the Medicis did it. I find it hard to believe Shakespeare didn't go to Italy too. Charles I invited Rubens to London. Van Dyck came and went and finally stayed. We have the landmarks of the Queen's House at Greenwich and the Banqueting House in Whitehall. What do we have in the way of gardens?

Hatfield House is the obvious place to look, and Mollie Salisbury, the late marchioness, managed to invoke their great gardener in her marvellous knots and parterres. I always think of Ham House in Richmond for the feel of the Stuart court, although in reality it was given its present rich patina after the Restoration – and by the National Trust. The truth is we don't have a Tradescant garden design, but Trad *père* would surely have been more Tudor than Stuart, and Trad Junior more in the Renaissance spirit.

February

CAPABILITIES

My forest walks – walks anywhere in fact – are always overlaid with visions of what could, or might, replace, and in my opinion improve, what I see around me. I expect Lancelot Brown felt just the same. In town I imagine scruffy jumbles of nondescript buildings replaced with well-proportioned terraces or gleaming towers. From the train I envisage rivers and woods and rolling pastures full of calm cattle. From our favourite bench in deepest France, with a huge view of undulating bocage, I used to imagine a snow-capped mountain range on the horizon.

There is a little valley in our Welsh woods where two lively streams converge. Two more little streams glide down through culverts to make a meeting of four waters. All this hydro-activity was hidden under dark smothering spruces until a gale last summer felled a great tangle of trunks and branches, and toppled two in a line of tall western hemlocks. The hemlock is not a tree foresters respect or sawmills want to buy, but in my view the most handsome of the potentially giant conifers we have from West Coast America.

Clearing up the resulting chaos revealed the potential beauty of this corner of the forest. The main stream comes crashing out of dense woodland higher on the hill, and springs from a gap in a mossy old sheep-wall into the new clearing, to bounce and splash down the black rocks, below five majestic grass-green hemlocks aligned like a guard of honour. Fifty metres on, it dives under the track to emerge again furiously into a much wider arena where we have cleared an acre of dark conifers. The three other streams meet it here, converging to form acute angles of rushing water in the mossy forest floor.

At the moment it is a picture of stumps and snags and the debris of logging. In my mind's eye it is something else: a mossy, ferny hollow under the beeches I will plant this year, where bluebells will rejoice in spring and in summer we will picnic in their dappled shade.

March

A DREAM

Here's my fantasy. A hackney cab picks up a nurseryman from his Brompton Road nursery. They call at a house in Park Lane to collect an important customer who is a fanatical collector of new plants from China. Together they rattle on, down to the Strand to take a wherry to the new docks at Blackwall, just opened in 1806 for the biggest merchant ships of all, the 1,000-ton East Indiamen. The *Cumberland*, her Captain Euen Campbell, has been signalled from Gravesend, where she had stopped to lighten her cargo. Her huge four-deck bulk is being handled through the dock gates into the Import Dock. Our plantsmen go aboard to collect their prize from the captain's hands: two new camellias never before seen in Britain.

Some of the camellias flowering in the Conservatory at Chiswick House this month are the plants brought over in the Company's ships. Looking at the towering bush of 'Rubra Plena', one of the first to arrive, you can see what the excitement was about: a shiny-leaved evergreen bearing countless double bright-red flowers. Moreover camellias are marvellously genetically unstable. You never knew what their seed might produce in the way of colours. You could pay £5,000 for a plant with brightly blotchy red-and-white flowers; its offspring could be indifferent pink. The plant named as 'Variegata' produced a seedling that is now called 'Alba Simplex' – the name describes it perfectly. Not variegated at all. Not even a double.

The Duke of Devonshire finished his beautiful 300-foot Chiswick conservatory in the 1820s, a few years after my fantasy starts. Some of the camellias flowering in it today are originals; have seen the Southern

Ocean. Most are their offspring, or at least descendants. Some have names referring to their importers, or the captains or the ships that carried them, like the ancient vintage madeiras, another precious cargo, still to be seen in Savannah, Georgia. Others lost their identity along the way. Some now have trunks two metres round.

Fifteen years ago they were on their last legs. The conservatory was falling to bits; they were starving and infested with scale. Then the Camellia Society rode to the rescue. Today they are worth travelling to see. This month the Society is coming to Holland Park to see the dozen veteran plants along the west wall of the Victorian orangery. It would be good to know their history, too.

— May —

CHILD'S PLAY

Children see gardens differently. How differently you appreciate only when you watch them at it: their alternative interpretations can be amusing – could actually be inspirational – or can be just plain annoying. It's the go-karts that get to me.

Our careful creation in the New Forest, 30 acres of it, has infinite play potential, from swimming and toy boats in the pond to tree-climbing, stream-damming and just plain mud pies. Small children stay closer at hand, of course, and wreak havoc in the herb garden by the kitchen door. At five or six they find steps amusing: how many can you jump at one go? At seven they (and their friends) are keen on leaping streams, and anything containing water. A flight of garden stairs branching to enclose a water tank and splashing spout is good for a running leap onto the path below, sending the gravel flying onto the lawn. It wasn't a good idea to plant primulas on the brink of a pond just at the take-off point for a jump to the little island, either. Building a dam in the carefully adjusted overflow from a pond comes naturally (irresistibly, in fact). Then the flooded margin makes a good splashing ground with excellent mud-pie potential.

Deer saw to it long ago that lots of our trees are multi-stemmed and prime for climbing. It's only natural to kick footballs at flowerbeds and try to hit the bedroom windows with them. The logpile is a builder's yard with intriguing construction possibilities, and the circle in the gravel drive is the perfect go-kart skidpan. In the decibel stakes a go-kart comes just below a leaf blower, but it's a close thing.

Did someone suggest planting beans? The magic of germination comes a poor second behind stream-damming in child-appeal.

BENIGN NEGLECT

Three years ago, in May 2015, I wrote an entry about staying in a Welsh country house hotel. We're here again, and everything I wrote is still true. I don't know any other garden where the tastes and sentiments of 100 years ago are so perfectly preserved. Benign neglect has done its work.

Clearly there were once many more incidents of structure and planting. Traces of abandoned stone paths wind up the steep slopes under the huge beeches and oaks. Where once there must have been beds of massed azaleas and camellias, only the sturdiest have survived, to reach an impressive size.

Some specimens of rhododendron arboreum are now 12-metre towers of deep green and bright red. Sheltering under one of them is a pure white camellia, intricately double, now six metres across, covered in perfect buttonholes. Across the granite path, plush with moss, the yellow azalea mollis and another, a peachy version, have opened up into graceful dancers in the dappled shade.

The phantom of an avenue leads straight on from the sunk parterre, rising with the hill from a meadow of bluebells, scattered with old orchard trees and on one side, beehives. A wavering stone wall, deep-brown and moss-green, divides it from the forest.

Above the house the rectangle of what was once the tennis court is now bluebell-spangled, with silver birches in place of netting. A cuckoo speaks above the background burble of streams; the hill is full of them, converging in black rocky channels on a long pond where gunneras are just expanding their elephant leaves.

There is a secular logic about this garden. It meanders with the contours of a mountain, trying tentatively to impose shapes on random slopes. Dark granite balustrades outline what was once formal. A rectangular lawn points away from the house at what seems an awkward angle until you look beyond; it is aimed squarely at the dome of Diffwys, purple or snow-covered, second-highest mountain in these parts after Cader Idris.

Time has engineered perfect integration here, of nature on the grand scale and the gardener's puny interventions. The result is tranquillity.

THEY BRING THEIR SANDWICHES

'If you have pleasant memories of these ancient capitals, I hope you will cherish them.' My Japanese correspondent is writing about Kyoto and Nara, Japan's most historic and beautiful cities.

Kyoto 'is one big busy theme park; centuries-old temples and shrines being attractions not unlike Sleeping Beauty's castle. The signs saying "No food", "Do not take photos", "Do not step on moss" are the only way of telling that this is a historic place of worship. Even "No drones".'

It's a serious problem, and it applies to all the world's most famous and accessible tourist honeypots. Have you been to Florence recently in summer? Have you seen the cruise liners towering above San Giorgio Maggiore, whose 5,000 disembarking passengers, notoriously, 'bring their sandwiches'?

Cambridge is another victim of its own success, recently made more acute by, of all things, a dead poet's fan club. Xu Zhimo studied at King's in 1922 and was moved by the beauty of the Backs to write a poem about the Cam, rather better, it must be said, than Rupert Brooke's *The Old Vicarage, Grantchester*, written ten years before. Two lines of the poem are inscribed on a white boulder by the bridge and willow he describes, perhaps unfortunately inviting the reader to go punting. He can hardly be blamed for the resulting queues.

June

HANOVERIAN SUMMER

'Three fine days and a thunderstorm.' I always wonder why this famous definition of an English summer is attributed to King George II, with the specific date of 1730 attached. He became King of England (as well as Duke of Brunswick) in 1727. Both 1730 and 1731 were famously hot summers; they apparently held the record for summer heat until 2006 (July 2006 was the warmest month in Britain since records began) – and then August was one of the cloudiest and wettest. Are we on to something here? Is this what happened in 1730? Maybe the new king was commenting on the actual weather in a very English way – even if there were far more than three fine days. More to the point, though, is why does this happen (as it just has this week)?

Here is a meteorological answer: a heatwave warms the sea. A warmer sea evaporates faster. The wetter atmosphere generates areas of low pressure. Moist air rises, cools, and dumps as rain. Are three hot days enough? They certainly seemed to be this week – and who would argue with the King?

IMPERIOUS MANNERS

Rhodies (it takes chutzpah to call them that) were never my thing until some acid soil came my way. I'm afraid we're all more interested in things we can join in ourselves. I gave myself an intensive course in them when I was writing *The Principles of Gardening*, even devising a family tree that probably provoked giggles in Rhodoland. But that was 40 years ago. I said then that the past 100 years (ie the 1870s–1970s) might well be called The Erica Dynasty; the family had imposed two whole new fashions on gardening, the heather garden and the woodland garden, which were both still going strong when I wrote.

They haven't died. Heathers may not have the hold they had (nor the 'dwarf' conifers that were usually married to them). Woodlands on sandy soil are still being adorned with luscious flowers, but the vogue is no longer dominant. If the Chelsea Flower Show is an indicator, the genus rhododendron has been relegated. I wrote then that 'they have imperious manners. They are not good mixers. They grow and look best in the company of their own kind.' With something like 800 species that should not be a problem – except to a gardener trying to keep track of them, and above all of their hybridization.

My rather pedagogic, let's-start-from-basics approach of the 1970s still holds good, but when you are in the thick of it, with a mixture of botanical names and nursery cultivars whizzing about, made no easier by the botanists' concepts of 'series' and 'grex', it is tempting to point to a juicy pink flower and say 'That'll do.' You'll be missing a lot, though: the scary adventures of Robert Fortune; the gritty thoroughness of E H Wilson; the patient ingenuity of such breeders as Waterer, Aberconway and de Rothschild in combining characters deemed garden-worthy – and finally bringing branches of improbable sumptuousness to battle for gongs in Vincent Square.

UNPREDICTABLE

What precise algorithm of sun and rain, of isobars and daytime averages, gave the auxins their instructions and the roots their rations we shall never know, but the roses read it, and so did all the other plants that have made this spring the floweriest in memory – at least in the South. Most noticeable of all were the trees: the Indian horse chestnuts lining Kensington Road are a wall of white flowers in June, lime trees gilded all over with flowers, their scent almost painfully powerful.

Gardeners' memories of the weather are not exactly reliable; nor are accurate recent records easy to find. Go to the Met Office and all you find is forecasts (with the same proviso about reliability). Backcasts, as it were, are seemingly either binned, or archived where access is awkward. We all remember a proper winter this year, after years of wondering whether that chilly weekend was supposed to count. Not a real old-fashioned one, but enough to make the headlines as 'The Beast from the East'.

August

LAND AND SEA

I suppose if there is an opposite to gardening, or rather an occupation as different as could be, it is sailing. What the two have in common, though, is of course their dependence on the weather. Both take their cue from it; absolutely depend on it for their functions.

To gardeners and sailors, weather is existential. Having just been blown about the Solent, on glorious days of blue skies perfect for admiring roses, I'll admit to being torn between the two. If sailing wins this time it is its added spice of excitement, the commotion of competition, the regatta rush of crowding boats in touching distance rounding buoys in churning water, setting a new course, the pull of the spinnaker and the flying foam astern.

Cowes Week brings together 800 boats, from dinghies to towering yachts and catamarans that slide along like skaters; thousands of sailors speaking their strange language. It is an alternative civilization. This August the garden, in contrast, is immobile. Cocooned in trees, the air barely stirs. The burning sun makes shadows too dark to penetrate. Streams have dried to an inaudible trickle. The suspense is palpable: when will it rain?

It is the time of hydrangeas; those dowdy pink knobs that clash happily with orange montbretias in dusty front gardens by the sea, and deep in the woodland the majestic domes, purple or sky-sapphire, nestling in deep-green leaves. Their name suggests water, although it seems Linnaeus was just fooling about with the Greek for a water jar they supposedly resemble. They certainly appreciate moisture in the soil. More important is its acidity – and much less easy to adjust than textbooks suggest. I have taken cuttings of a truly sky-blue one and grown them in compost identical to the parent, only to achieve a washed-out mauve. You see *H.* 'Annabel' everywhere these days; such an eruption of foamy white that without support it collapses in a heap. Now I've taken to planting the rather more realistic *H. paniculata*: no Fra Angelico colours, but eventually something approaching a small tree. In fact the arborescent version on a one-metre trunk makes one of the great summer eye-catchers.

September

A MACROGARDEN

I have sometimes got funny looks from committed gardeners when I mention forestry; the word no doubt summons up for them a picture of hills black with spiky spruce.

It is 30 years now since I first planted what was destined to become woodland (the respectable, even cuddly word, if forest is too aggressive). That first essay was on fields of dreadful, shallow, acid soil roamed by feral sheep in the centre of France. The French government, or its Office National des Forêts, was incredibly efficient and generous with advice (and grants – though why a country which is already more than ten percent oak woods should want to pay for more, I never understood).

For the past 25 years our planting (and of course felling) has been in the wildly beautiful Snowdonia National Park. It has a different purpose from gardening, of course, with economics at its heart. I am unusual but by no means unique as a forester in putting landscape above profit in my priorities. The two in any case can be perfectly compatible – so long as you have a taste for the beauty of conifers.

This Welsh landscape was dedicated to sheep, criss-crossed with monumental stone walls, dotted with little stone farms, barns and pens. Along streams and wherever there was deeper soil grew thrusting ash and old bent oaks. Everywhere else it was heather and bilberry – or rushes. And far too much bracken.

In the 1960s the Forestry Commission, and an industrial pension fund, invaded it with conifers: larch and pine in drier places, here and there western hemlock, and almost everywhere Sitka spruce. They planted regardless, up hill and down even where there were already groves of oaks or ashes – the idea being that the quick-growing conifers (they can easily manage a metre a year) would simply grow through and shade out the broadleaves. In some cases we arrived just in time, almost 40 years later, with many of the conifers mature, in sawmill terms, and ripe for felling. Above the battlefield of a clear-felled site rose disfigured, spindly oaks gulping for light and air. When we released them, some broke or blew down; many others burst into rugged towers of leaves.

There were planted plots of oak and beech, too, at 40 years old just forming proper little woods. These and the veteran trees became our guide and the sketch for our future landscape. Down came the dark masses of spruce, 20 acres or more at a time, revealing the streams, walls and tracks that shaped the landscape, and providing the income to put it back together again as distinctive and Welsh.

This is where a gardener's eye comes in. There are places where deliberate simplicity sets up a strong line or mass; where in a garden you would plant a hedge or an avenue. There are tracks and paths that lead the eye into the distance or into a concealing bend. There are effective and appropriate places for water; 'flood the hollows', as Repton prescribed. There are prompts for open space – for instance to reveal a significant rock or a dramatic change of level. On the hills there are streams to reveal for the sparkle of their water through peat or over rock. There are boring bits where the best solution is to grow something productive: in the garden, veg; in the forest, Sitka spruce. You can contrast the dark bulk of conifers with the open arcades of broadleaves shorn of their lower branches. Eventually the necessary thinning of larches, when they are 40 feet high, produces one of the loveliest effects in the forest: their soaring straight trunks carrying graceful light canopies above what can be a fascinating understorey of seedlings and shrubby plants. Old stone walls are all the sculpture and statuary you need.

TIME'S UP

It's *la rentrée* (taken so seriously in France that on August 31st there's gridlock on every autoroute) that snaps the garden back into focus. In our case *rentrée* from a week in Provence at its most perfect: cool in the morning, hot in the afternoon and warm at dinner-time. No need for shawls on the terrace. I expected the countryside to be as brown as the England we saw from the plane, but most of it looked relatively fresh. The plane trees (to me one of the great sights and principal glories of Provence) were in full green leaf; very few crackling brown cast-offs on the ground. Where they have water at their roots they can grow into ivory monsters, spilling obesely over kerbs, walls, rocks. Closely set in avenues they can soar cathedral-high, pale pillars to a pale-green roof. They are the glory of (for instance) the Cours Mirabeau, the Champs Elysée of Aix. Some insane official has replaced a few of them with red-leafed maples. The guillotine is too good for him.

Gardening has to be simple near the Mediterranean. You can add such routine exotics as mimosa, palm trees, oleander of course, but the basic ingredients scarcely need the gardener's help. Pines, planes, cypresses, holm oaks, olives, an azure sky and pale stone are a full palette. The true pine of Provence is *Pinus halepensis*, the Aleppo pine, though why we don't call it the Provence pine I don't know. By nature it is tall and slender, and even at the end of summer a pure, piercing, almost apple-peel green.

A week away sharpens your focus when you get home. There is far more to enjoy than I expected; new flushes of roses, invigorated *Clematis orientalis*, yellow among the purple of the now-towering *Solanum rantonettii*. *Phlox* 'White Admiral' with a new lease of life, agapanthus fully out, more geraniums, but above all the incomparable (however common) *Anemone* 'Honorine Jobert'. Jobert was a nurseryman at Verdun in the 1850s. Was Honorine his wife? For such a simple white flower, a nine-petal daisy, it has extraordinary presence and grace – and persistence. In Provence as in London.

PEACE IN THE VAL D'ORCIA

London was worryingly as warm as Tuscany when we got home from staying with friends in the most perfect summer-cool garden near Montalcino. Their house, vineyards on one side, olives on another and an oak wood on a third, is blessed with a gushing, crystalline, never-failing spring. I have always dreamed – really dreamed – of living where water springs from the ground. Here it flows down little stone channels into glinting basins, chuckling as it goes, then takes another run and spouts in crystal arcs into basins big enough to plunge and wallow in. It's cold of course, but under a Tuscan sun, the ultimate luxury.

It is not easy to keep your bearings on the endlessly winding roads of Tuscany. All the ancient settlements are perched on hilltops reached by a series of hairpin bends. The *campanile* or farm or orderly olive grove you take as a landmark gyrates around you as you follow the road in countless twists, in and out of the shade of oak or pines, then dazzling sunlight. The wide Val d'Orcia comes as welcome relief, a definitive break, a broad pause in the confusion with the signature profile of Monte Amiata blocking the way to the South.

Villa La Foce is perhaps the nearest Tuscany comes to a stately home, at least in its setting, a near-English garden poised like a balcony looking south across the valley with the summit of Monte Amiata in its crosshairs. It is famous as the home of the Origo family, where the author Iris Origo lived through World War II and wrote *War in the Val d'Orcia*. She wrote *The Merchant of Prato*, a unique account of a Tuscan merchant's life in the 14th century, after she found his correspondence in the 1950s.

The Origos employed Cecil Pinsent as their architect, as Bernard Berenson had at Villa I Tatti, so they can hardly have been looking for a totally Tuscan result. To blend the orderly intimacy of English tradition with the wild breadth of the Tuscan landscape, where distances are measured in purple ranges of receding hills, is a challenge – which he overcame with the almost inevitable staircases, alleys of cypresses, and hedges. In steep hillside gardens, which almost all Italian gardens are, changes of level are the key decisions. Slopes are usually a mistake: you need to cut and construct terraces. Then you can contrast and balance intimacy and wide skies, detail and bravura. French windows (is there anything more English?) on to rose beds, cloistered plots, vine pergolas, lemon pots, fuchsias and hydrangeas ... the ingredients may be universal, but the scale and sentiment are something an Italian would not conceive. And the upkeep, the planting and the tidiness: utterly English.

October

HIS LORDSHIP'S GRAPES

It's a sign of advancing years, I know, when you start to research your family history. In my family there's a surprising amount to go on: assorted letters and papers covering, in all, 400 years. It's not that any of us were grand or landed; there has clearly been an itch to record passed down from, on my mother's side, farmers in Saxony who were anxious to be considered 'respectable', which seems to have meant owning something; and on my father's side someone described as 'a gardener' – which has naturally intrigued me.

The gardener lived near Waterford. That much we knew. There was also a family legend that he had smart connections involving the Marchioness of Waterford. My sister has the itch, too, and did something about it. She took the miniature portrait we have of a soldier in a red coat, the subject of the legend, to Curraghmore, now as then the palatial seat of the marquesses of Waterford. She met his land agent, told the story, and was rewarded with a copy of *A Common Country: The angler in Ireland or An Englishman's ramble through Connaught and Munster, during the summer of 1833* by William Bilton.

Bilton was one of those inquisitive travellers who noted everything and spoke to everyone. One of his visits was to the country round Waterford, where he introduced himself at Curraghmore and was taken round the demesne, of 'nearly five thousand Irish acres' by 'the very intelligent gardener, Mr Johnson' – at which my sister naturally pricked up her ears. This is what Bilton has to say about Mr Johnson:

'I have nowhere seen a garden conducted on so liberal a scale. The hothouses are filled with all the choicest varieties of grapes, and there are large and numerous succession houses for pines. Of outdoor fruit I was shown a very complete collection of apples, both of the many excellent kinds peculiar to Ireland and of those lately obtained by the Horticultural Society, &c. Among the flowers, I noticed above two hundred specimens of the best and rarest sorts of dahlias, each of them displaying a profusion of prize-flowers. There seems no limit, in point of expense, to this department; and the whole management is left in the uncontrolled hands of Mr. Johnson, who generally has about fifty men and women employed in the gardens and adjoining pleasure-grounds, besides a score of carpenters and glaziers, all equally under his orders. I wonder what his Lordship's grapes cost him per pound!'

Almost the Irish Paxton, in fact. He was Owen Johnson, and apparently my great-great-great-great grandfather. So that's where Trad's love of gardening comes from.

November

NIWAKI

Since I first went to Japan, in the autumn of 1976, there has been a part of my brain (on the right, I imagine) that manages to keep a sort of focus I learned on that visit. I went when I was writing my most ambitious book, *The Principles of Gardening*. The uber-pretentious title was not my idea, but it made me reflect: English gardening ideas are virtually unchallenged in this country, and admired round the world, but do they constitute 'principles'? I had already taken Arab, French, Dutch and Italian traditions into account (however summarily); what was missing was the Japanese (and indeed Chinese) view.

My right brain swims into action now and then when I am thinking about, or looking at, a garden, and reminds me that there is another vision; an alternative, more precise concept of gardening, with poetry at its heart and craftsmanship as its medium. It came into focus this morning when I was cleaning my shears – the single-handed kind used for trimming topiary. They come from the Dorset-based importer Niwaki, the word for garden trees, ie sculpted trees as opposed to natural ones. The French *élague* their trees remorselessly in something of the same spirit, but without the artistry.

Jake Hobson, founder of Niwaki and probably England's number-one niwakist, has a simple message: KEEP THEM CLEAN. It's the tools he's talking about, not the trees. So I sit here, with wire-wool and 3 in 1 oil (Jake says camellia oil) scrubbing blades I have allowed to get disgracefully dirty. What reminded me to do it was an extraordinary exhibition at Japan House, a new showroom near Kensington High Street Station, which is worth visiting at any time. In an exhibition of all sorts of tools downstairs, they have a whole wall of scores of hoes forged by blacksmiths all over Japan, no two alike, designed or evolved for different local soils and crops. Can you imagine such a thing in this country, where there is only one design of spade? I can think of no better example of craftsmanship, practicality and precision.

December

REPTON AND THE PRINCE

Repton has always been the landscaper for me. He seems more human (and of course marginally more modern) than Brown. For one thing he writes clearly and eloquently about his aims and methods. I often find myself quoting the sound sense of his 'Observations'. For another he seems to have a gardener's weakness for the beauty of flowers and the pleasure of wandering among different plants.

All this comes across in the brilliant little exhibition at the Garden Museum that commemorates 200 years since he died. And then yesterday I came across a description of what sounds very like one of his gardens in the letters of Prince Pückler-Muskau. The prince has just spent a long hot day at Ascot races. He rides off with an army friend to visit a fashionable lady who lives at Windsor. They arrive at her house and find no one there:

'It was like the enchanted dwelling of a fairy. If only you could have seen it! The house stood on a hill, half hidden beneath magnificent old trees. Its various projections, dating from different eras, were concealed by shrubs here and there, so there was no possibility of getting an impression of the whole. A gallery-like rose arbour bursting with hundreds of flowers led directly to the entrance hall, and passing through a few other rooms and then a corridor, we arrived in the dining room, where the table had already been handsomely laid. But there was still no one to be seen.

'From here the gardens extended before us, a true paradise, brilliantly illuminated by the evening sun. Verandahs of varying shapes and sizes ran along the whole length of the house; some jutted forward, some retreated, and all were covered with different blossoming vines. These served as a border for the colourful flower garden that extended all across the hillside. A meadowy valley, deep and narrow, adjoined this, and behind the terrain rose again to a higher crest, its slopes appointed with ancient beeches. To the left, at the valley's end, the view was closed by water, and in the distance, over the tops of the trees, we could see the Round Tower of Windsor Castle, with its colossal royal flag rising into the blue sky.'

If you haven't met Prince Pückler, his letters to his wife in Germany are the most vivid and entertaining account of fashionable England in the 1820s. They were published (a very fat book) by Dumbarton Oaks in 2016 under the rather odd title of *Letters of a Dead Man*. He was determined to transform his inheritance of a mansion and its large park in Germany into an English landscape garden. The question was, how to find the money. His wife agreed to an amicable divorce if he could find a rich English bride. The letters to the princess are his account of his (finally fruitless) search, while he explores England from palace to pub, enjoying every minute.

2019

January

RENEWAL AT KEW

I always thought it sounds a bit preachy to say you prefer natural species to the catwalk versions that are often all one finds in nurseries – certainly in garden centres. But then you see, in all its purity and innocence, a parent of an all-too-familiar nursery favourite.

The little alpine house at Kew is my favourite excursion at this time of year. I missed my special pin-up today: there was no *Scilla maderensis*, the exquisite oversized squill from Madeira. Squill, they tell me, has been used as a tonic for fluttering hearts; perhaps it was a visitor to Kew who discovered its properties. The plant that moved me this time was a cyclamen of heart-stopping purity and grace. The label was hidden, so I couldn't see which Mediterranean country it comes from, but it makes the florist's 'Persicum' look like what a Victorian would call a fallen woman.

TIME MACHINE

It's pure escapism, but this month there is plenty to escape from: politics above all, and on days like today, the weather. I escape into the past – specifically the gardening past.

The Gardener's Magazine had not started 200 years ago, so 190 years would have to do. The volume starts with the editor's – or 'Conductor's – four-month tour through France and Germany in the previous autumn. It was typically rigorous. 'The knowledge required by the traveller should extend to all that has been done or written in his own country [...] on the subject of his pursuits.' All? (And he was interested in agriculture, too.) But before long he is off on another hobby horse, the education of children, which he finds so much better in Württemberg and Bavaria (and also France) that the manners and morals of 'all classes of society' are superior to those of the British. 'There are no mendicants among them, and very few imprisoned.'

He sets off, oddly enough, from Brighton and sails to Dieppe, which he clearly prefers. He was a socialist at heart, feels alienated by the obvious wealth, display and novelty of Brighton, and attracted by the accumulated culture of a relatively poor town, where people build (and dress) with respect for economy and durability. Dieppe, in today's terms, was relatively 'sustainable'.

J C Loudon's tour via Paris, Strasbourg, Ulm, Augsburg, Munich, Ratisbon (or Regensburg), Nuremberg, Stuttgart, Baden and back via Metz makes many pages of escapist reading. Even more escapist though, is the next article, 'A Landscape Gardener On the Siting of Palaces, Royal and Episcopal, Abbeys, Priories, Castellated Mansions, Cottages Ornés ... ' each with its appropriate landscape treatment. (On siting a bishop's palace, 'Seclusion and solemn quiet' are what to look for.)

The Conductor's range always astonishes me. In a few pages he tackles palms, mealy bug and white scale, the flora of Choco (where? In Colombia, and as poor and remote as they come), the pay and workload of a journeyman gardener ('A man for every acre') and a plant I should love to see: the Jersey Cow Cabbage. Fact or fantasy, I don't know, though one might want to escape the smell.

March

RETICENT? MOI?

Few will have noticed, and none I hope been concerned by, a certain reticence from Trad over the past few weeks. He (I slip back easily into the third person I used for Trad's first decade, 40 years ago) has been submerged in the creation of the eighth edition of *The World Atlas of Wine*. Once every six years, for the past 48 years, this work has been growing and growing to keep pace with a world of wine we once thought was mature, but now realize was still in short pants.

So what does wine have to do with gardening, apart from a glass after a day with the hoe? Both have been my preoccupation, and delight, over the 45 years since I wrote a book on trees (having, as I then thought, shot my bolt on wine) and became embroiled with the RHS and gardening. Besides, they have much in common. They are both sensual pleasures with a strong tincture of the intellectual. They call for understanding, reward curiosity, and satisfy several senses. They demand a working memory. They repay acute observation. They can bring moments of intense pleasure.

A certain sensibility, it seems to me, applies to both. You look at a flower with focused vision, to delight in its texture, its structure, the originality of its form, its colours, and perhaps its scent. The glass of wine in my hand brings on the same close attention: to its colour, its denser or more delicate substance, its scent as it develops in my glass and its flavours, simpler or more complex, as they develop in my mouth, ending abruptly or dying gradually away to leave me savouring some elusive sweetness.

Plants and wine both bring on the human urge to name and classify. We find pleasure hardly justified on any grounds of utility in dividing and subdividing and naming categories of both. Do we need three thousand varieties of rose? Do we need to name and classify and attribute different and precise qualities to each of the little fields of vines in Burgundy? Six hundred are named, ranked and priced separately. They are not natural species, like birds or butterflies. They are not the same sort of deliberate creations as, for example, postage stamps. They are collaborations of man and nature to an essentially aesthetic end. They engage the senses and the intellect together. They also call for patience – in growing, nurturing and waiting (sometimes for years) for maturity.

April

PERSONAL GEOGRAPHIES

How often do you see an artist's work that so draws you in that you begin to see – or try to see – in their way? Eileen Hogan's paintings do this for me. I first met them when in 2016 she was 'artist-in-non-residence' at the Garden Museum and her personal vision filled the walls. Her paintings, large or small, are done in combinations of paints and wax that allow her effects of ghostlike fading and focusing. She appears to divine and absorb an atmosphere or a mood before she homes in on the particularities, then paints the details – some details – with pin-sharp precision. Isn't that the way your mind works: changing focus as objects, or ideas or associations swim to the surface of your consciousness, or indeed unconsciousness?

Hogan's work is often in twilight, or mist, or under a sheen of rain or cloak of snow. Then something comes into focus – perhaps something physically quite inconsequential. The chalk lines marking out a football pitch on scrubby grey grass, a snatch of lettering, a walking figure seen from behind. She seems to like parallel lines, whether sunshine through a slatted blind or the Order Beds in the Physic Garden, where a sprinkler makes a small explosion of white shards of water against the green. She likes empty chairs and their shadows scattered in a café when everyone has left. Absence, in fact, is a sort of presence in her work. In a few paintings the degree of detail almost amounts to hyper-realism; others remain impressions.

All this is in a remarkable new book, published by the Yale Center for British Art. It chronicles, in her words and several others', her creative life as painter, calligrapher, printer and publisher – and almost as an afterthought reveals her as a masterly portrait-painter. Her portrait of the Duchess of Cornwall, for one, is so sensitive it seems almost an intrusion to look at it.

In her essay she explains her methods of sketching, note-taking and repeated looking; obsessive observation. This is figurative painting involving not just the eyes but the whole intellect, memory and emotions. Could abstract painting ever capture your vision like this?

A BORDER TOO FAR

When you know a public park as well as your own garden it can be difficult to keep quiet about the way it's run. Holland Park is our backyard. You couldn't ask for more variety in a mere 50 acres. Besides the remains of Holland House, firebombed in the war and now used as the setting for Holland Park Opera, there is a generous playing field and tennis courts, a wild woodland (popular with foxes) covering a third of the area, a formal Dutch Garden, well-known for its tulips, a historic camellia walk, peacocks, iris beds, a maple-and-hellebore walk, two playgrounds and an ecology centre, an orangery, a café, a restaurant, and London's best Japanese garden. The idea has always been to keep as much as possible of the country house garden as it was in Lord Holland's and Lord Ilchester's times. On the whole it is a credit to the Kensington and Chelsea Parks Department and the park's Friends. You're waiting for a 'but'; here it comes.

The remains of Holland House are dreadfully neglected. The east wing, the only wing still standing and now used as a hostel, has crumbling stonework and woodwork that has not been repainted in 15 years; a shameful sight. Last year the house was promoted, if that's the word, to the register of Historic Buildings At Risk.

Its south terrace, recently elaborately repaved, fronts the park on an eight-foot wall with gate piers attributed to Inigo Jones. At its foot, until now, innocuous grass and a couple of benches. But now the grass has been done away with and in its place is a sort of mixed border a hundred yards long, mixed enough to contain alliums and bay trees; the bare earth, one would think, a maintenance nightmare to the small, keen but stretched team of gardeners. There is no sign of a rational plan. The bay and holly trees will in due course hide the house from the park and vice versa. But oddest of all, the border is surrounded by a four-foot post and wire-mesh fence. True there are lots of dogs running around; is this the reason? The result is hideous, the absurdity laughable, but the waste of resources is simply a scandal.

FENCE AND GUN

Is there anything rabbits won't eat? I asked a local Mr McGregor the other day in our New Forest garden. 'Well', he said, 'There's the roller ....' Lettuces may be first on bunnies' menus, but they show little sign of much discrimination. The deer come to their aid of course, when there is something interesting out of their reach. The roe deer take care of the higher stuff while the muntjac are usually available for the mid-level.

There is a particular bed near the front door I would like to take off the menu, but so far no luck. My first idea was to fence it off, as it were, with a low yew hedge. Isn't yew poisonous? Not to our customers. The little plants were immediately gnawed down to their stalks, and further into the bed, the rugosa roses (pretty thorny, I'd thought) were thoroughly investigated, if not destroyed.

Plants with aromatic leaves, or hairy ones, folklore says, are a turn-off. We tried lavender (nibbled to bits) and rosemary (ditto). Daffodils, say the books, are pretty unpalatable. Fair enough, but that only takes care of March. Bluebells are not usually destroyed; but neither are they in the garden; they belong in the wood. The list of less-delicious plants goes on, but a garden composed of them would look pretty odd: daffs, daphnes, buddlejas, bay, nerines, kniphofias, rhubarb .... Tulips are caviar. Roses, rhodies, camellias, hollies ... the essential woodland garden plants are all popular menu items.

We'll go on experimenting, but at the moment fence and gun seem to be the only realistic solution.

STOP PRESS: They don't seem to relish sage.

CORNUCOPIA

From the day he walked into a brasserie in Besançon to be a washer-up to his seriously senior status today, Raymond Blanc has exuded a special sort of focused enthusiasm. It has made his Manoir aux Quat' Saisons, near Oxford, one of the best restaurants (and most expensive hotels) in the country. It has made him the most convincing television chef, and it powers his no-holds-barred gardening.

He employs 12 gardeners at Le Manoir, not because of the size of his gardens, but their intensity. In April the sight of perhaps half an acre of perfect tilth scored in immaculate straight rows (this is his veg plot) is pretty striking. Its produce, via the kitchen, is irresistible. But most impressive of all is the orchard, where more than 800 varieties of both British and French apples and pears are arranged in perfectly pruned files round a central circle. The famous Potager du Roi at Versailles, it seems, had 400 varieties.

Blanc works in collaboration with the celebrated Delbard nursery at Malicorne, near Montluçon in the Allier, the very centre of France. Henri Delbard is famous for rose-breeding, too, having created a series of flowers matching, more or less, the palettes of Impressionist painters. His collection of historic varieties of fruit is a national reference, trained, cordoned and espaliered in wonderful ways, double and quadruple candelabras among them.

The art of pruning and 'training' trees is a French speciality, obsession indeed, which can have pretty ugly results. The British way, of letting a tree grow to its natural shape and size, is not at all the thing. '*Elagueurs*' with their saws and axes even scale tall hedge trees between fields, though here the purpose is harvesting fodder for cattle. (Cattle love elm leaves in particular.)

In French orchards – and here at the Manoir – pruning becomes an art of almost Japanese intensity. Apples and pears are given the same precision treatment as vines; each bud to be retained carefully chosen, the rest removed. How many pairs of secateurs does it take, I wondered, to reduce nearly a thousand fruit trees to perfect parade order?

Not only is Raymond growing them, he is testing them in the kitchen, compiling notes on the best method of preparation for each variety; whether it is best poached, roasted, steamed, baked or puréed. How many cooks?

EASTER TRANCE

London (or at any rate Kensington) was in a trance over Easter. It was summer weather, London was radiant, but everyone had gone away. The streets were quiet, and in the enclosure formed by the terraces around us, nobody had a party: no music, conversation or barbecue smoke. I spent the afternoon writing a list of all the plants in the garden: 120, plus pots in the greenhouse. Then in the evening, after supper outside (this is still April), I sat with all the lights out, gazing at something I have scarcely ever seen in London: the stars. Nothing stirred: no wind, no birds, no sound of even distant traffic. Surely with such a clear sky and an almost full moon there'll be a frost? Warm air was pouring up from Africa; we were in an atmospheric duvet.

I had switched off the rather spasmodic pump that trickles into our tiny fish tank. For two weeks now I've been worried about our two Comets and a tiddler. The water has needed changing and the tank emptying of a winter's worth of detritus. Only one of the fish has been coming up to feed, and that with little appetite. Over the weekend we found out why: he (she?) is alone. What could have taken the others?

There was a heron standing on the greenhouse ridge, I remember, a year or two ago. He flapped off over the garden wall when I showed up. So herons not only sail past, they come down to investigate. In most gardens they are as likely to find a frog as a fish. How can we baffle them? I'd hate a net over the water; maybe just a cunningly placed wire? For all the serenity this little space encloses, nature is still red in beak and claw.

TEA AND BOTANY

Last year we went to Cornwall to see magnolias and saw nothing through the driving snow. (Camellias at eye level, snow on their flowers, looked wonderful.) This year the view was perfect, the magnolias magnificent, and the garden at Tregothnan glorious: from the house over the grandly austere parterre into the combe that zig-zags down to the River Fal, with a ship moored exactly where you might build an eye-catcher.

It is an understatement to say that Tregothnan is spacious. There are walks and glades among huge trees, magnolias and rhododendrons of course, but all the things you go to Cornwall to admire stretch down valleys and over plateaux, follow streams and sneak into woods, it seems without limit.

Then there is the startling sight of a hillside, trim and trained as a vineyard, with long lines of shining green: *Camellia sinensis*, producing Tregothnan tea, the only tea, as far as I know, grown commercially in England. The Boscawen family, with Viscount Falmouth at its head, has been at Tregothnan for 700 years, and is still having new ideas.

I went down to ransack the archives of The Garden Society, the dining club formed one hundred years ago by such horticultural legends as Gerald Loder, Reginald Cory, Frederick Stern and Lionel de Rothschild to meet after RHS Show Days and discuss their new plants. Show Days at Vincent Square are alas almost extinct, and new plants much rarer now than in the days of the great plant explorers. Today they would be accused of cultural appropriation or worse. The urge of gardeners to talk about their favourite plants is not so easily suppressed. The Garden Society dines on.

May

OF ROCKS AND WEED

More news from Japan. I happened to mention that I love oysters, the smaller and sweeter the better, and best of all the curiously named Kumamoto. Curious because these days they come, I understand, from Puget Sound.

Where, then, is Kumamoto? It is a prefecture in the Kyushu archipelago in southwest Japan, important as the prime source of the nori seaweed essential for making sushi. We had been discussing rocks, and how the Japanese choose them for their gardens. We have granite outcrops in the Welsh woods that split to make splendid three-metre splinters. There is one deeply embedded (and much regretted) still in our former Essex garden. Wales, said my pen friend, has connections, and not only rocky ones, with Japan.

Laver is not quite as essential to the Welsh diet as nori is to the Japanese, but it is the same plant. Its unpredictable life cycle had baffled botanists in both countries until Dr Kathleen Drew-Baker, at Bangor University, discovered that at its 'seed' stage, as a single-celled alga, it relies on vacant seashells as shelter. In the 1950s Japan was suffering a critical shortage of nori; here was the solution. And to this day the people of Uto, a town in Kumamoto, celebrate an annual 'Drew Day' around a monument to the Welsh doctor on the shore.

And à propos of rocks and the acknowledged 20th-century master of the Japanese garden, Mirei Shigemori. His parents were admirers of French painters of the Barbizon School – in particular, Millet. Hence their son's name. Another of their children was named Bailon after the author of 'Childe Harold'.

June

PEAK PONTICUM

Few species have been as demonized as *Rhododendron ponticum*. Among foresters it is a hissing and a byword; among conservationists not much better. The charge sheet: it self-sows with prodigious energy and success in typical forest land, which is often acid and rained-on. The seedlings then grow with villainous vigour and smother other seedlings and saplings. They create a damp shade, which is no bad thing in many woods, until it falls under a new suspicion: of harbouring and encouraging *Phytophthora ramorum*, or *P. kernowiae*, pathogens responsible for the death of among other things, larches.

For years there were grants available for the thanklessly repetitive tasks of spraying, or better injecting, it with herbicide. The grants systems change but the problem remains. Foresters still shudder at the sight of mauve blooms in the woods in May, however pretty they may be. Tourists crowd buses to visit the hotspots. There is no denying the spectacle of hillsides aglow with it. Nothing shows up the shades of purple more vividly than the old slate mines of North Wales, where whole mountainsides are slate-black and ponticum-purple.

I am ambivalent about it. Last week in Snowdonia no one could deny its beauty. It can form phalanxes of flowers by the roadside or peep from high among forest trees where flowers are the last thing you expect to see. Its shades of purple, or mauve, sometimes intense, sometimes much paler, are always a startling contrast with woodland green. Yet the sight of it among our trees, flowering when a mere stripling two or three years old (as weeds often do), makes me shudder. There is no alternative to costly destruction.

One botanist has been convinced by its supernatural vigour to declare it a new species, and baptised it *R. × superponticum*. Other authorities say that's rubbish. Although it may possibly have swapped a few genes with other species, such as the American *R. catawbiense*, it remains true to the *R. ponticum* standard – or rather one of them: the strictly pontic one is from northern Turkey, the other (oddly enough) from Portugal. They are apparently not physically different enough to be two species, but the one that spreads is consistently the Iberian strain. So 'super' is fair enough for its performance but doesn't make it a distinct species. Just a super one.

SKETCH INTO PAINTING

Back from a fortnight in France: Brittany Ferries to Bilbao, then a circuitous drive north via Bordeaux, the Centre and the Loire, back home to a London garden transformed by the rain. However assiduously you water your plants it's only drenching rain that brings such surges of growth. I thought the garden was pretty full before, of shoots and sheaves and swags of burgeoning green. We came home to the steps nearly blocked, the path jungled over. All morning I was chopping away.

The high point of our trip was going back to the garden and the woods in the centre of France, which we left 15 years ago – happily in the most sympathetic and energetic hands we could have hoped for. Our successors have become family friends. The continental climate of the Centre can produce growth we never see in England, despite its mean acid soil and stingy rainfall. Things that were merely sketched (parterre, arboretum, woodland rides) are fully painted pictures. Can a gardener have any deeper pleasure than revisiting his work years later to find it continuing as he planned? Even completed (except that gardens never are).

Above all, of course, it's the trees, twice or three times the size they were when we left in 2004. American scarlet, pin and willow oaks, sugar and red maples and the tupelo, *Nyssa sylvatica*, exotics we planted to blaze up as they never quite do here, are almost full-grown, sumptuous volumes of leaves. A tulip tree is invading the barn with long low branches and Italian cypresses have grown almost comically tall. Our survivor elm (always a puzzle; its companions get the disease) has become a landmark from across the valley. And the broad rides we made to define and connect the different plantations are grazed by horses that we imagined, but never acquired.

July

RUS IN URBE

Was ever a little terrace house as sylvan as ours? In front a magnolia, a myrtle, the 12-metre double-flowered white cherry in the street and an exceptional rarity, our neighbour's weeping *Cercidiphyllum*, alias Japan's Katsura. The katsura was already my favourite tree: to find one cascading its exquisite light-green leaves outside our windows is outrageous good fortune, and when in autumn it turns a motley red, yellow and crimson and smells like strawberry jam, I have to pinch myself. Not even Kew has a weeping one this size; people on the pavement stoop to walk under its great umbrella of green and seem to love it.

At the back we look at our own park-size sycamore, a dark tower far higher than the house, our neighbour's walnut, rapidly catching the sycamore in height and exceeding it in the extent of its shadow. Beyond the walnut is a golden catalpa, an apple tree and a row of limes. Beyond the sycamore a house-high bay tree, beyond that an acacia ... in sum, nothing but leaves.

London provides a sound-track, of course: builders, sirens, helicopters, but in summer the houses around are hidden; we might be in the country. The Meyer lemon on the verandah is in full flower (and also fruit, the wonder of the citrus family). There is no more piercing, nose-grabbing scent; it drowns all others. The tinkle of water in the basin below joins the scent to seal the garden off from the world.

CALL ME A COTTAGE GARDENER

Friends are too kind to say anything, but I do sometimes sense a touch of disappointment when they look in my greenhouse, 'Grandpa's Shed'. My pelargoniums, they hint, should be blazing away in unison – or discord, rather: 'Voodoo' and 'Rocky Mountain Orange' can hardly be said to harmonize. Instead I have a forest of green leaves, some lovely smells, but only a scattering of flowers.

I love flowers – but as individuals. I can focus much better on plants and their flowers as individuals or as small groups than on a brilliant mass. And for that matter it's not only in the greenhouse: leaf-greens are the theme of this whole garden, with the plants that are celebrating their flowering season standing out as eye-catchers. Now it's *Clematis viticella*, unruly outbursts of purple, white and crimson scrambling up whatever plant they meet. A few plants have been planned to harmonize or contrast with their neighbours. Some (the neighbour's roses, for example) are unplanned intrusions, others – such as the wisteria and magnolia now taking a curtain call – are nice surprises. Call me a cottage gardener. Massed colours in formal herbaceous borders usually leave me underwhelmed. I admire their technical skills, but do they celebrate the beauty of flowers, or is it just the excitement of the colour spectrum? The prairie look, so successfully promoted by Piet Oudolf, where mauve and brown daisies form islands in the waving grasses, leaves me longing for green – but most of all for structure: roses, hedges, arches, and all the unfashionable apparatus of yesterday's gardens.

QUEUES AT KEW

A visit to Kew used to be a quiet affair, even contemplative. There was time for a word with the gatekeeper, who said he'd heard the camassias were looking good down in the oak collection by the river. Off to the left the camellias were getting on with their business; there were a few visitors, but nowhere anything like a crowd or a queue.

Yesterday, a Monday, the queue at the turnstiles reached far outside the gates; the shop, the little train, were packed, and everywhere you went there were couples, families, rugs and picnics. Kew has come alive. The main attractions, undoubtedly, are the new features – above all the Children's Garden near Kew Palace. An area of several acres has been screened off with new hedges, but no one can doubt what goes on inside. The excited voices carry round the gardens. There is already a booking system for 75-minute slots, and a queue at the entrance. Next time I must take a grandchild with me to see all the ingenious dodges aimed at showing children that plants are fun.

Dale Chihuly's glowing glass sculptures first appeared at Kew six or seven years ago. Their reception was rapturous. He is back with even more ambitious towers and chandeliers and plant-like creations scattered through the gardens and conservatories. Last month we watched some of them being built, a process involving scaffolding and a team of a dozen, unpacking the huge glass tubes and spikes and spirals, and fitting them with laborious care into their slots; hundreds of pieces in shining fruit-gum colours. They are particularly effective, in my view, in the Temperate House, where they mingle with the exotic plants in a glorious jungle, peering from undergrowth or floating on the ponds, plant-like enough to make you wonder. Four months ago, when it reopened in spring, the Temperate House looked rather bare. Today in places it already feels almost overgrown.

There is the restored pagoda, of course, with its Disney dragons, and there is the refreshed Pavilion Restaurant nearby. Most rewarding of all, for anyone botanically bent, is the new Agius Evolution Garden replacing the old Order Beds. It makes a start at explaining how DNA and other dark arts are making a macedoine of plant-family relationships, to the confusion of the old Linnaean guard.

August

THE PLACE OF PIETY

Is it the garden you respect, or the gardener? The question hardly arises in the other arts. The painter leaves a unique image, the composer a score. The performer of course interprets it, but the score is at least a clear instruction.

There is no score for a garden or a gardener. When a garden changes hands, its creator moves or dies, what the new owner inherits is basically a plot of land – cluttered, to be sure, with plants, paths, every sort of feature, and a maze of ideas. The successor may think, or assume, that its creator was happy with the result. He or she may, for example, feel obliged to retain some feature the original gardener regretted, but never got round to changing. Could that cypress really have been planted there deliberately, when it throws the whole view out of balance? And that protruding bit of bed everyone has to walk around? Wasn't it rather peculiar to plant pink roses with pink rhododendrons?

It is very easy, and often tempting, to build on the mistakes of our predecessors. Which raises the question: is there a place for piety in gardening at all, or should we always return to basics, analyse the site, survey the surroundings, assess the value of anything predominant, be it a tree or a pergola, and start from there?

The National Trust has to answer this question all the time. Where do you draw the line between garden and museum? How many history lessons do we need about Brown's obsession with water and grass? The answer often lies with the house, if there is one.

No one will argue with the classic picture: pillared façade, sweep of sheep-shorn grass, clutch of cedars, framing woods, water at the bottom of the slope. If a Victorian enthusiast knocked down the Palladian house and built a fantasy of turrets and pinnacles, what then? Gothic buildings need gothic surroundings: fir trees, gloomy shrubberies, exotic follies in keeping. The third viscount, let's say, had a thing about animals: their likenesses crop up in various materials all over the place. Must they stay, all the monkeys and crocodiles? On a smaller scale, you inherit a rockery full of alpine rarities. Do you have moral obligations? Horticultural ones? Which values should we inherit from the previous generation? Judging by the social media conventions of today, none.

I stand with the late and much-missed philosopher Roger Scruton: we have everything to learn from where our forebears have been, if only so as not to copy their mistakes. If we recognize them.

HEDERADOXY

When did the tide turn on ivy? Early photographs of country houses and churches prove that it was generally accepted as a natural, and presumably desirable, 'mantle' for old buildings. Engravings in William Robinson's *The English Flower Garden* show it blurring the outlines of great houses, clothing the ground and shinning up trees. In Gray's elegiac country churchyard, the owl-haunted tower is 'ivy-mantl'd'.

There have often been arguments about whether or not ivy harms trees, by strangulation, or as a parasite, or by making sails in the upper branches that catch the wind. Officialdom seems, if anything, anti-ivy. The Ministry of Works, when it owned what is now English Heritage (unless I've missed another change of name), laboriously cut and scraped it off its hallowed walls. I remember visiting a freshly stripped Bury St Edmunds Abbey, where every craggy ruined wall was in the nude with a little pebble border at the base. It had lost all its dignity and all its romance.

The conservation argument is clear: ivy degrades walls. It roots in mortar, blurs profiles and hides details. I have just spent a morning finger-nailing it off the rubble-stone walls of our Welsh gold mine building. We had renamed it Myrtle Mansions in honour of the big myrtle tree by the door, but on second thoughts now call it the Banqueting House after its function, as the Tudors did their garden buildings. I dare say most of their 'banquets' were picnics too, if a little more stately than ours.

Stripping the ivy is a satisfying pastime. The trick is to look for a loose stem, detached from the wall (or tree) in a loop large enough to take your finger or your hand (a tool is also permitted). You grasp the loop and pull, not outwards but down. Ivy seems to resist an outwards pull but succumb to a tug on the plane on which it is growing. A longer or shorter length comes away in your hand, usually leaving a loose end for another tug. By the end of the morning much of the stonework was bare. I was standing in a green heap, covered in crumbled mortar and teasing it out of my eyes and ears and hair. Dignity the building never had; its romance survives.

September

TEMPS PERDU

I hadn't been back to Selsey for 30, perhaps 40, years. My parents had a seaside house there before and during World War II, when we were obliged to leave. A promontory into the Channel, Selsey Bill needed defending from Hitler, and certainly in 1940 preparations were made to receive him: vast concrete blocks and thickets of barbed wire.

When I went back last month I didn't recognize it. Selsey Bill is now largely covered with expensive-looking houses. One notable Arts and Crafts house, The Bill House, designed in 1907 by Hugh Baillie Scott, is now a nursing home. I walked along the pebble beach (where I once earned half a crown) looking inland, trying to picture the exact shape of a remembered gable. And there it was, clustered round with new ones, still looking down its half-acre out to sea. They were selling crab sandwiches on the beach. I ate one in a deep reverie.

Memories drifted back. Would I be able to find the farmhouse my father painted, an oil that still hangs by my bed? Was it at Sidlesham, on Pagham Harbour (where, a 16th-century map tells us, 'a barque of 40 tonnes may flote'. Not any more)? The grove of elms in the painting would have died in the 1970s. I searched in vain. I tried all the roads in what I learned is called the Manhood Peninsula. A little chapel stands where St Wilfred, the first bishop of Selsey, reputedly landed to preach to the South Saxons. I remembered being told as a small boy that Selsey Cathedral was still out there somewhere, under the waves. Some said you could even hear its bells.

My madeleine moment, though, was when I went on to Itchenor to look for an uncle and aunt's house. We used to sail with him in Chichester Harbour; more potent memories. The house has gone, but the lane beside it still leads to the cottage where my first girlfriend lived. I was about 12 when I stole out on summer nights to hold her hand. As I passed the cottage door I was suddenly overcome by a positive blast of memory. There beside the door was a wizened old honeysuckle in flower, the very one that still defines a tender moment 70 years later.

DE MORTUIS ...

With alarms about ash disease, oak dieback, phytophthora, and now problems with planes, it seems I have dying trees on the brain. So two visits I have just made may have been grimly apposite, but were nonetheless inspiring.

How long can a dead tree stand as a feature in the landscape? Conservationists urge us not to cut them down, or at least to leave them on the ground as bug hotels. C Brown was apparently in favour of leaving a few in his parks, and even of erecting (transplanting?) them. Most dead trees, of course, fall apart quite quickly; the elm cadavers of the 1970s were mere branchless rotting trunks ten years later. So what do we make of the oaks and (particularly) sweet chestnuts that decline to disintegrate and stand as skeletons for decades after the last leaf has gone?

There is a field near Englefield in Berkshire, and another near Forthampton in Gloucestershire, where dozens of huge tree skeletons stand like an orchard of monuments, their trunks monstrous with carbuncles, often hollow, rising barkless as bones to a full head of branches, and not only the main branches, but sometimes quite a spread of principal twigs. Sweet chestnuts seem particularly prone to hanging on intact, even more than oaks. It must be that the lignin they produce is more dense and durable. My camera is assembling a beauty competition for ghost trees.

October

TAKING THE LONG VIEW

We've just been doing a spot of picture-hanging. Rehanging, rather, to welcome a new painting. In the bedrooms, up the stairs. And suddenly I am seeing them afresh, the way we did six years ago when we moved here. Inertia saps the senses. Pass something several times a day and it ceases to register.

Gardens of course are not pictures; they are processes. The seasons take care of that – and so do the times of day. I have always tried to imprint something permanently satisfying on our main views: structure and proportion in harmony that looks right summer and winter (and morning and evening). The main plan is to concentrate on the longest view available – right to the boundary and preferably beyond.

Our Saling Hall garden was long enough (though relatively narrow) to allow a 150-yard view in the front over the duck pond and along a poplar alley. More park, I admit, than garden. Toward the far end I put a Chilstone Pope's Urn. Alexander Pope wrote the wittiest couplets in the language. He also commissioned William Kent to design the most perfect urn, with spiral grooves that give something lively to its surface in all lights. Behind the house, where we planted a sort of landscape arboretum with watery distractions, the central, longest view was even longer, nearly 200 yards to the inevitable eye-catcher, a Haddonstone temple, which we dedicated to Bacchus. The pediment bears two gambolling carp and an inscription that perplexes everyone. Can you figure out *Innumerae Veniunt Artes*?

Now, with a garden a mere 55 feet long, the principles are the same: a central view to the boundary. Not quite central, in this case, because the greenhouse takes up half the width. Trees (or now shrubs) pace out the distance, one-third of them evergreens. Their differences of height, colour, density and bulk are the subplots that keep it interesting. At the same time, with the seasons and the times of day, shadows keep shifting and emphasis changing. All this is the framework for a changing scene of leaves and flowers. Movable pots are the sideshows to attract attention to different corners. Two changes of level with stone steps certainly help; the far end is six feet higher, which somehow flatters the modest length of the garden. But the principle is the same, town or country: keep the centre open.

IN THE NIGHT GARDEN

Deep down perhaps I'm a Teletubby. Certainly at this time of year, when the Day Garden is reduced to a few hours, the sun so low as to be confusing and teatime a fireside feast. I tend to draw the curtains and curl up with a book.

There is an alternative, though. A relatively small amount of well-aimed electricity can give you garden pictures quite different from those of daytime. In our tiny London garden our predecessors had the idea, and did a good job. There is a valid garden picture day and night. Invite Maud 24/7. (Her tryst at the gate, remember, was a daybreak date: 'the black bat night' had flown.)

In our little patch four spotlights, high up on each of the side walls, unequally spaced, can be swivelled to point downwards or sideways. They light the steps (essential), a table, and whatever plants are eye-catching when picked out against blackness. Certain ferns, for example, a generously yellow-splotched ivy, a camellia (mainly for the shine of its leaves), the bleached flower heads of a hydrangea, the trunk of our oversized sycamore, a vase or a balustrade. And, of course, the greenhouse, which becomes a Crystal Palace on a black night. There is the gleam of paving in the rain, and very occasionally the magic of snow. Just outside the French windows on the covered verandah, the lemon tree can be spotlit. It is always doing something; often in winter flowers and fruit intriguingly at the same time. The surroundings become invisible, cast into mysterious blackness.

Goodnight, Macca Pacca. Good night, Iggle Piggle. You go to sleep; I'll watch the night garden.

THE T WORD

Somehow hydrangeas always pop up in Trad at this time of year. It's partly their duration; what flower is so much in evidence for so many weeks? Even spent and faded flowers keep their shape and remain a presence in the garden.

But it's also the conundrum of their colours. It's all very well saying they will be blue in acid soil, pink in alkaline. You can control this, they say, with aluminium salts. Oh, yeah?

They have minds of their own. Our Welsh resort has ancient clumps that have settled down over the years to a marvellous medley of colours, by autumn principally maroon and dusky purple, but with individual flowers still at extremes of the blue/pink spectrum. And this is rain-soaked acid soil. So is the soil the answer? If it were grapes and wine we were talking about, we'd be discussing terroir.

The British shy away from this essentially French concept; both the word, which has no precise English translation, and the idea that certain soils in certain situations can affect the qualities of the fruit they produce. There's a suspicion that terroir is just muck and magic with a French accent, designed to prove that only La Belle France has the conditions for great wines.

If soil can affect the colour of flowers, though, can it not affect the flavour of fruit? Plant a vine of, say, Chardonnay, on chalk or on slate and you will get two quite different wines. Plant it on the Jurassic lime-stone of Chablis, a pale, quite heavy, soil visibly made up of minuscule ancient seashells, and you will get wine of a recognizable flavour that no other vineyard has ever, as far as I know, achieved.

Scientists have been keen to show that vine roots have no way of abstracting minerals directly from the soil they encounter. The only demonstrable difference between soils, as they affect the plant, comes from their permeability; how fast they drain, which in turn affects their temperature. Warmer soils equal riper grapes. If claret from St-Estèphe has more acidity and 'structure' (or less perfume) than claret from Margaux it's because St-Estèphe is lower down the Gironde Estuary; the river has deposited more stones in Margaux and carried more silt down to St-Estèphe. Silt equals clay, equals slower drainage, equals cooler soil.

How simplistic that is. How does it account for Château Calon-Ségur and Château Cos d'Estournel consistently tasting different? It's not that simple. If there were an analogy between vines and hydrangeas our wines could all end up somewhere between maroon and purple.

November

MORE THAN NATURAL GRACE

Just home from a week in New York, at its October best. My lodging is as near Central Park as you can get, and I spent all my spare hours walking in this extraordinary playground landscape. Thirty years ago it was a crime-ridden wasteland. To walk there after dark (or even before) was not advised. Then in 1980 mayor Ed Koch initiated The Park Conservatory and put Betsy Barlow Rogers in charge as its first administrator.

The park, covering 840 acres, was created in the heart of Manhattan, pretty much with shovel and barrow. Frederick Law Olmsted and the English architect Calvert Vaux, its creators, were inspired by the new park at Birkenhead on Merseyside, designed by Joseph Paxton, one of the first to be created for the public to enjoy.

Birkenhead was finished in 1847. Olmsted arrived in Liverpool in 1850. He wrote: 'I cannot undertake to describe the effect of so much taste and skill as has evidently been employed. I will only tell you that we passed by winding paths, over acres and acres, with a constantly varying surface, where on all sides were growing every variety of shrubs and flowers, with more than natural grace, all set in borders of greenest, closest turf, and all kept with exemplary neatness! In democratic America there is nothing to be thought of as comparable to this people's garden.'

Olmsted's Manhattan site was more problematic: marshy, among huge up-rearing grey rocks, partly built over in the voracious development of the city, almost desolate of vegetation. His vision was a pleasure ground on an unprecedented scale, shaded with the glorious variety of America's trees, embracing the pastoral (the sheep meadow), the romantic (a castle overlooking a lake), the monumental, the frivolous, the untamed, the useful, the whimsical ... every genre and mood of gardening. Among the early visitors was the essayist Oliver Wendell Holmes, who wrote: 'The Central Park is an expanse of wild country well crumpled so as to form ridges which will give views, and hollows that will hold water. The hips and elbows and other bones of nature stick out here and there in the shape of rocks which give character to the scenery, and an unchangeable, unpurchasable look to a landscape that without them would have been in danger of being fattened by art and money out of all its native features. The roads were fine, the sheets of water beautiful, the bridges handsome, the swans elegant in their deportment, the grass green and as short as a fast horse's winter coat ....'

It was a stupendous task to construct, and is even more of a challenge to maintain. So its current state, a bustling resort where every visitor feels at home, safe, stimulated, active, absorbed, pop-eyed with discoveries, is an extraordinary achievement – for which Betsy deserves much of the credit.

BUBBLY IN THE GARDEN OF ENGLAND

Did you ever expect to see the neat green corrugation of vineyards tilting down the South Downs? The North ones? Or in the Chilterns or along the South Coast? Last week, in their yellow autumn suits, they looked quite at home, even beautiful in their leafy English context.

I was in Kent, visiting three wine estates that are already making wonderful wines. Wonder is the relevant word: ten years ago I was still a sceptic. The best, and most, of what they make is sparkling. At last Champagne really has a run for its money. No other region anywhere has been able to challenge it as England now does.

How has this suddenly happened? Climate change has a lot to do with it. The average temperature of the South of England has climbed one-and-a-half degrees in a generation. Ripening grapes outdoors here used to be a chancy business; now, in a reasonable summer, it is a given. Just as important is the adoption, by most English wine-growers, of what you might call 'serious' grape varieties. In the experimental years of the '70s and '80s it was thought prudent to plant crosses bred in Germany specifically for early ripening. Their wines, unfortunately, were unconvincing. It was the analogy of champagne that made all the difference.

Two hundred miles away over the Channel they make the world's best bubbly on the same chalk formation as our Downs. Their grapes are often on the margin of ripeness – and high in acid. But it's their acidity that makes them so drinkable in their sparkling form. Once that penny dropped, and English farmers had the confidence to plant Pinot Noir, Chardonnay and Pinot Meunier, and their flavours emerged in the wine they produced, the word spread. (Pinot Meunier, incidentally, has a synonym: Wrotham Pinot. And Wrotham is in Kent.) The champagne method is not cheap; it needed investment in plant, training, and time – at least a year more than still wine to be ready to drink, and preferably very much longer.

But now there is nothing left to prove. Even famous champagne houses are convinced. Tattinger and Pommery have already bought and planted land in England. The next question is where will our best terroir turn out to be? And the apparent answers are full of surprises. There are good English sparkling wines from Kent, Sussex, Hampshire, Dorset, Cornwall, Oxfordshire, Bucks, Essex ... and not all of them, by any means, are grown on our Champagne-like chalk. Some of our best examples are grown on greensand, often on unpromising-looking clay, or on flinty ground where you wouldn't want to garden. Wine-growing, in fact, is gardening on an industrial scale. Which is why a vineyard is beautiful.

RAKING LEAVES

What are the words for these rejects, these fragments of plant-flesh, designed, precision-cut, palmate or pinnate, extruded into air by a mysterious subterranean pump? Sun coloured them, rain polished them, wind rattled them, time tired them.

Some let go, some hung till frost forced abscission. Was that hard, breaking the cord of life to float some seconds free, the ground coming up, choosing to land on the hedge, in the currant bush, tangled in ivy or safe on the path?

I scratch you out with my rake, wherever you land, admire your yolk-yellow, your dappled apple in a glance and drag you into my soggy pile.

MORE LEAVES

I've been totally absorbed all morning in the childish pleasure of playing with water. Its most joyous form, for me, is encouraging a trickle to become a stream. In Wales it's easy; on the hills there is always a head of water to be released by shifting a rock, some earth, even a few leaves. The most satisfying result is when a single leaf is blocking a potential leak. Once let a trickle feel the force of gravity and it soon swells. 'Freshet' is the word for a sudden tide of overflowing water; miniature it may be, but the sense of inevitability, of unlocking a predictable process is deeply satisfying.

The first leaf moves, two more follow it, six more stir on the surface and the water gathers speed. A clump of fallen leaves dams the tiny stream until I poke it with my stick. The streamlet gushes on, the flow accumulates, I nudge more leaves aside; now the flow has the momentum to push an obstruction away. It reaches a tiny cliff-edge, breaks over it and charges on, feeling the contours, hesitates when they flatten out, finds the lowest way and soaks the surface while it gathers weight to push on again. I look back; there is a little silver line where my stick and I have been.

2020

January

HUSH

Cabin cruises on Grasmere, 4 x 4s in Tilberthwaite ... the Lakes are in an uproar about inclusiveness. Nobody goes there, apparently, who isn't white, middle-class, and probably male as well. What the Lake District needs is visitors of all ages, races, genders, socio-economic classes, religious affiliations, blah, blah, blah. Not just people who have read about them, looked at maps, and have a taste for scenery and silence.

Silence. Is it elitist, racist, or anything more than just noisist to want to get away from intrusive sounds? Irrelevant sounds; that's the point. Wind, birdsong, sheep, even a tractor across the valley are the natural sounds of the countryside. Radios and revving engines are intrusions. Forestry is admittedly noisy – occasionally. Chainsaws and bulldozers are no friends of quiet enjoyment. But they only break the silence in working hours during felling and thinning operations. Not at weekends, and for limited and predictable times.

On our hillsides in Snowdonia we have narrow gates with stones to frustrate off-roaders. We have signs that say *Dim Modurs*, and don't often see or hear intruders. But we are far off the beaten track and our terrain would seem tame to serious petrolheads. In the Lakes, where millions go to breathe deep of mountain air and cock their ears at country sounds, can anyone argue that the general good is enhanced by revving motors?

THE ROAD TO WALES

We're off to Wales in the morning; a journey we make four times a year. Boots in the car, a scratch picnic just in case, clothes for one evening out and three probably wet days. Out of London past Westfield, the mammoth shopping centre I've never penetrated, onto the A40, past Hendon, where Uncle Pat, Flight-Lieutenant W E P Johnson, taught RAF pilots (and was, in 1931, the first person to take off, fly round and land with a blanked-out windscreen, on instruments alone).

You're soon in the woods, or apparent woods, where the tree-planting to screen the new motorway has come of age. An unnoticed climb through the Chilterns until suddenly a deep chalk cutting reveals the rest of England, or at least the broad Thames Valley, stretching off to the north. Oxford, Banbury, Warwick seem to be among unremarkable fields and occasional herds. It's amazing how empty England is ... until the lorries thicken, gantries come up one after another: Birmingham, M6 north, airport, NEC, and England is suddenly modern and unfriendly.

The M6 Toll Road is a luxury break, then more queues until the M54 cuts loose, heads west, and you feel you're leaving it all behind. Telford, signs for Shrewsbury, across the sluggish Severn and the signs say Wales. And we see it. There is a grey hill on the horizon that is not English-shaped. Left at the roundabout for Welshpool, the road narrows, and now its 50 miles of bends and steeper, greener hills, and sheep instead of cows, and bigger beeches, then hills high enough for heather. Miles of bends behind trundling caravans, grey villages with ARAF/SLOW painted on the road and names too long to read as you drive through.

The windscreen wipers are going, the houses are scattered and the hills rise above the car windows. The river below the road is black and white with foam, then the climb begins, a high waterfall to the right, winding into bare turf and rock, sheep and heather and bracken to a pass that changes everything. Light floods from under black clouds to the west, Cader Idris crouches grey in grey gauze through the raindrops. The road swerves down and down towards the sea. We're ready for the orderly market square of Dolgellau, its trim charcoal stone shining with rain. It feels like home.

February

DA CAPO

It happens every time I start on a job that needs only moderate concentration. Today it's tidying a trellis above the wall, pruning a *Clematis viticella* right back, disentangling last year's sprawling growth, finding, pruning and tying the rose ('Bantry Bay') in the middle of it and tying in the *Viburnum* × *burkwoodii* that shares the wall. What happens? I find words and music recycling on a loop in my brain. Often from *Hymns Ancient and Modern*. Today 'Lead kindly light, amid the encircling gloom ...' round and round and round. It's often Bach (usually the B Minor Mass) or something of Stanford's.

It can be words without music. King Lear, for some reason, keeps popping up – but then I do keep quoting the bit where Goneril (or is it Regan?) asks him why he needs 25, or 12, or five, or even one knight to serve him, when her whole household is at his disposal. His response is 'Oh reason not the need', with heavy emphasis on the last word. And mine when my wife questions my buying a new ... almost anything. I don't *need* a new trowel, but I saw a jolly nice one in Rassells over the road.

The *da capo* in my head is apparently called an earworm, and can be so persistent, says Google, that it rivals tinnitus as a problem. To me (touch wood) it's more of a pleasant distraction. To turn it off I just got out the ladder and tackled the high bits. That called my brain away to more serious business.

NEW WINE IN OLD BOTTLES

It's not always easy to say when a plant has had its chips. We've all learned to lift and divide border stuff now and then, but when is the now? Your proper professional will have a routine and keep a diary. Besotted amateurs (I'm making a confession) will merely observe and enjoy – even the onset of senility. It gives a border an established look.

When to ditch a shrub can be a much harder question. 'The slower it grows, the longer it lasts' is a fair rule of thumb: a broom or a mallow that gallops away is soon a diminishing asset; a well-managed rose can go on practically for ever. The real question is not how long it will live, but how long will it remain an ornament?

One of the terraces in our daughter's garden on the Riviera clearly begs to be refreshed. There are shrubs with more wood than leaf and flower. An old plumbago has become a thicket, cistus stands stodgy and flowerless, hydrangeas are gracelessly stumpy or leggy, my favourite *Solanum laciniatum* waves thin flowering shoots above amputated limbs. Only perovskia flourishes in straggly masses of lavender blue.

Is the answer piecemeal chopping, and planting in the gaps? The mixture of old plants and new is rarely a good one. Encouraging the ground-covering herbaceous plants, in this case mainly agapanthus and 'Society garlic', as they used to call *Tulbaghia violacea*, keeps the borders looking filled, but the proportions of height and lower mass soon get out of kilter. You see the bones; it all looks senile. Much better to pull it all out and start again. Then the real foundations of the garden become apparent; the olive and lemon trees, stone walls blanketed with trailing rosemary, the pergola with its vines and the sentinel cypresses state their simple case. Do we need more furnishing?

March

ELF & SAFETY

Pootling around on the Internet the other evening, looking for information about splitting logs, I stumbled on a surprising source:

a series of films (some new, some very old) made in different parts of France on their country crafts. Log-splitting is there all right: the ancient art of the *merrandier*, the forester who renders a solid oak log into perfect slabs for conversion into, for example, barrel staves. Coopers are there, too: the ancestral barrel-makers who fashion a whole barrel from scratch by hand. Their tools alone are a study in practical evolution: planes, chisels, draw-knives, drills, clamps, mallets and the massive beetle so brilliantly called a 'persuader'.

A barrel, when you think of it, is hardly an obvious container. Who thought of flexing planks and constraining them with hoops to keep them tight together and watertight? The Romans didn't. They used heavy two-handled clay amphoras for anything you could pour, from wine to corn. It was the Gauls who invented the barrel: weight is no problem when you can roll it.

There are films on thatching, tiling, charcoal-burning, puddling clay and carving sabots (usually from alder). There is the forgotten drama of using rivers for transporting timber, when labourers worked all day in the water up to their thighs in threadbare trousers, in ordinary shoes (and some with waistcoats and watch chains), fishing logs out, stacking them, lashing them into rafts and braving rapids on them.

It is the direct physicality of all these crafts that makes them so familiar, yet so alarmingly remote from modern life. Limbs were limbs; strength was strength: you lifted, you pulled, you carried, you shoved. A pulley or a lever was the only mechanical advantage or way of increasing the force you could apply with your muscles. Your hands were your basic tools, vulnerable as they are. There are no gloves in these films; I flinch as I watch a blade coming down repeatedly within an inch of bare fingers. But that is how we got to where we are.

MARKS OUT OF TEN?

We've had to scrap a long-planned visit to Japan to follow the spring, from the small southernmost islands (one is Yakushima, home of the little felty-leaved rhododendron) north via Kyushu to Honshu across the Inland Sea, ending in Kobe. We were to take one of the little ships of the Noble Caledonia fleet, and were all ready to leave, when news of the new virus came from Wuhan, and gradually the Far East began to shut down.

We were to have started in Taiwan, which soon followed China in closing its doors. The voyage was then adjusted, to start in Okinawa in the southern islands, and visit South Korea. When South Korea shut down, the problem became the long-established laws of cabotage. No ship foreign to a country can trade between two of its ports without calling in at another country. So where was the nearest abroad? Russia. Instead of blossom-viewing we would have to spend four days steaming to Vladivostok and back over 1,000 miles on the North Pacific, in March. I'm afraid we cried off – and within ten days the voyage was cancelled altogether.

Our consolation has been England's most glorious spring. It has been hard to keep away from Kew; the magnolias are as fine as I've ever seen them. If only I'd planted *M. kobus* 30 years ago .... We've seen the last of them, though, for this year; even the Royal Botanic Garden has been closed.

As consolation for Japan's no-show I have been testing myself on the names of cherry trees around us and realize how rusty I've become. Once upon time I could tell a 'Jo-nioi' from a 'Taki-nioi' or a 'Shirotae' from a 'Shirofugen' at a glance. Now, shame-faced, I often have to resort to Picture This, an App that recognizes whatever plant you point your camera at (though Japanese names are not its strongest point).

It's tempting to have a beauty contest and give marks out of ten. Far better, though, just to marvel at their wonderfully lovely variations on a theme.

April

IN THE STILLNESS

We can hear the church bell striking three streets away. The wren in the walnut is deafening – and a poor performer, it seems to me: the same shout again and again. These are the sounds of locked-down London, where normally the rush of cars is endless, punctuated by motorbikes, sirens and drills. There are no planes overhead. We hear conversations in the street outside. The world we know has stopped, and we have time to think – and look.

I have never followed spring before as a full-time observer. Other years we catch sight of a magnolia or camellia, admire it for a moment, perhaps try to name it, and move on. There's no moving now; our plants are our companions, up close and personal. Spring is happening too fast. I often say that; there are too many climactic moments packed in a few distracted weeks. But we're not distracted now, except by the virus; we have all the time in the world to watch and enjoy nature's renewal.

The leafing of the trees is the greatest change, from the early greening of willows (weeping willows earliest of all; dry-grass green while everything else is still dormant) to the long-drawn-out colouring of the planes, their high traceries suspended for two weeks or so in a sort of pale olive mist. The limes are slow, first hanging out limp-wristed baby leaves that soon unfurl in brilliant varnished green. Oaks are individuals; one will be in full leaf long before its neighbour. Horse chestnuts' shiny buds split quickly to release limp rags. Elms fool you into thinking they're in leaf when the green is just their new fruit.

We watch two tall cherry trees in the street from our bedroom window, geans (a name no one seems to use for our native cherry) with double flowers that cover their lanky pliant branches with snow. One came out just before three days of hot sun; in that short spell its flowers were fried brown. The other tree timed it perfectly and is still alpine-white. It's Peak Wistaria too, and Kensington has aspiring champions in every street, from one that spans seven houses to others bonsaied up to the roof.

The focus moves on to crab apples and handsome old pear trees, while on the ground the blue of scillas and grape hyacinths gives way to bluebells and soon the pale *Campanula poscharskyana*, the London weed, and I can't take my eyes off the falling spray of double white

roses where 'Mad Alf' throws herself out of our oversize sycamore.
All in uncanny silence. I can't say I look forward to the returning roar.

SHARE OF SWEETNESS

Until the last few years, tulips had never really grabbed me. I seem
to have rather discounted the shiny flowers in brilliant colours that
come and go so spectacularly after the daffodils have made their golden
statement. I think the reason is the way they are sold. They are almost
always pictured nursery-perfect, as sleek and immaculate goblets
just starting to open. Scarcely more than gravid buds, in fact. Dutch
nurseries show miles of eye-wearying colour. Would you cross the sea
just to see a hectare of scarlet? Nor me.

Tulips had their moment in history in 1637, in Charles I's reign,
when immoderate enthusiasm for and speculation in 'broken' colours
caused the first great financial crash, 80 years before our equally dotty
South Sea Bubble. It was when tulips and Holland were so much in the
news that one of my favourite poets, Andrew Marvell, wrote about a
little girl 'in a Prospect of Flowers':

> *Reform the errors of the spring;*
> *Make that the tulips may have share*
> *Of sweetness, seeing they are fair;*
> *And roses of their thorns disarm:*
> *But most, procure*
> *That violets may a longer age endure.*

'The errors of the spring'; he sounds like a gardener. 'Give the tulips
some scent', is what he is saying. I always think the same about the
camellias: I want to get closer to these lovely nests of petals, to
commune with them. I put my nose to them; no response. Today
there is at least one scented tulip – and one of the very best: 'Ballerina',
slim, tall, warm orange and smelling of freesias, wallflowers ... roses
... I can't pin it down. But back to their usual image; too prim and
buttoned up. Tulips become loveliest when they blow, in post-

coital repose, their petals widespread, dishevelled, their stems in wanton curves, scented or not.

COVIDIA NONSENSIA

It's not considered prudent or polite, it may even be treasonous, to question the government's priorities during the Covid lockdown. But what on earth do they think they're doing shutting down plant nurseries, and at the height of the planting season, when they're bursting with stock that must either be planted out soon or condemned to rot? I'm peering through the fence at our local nursery, Rassells, at a feast of plants at their peak of beauty. The owner Richard Hood (who is watering everything, every evening) tells me he understands that if he sold fruit we could go in to buy it. Not a pansy, though.

What's the difference between a nursery and a supermarket? You can do social distancing as well in one as the other. What's more nurseries are outdoors, and locked-down gardeners are longing to be up and doing. Are they confusing plant nurseries with garden centres that sell more burgers and barbecue kits than living plants? By all means shut the hardware departments, but isn't it essential to nurture living things?

There is a well-publicised consensus at present that nature is good for you: gardening is good for the nerves, not to mention the soul. We haven't heard much from Number Ten about souls. I am longing to sit in our parish church, 16 feet away from the next person if necessary, if only to absorb its atmosphere of holiness. Archbishop Welby should understand that, even if Whitehall is oblivious.

May

OUT OF SCALE

I think I've worked out why this little London garden has a tree in it as tall as the garden is long. It lends a certain gravitas to a modest patch to boast a tree the size of a Hyde Park plane, even if a sycamore is a rather lower form of life. But it was here when we bought the house and we would certainly not be allowed to cut it down. Indeed it's an annual struggle getting the council's permission to prune it.

At least I've discovered its probable story. It's a war baby. We just measured its girth at breast height: 7' 3" (2.2 metres). Following the rule of thumb that most trees put on an inch of girth a year, that makes it 87 years old. Oddly, its ground level is a metre higher than the rest of our garden, and the neighbours'. Its end of the garden has now been paved, with steps up to it. I suspect it was a weed seedling on a compost heap, ignored during the war and now formally incorporated, and an object of rather wry pride.

THE URGE TO KNOW

Confession: I've never been a fan of most modern poetry, Ogden Nash apart. T S Eliot? I reckon he made it up as he went along. 'Peach' rhymes with 'beach'; couldn't we all do that? Now and then, though, I meet a poet with no great pretentions who says something directly and neatly and memorably; something Alexander Pope would approve. (Pope wrote 'What oft was thought, but ne'er so well exprest'.)

Six or seven years ago I wrote about Jay Appleton, the geographer and landscape philosopher who coined the idea of Prospect and Refuge. To recap, he said certain views are inherently pleasurable because they answer to basic instincts. They give us notice of approaching threats (and opportunities) and at the same time give us the sense of being protected from behind. The view of a valley from a cave-mouth, for example. Or indeed a Palladian temple.

Appleton's verse, 'Deflected Vista', was published in 2009 by The Wildhern Press in a little book called *A Love Affair with Landscape*. Wordsworth he is not, but any gardener would like – and indeed learn from – his poem. Sadly the strict laws of copyright (and the strange elusiveness of his publisher) prevent me from quoting more than short extracts.

'The thing I like about an avenue', it starts, 'is how it takes possession of the eye'. It draws you to 'a faraway, magnetic patch of sky'.

But if the avenue curves and you lose sight of the sky at the end, says Appleton, it merely 'feeds our curiosity'. The poem ends:

> *Deflected vistas therefore serve to show*
> *How overwhelming is the urge to know.*

July

A WOODLAND CREATURE

When it started to rain last week, a good month into a drought that had begun to hurt, it felt like autumn. By midsummer's day (according to one calendar) or the first day of summer (according to another) we'd already had more than a year's average summer weather. Twenty lunches in the garden in succession breaks all records.

With the afternoon sun just perceptibly lower in the sky, the rain clouds and the cool damp air, it felt like a different season or another place. Wales, for example. In the four months we have been stuck at home I have dreamed about our woods and the walks I know by heart after 25 years, not alas of residence, but of passionate engagement. Next month we will be able to go back to see hundreds of new trees planted.

The Snowdonia National Park (we are in it) has a project to get rid of the *Rhododendron ponticum* that springs up everywhere in the woods, smothering young trees and creating ideal conditions for the *Phytophthora* that is killing our larches. They undertook to poison all our ponticum. To my fury I have just heard that they have also poisoned the most prized plant on the property. I planted *R. augustinii* for its blue flowers, to match the bluebells in May, 25 years ago. *Augustinii* doesn't look remotely like ponticum. It is a delicate, transparent plant with leaves a fraction of the size and entirely matt, with no shine. The plant was in a prominent place by a waterfall where a simpleton could see it was a deliberate feature. I was beginning to compare it with the beauty by the river at Bodnant. It is now a stump stained blue with glyphosate. The park authorities apologized profusely, but 25 years is not something you can refund.

As soon as we're in the woods, though, under the beeches with the river rattling by and a whiff of woodsmoke from the chimney of our old stone building, cares will evaporate. I am at heart a woodland creature.

THE VOICE OF AN OLD FRIEND

I am looking for a recipe in Elizabeth David and reading her old magazine articles, the voice of an old friend, when I stumble on one of her descriptions of an August holiday. 'I have a *nostalgie de la pluie*', she writes. 'North Cornwall and its leafy lanes dripping, dripping, to walk in a dressing gown and gumboots through squelching grass to the stream to fetch water for our breakfast coffee ....'

She suffers August rain in the west coast of Scotland, 'drumming on the corrugated-iron roof' and on Tory Island, 'on what the Irish describe as a nice soft day, the Scots as a bit mixed, and I as a hurricane ....' Next came 'sodden Surrey woods' – at least a change from a Celtic soaking.

I have a *nostalgie de la pluie*, too, and seek assurance in the statistics that say August is indeed one of our wettest months. Walking on grass worn, grey and brown, patchy and without a fresh leaf, ankle-twisting, I wonder how many wet days it needs to bring life back. In the uncut meadow the grass was sere but soft, brushing your knees, dotted with purple knapweed and yellow rattle. The stream was clogged with dead leaves, the earth cracking. Roll on August; wet my face and hands.

We didn't have to wait for the calendar. We went to the seaside, and the children sailed to Cornwall. Down it came, the wind rose, they found a sheltered anchorage and I opened the French windows and listened, and watched, and saw leaves shining, and tipping their little brimfuls onto the leaf below till the branch shook.

What weight does rain add to a big oak with half a million leaves? A branch reaching 40 feet horizontally from the trunk must have to support several hundredweight of water. Why doesn't it split from the trunk? An ingenious American woodsman spent his life carving up trees to find the answer. The growth rings of the trunk and a branch springing from it alternate and overlap, splicing the two together in a union almost impossible to break.

In a day or two the tawny hide of Kensington Gardens will be overlaid with tender green. Already oaks have shot out pinkish and buff Lammas shoots, their instant reaction to a deep drink in mid-summer. My own Lammas shoots, meanwhile, spur me to celebrate this liberating moment.

August

OMBRA MAI FU

It was not far off 100 old-style degrees yesterday, and not a breath of wind. How did our ancestors in the 18th century, periwigged or corseted, survive the summer? Handel left some clues in two of his most successful and memorable arias. '*Ombra mai fu*', his largo in *Serse*, of 1738, is King Xerxes' love song to a plane tree and its 'soave' shade; 'Where'er you walk' (*Semele*, 1743) is Jupiter's promise to his mistress, Semele (the mother of Bacchus), that her life with him will be a (shady) paradise; 'Cool gales shall fan the shade'. Our garden is permanently shady, but you need a breeze as well; close and airless shade is no pleasure.

For months already this summer I have been crossing to (even planning my walks for) the shady side of London streets: east in the morning, west in the afternoon, or the south side of east–west streets. Avoid north–south streets around noon.

Am I unusual in shunning the sun? I shudder when I see photos of crowds fully exposed on shadeless beaches. Summer sun without a shady refuge is my idea of hell. I suspect that plants feel the same. Why do they flower in sunshine, and vegetate in shade? Shade gives them the opportunity to grow, to breathe freely, open their stomata and pump carbon dioxide, using the carbon to multiply their cells and expand. Sun, I imagine, constrains them, makes them hoard their juices, induces the sense of mortality and the urge to reproduce; hence make flowers, mate and produce their fruit.

This is no way to think of a plant, I'm often told. They don't have feelings, sensations or urges; let alone a concept of the future and the need to provide for future generations. I'm not so sure. They can't book holidays in a climate that suits them better. Nor, while this poxy virus is among us, can we.

SOCIAL DISTANCING

I came across a sentence the other day in a pre-Victorian memoir that made me wonder who exactly did all the work in the huge gardens of the day. Brownism, of course, greatly reduced the detailed gardening of parterres and topiary. Sheep did a lot of mowing. We have seen photos of garden teams 50-strong, the men all wearing hats, waistcoats and watch chains, the boys caps (the weeder women not even in shot). But here is Prince Pückler-Muskau, in a house-party at Lord Darnley's Cobham Hall in July 1828:

'Today I diligently helped clear a few new vistas through the brush, to which everyone lent a hand.' This is something Jane Austen left out: the gentlemen in their shirt sleeves, the ladies in ... what, I wonder? Pinafores? And where did the sons of toil fit in? Did they set to, competing to impress with their brawny bending, or watch from the wings, concealing their giggles, or pitch the branches on a bonfire? Did the cider-flagon go round the party, ending with a shanty and a jig, or did they practise social distancing?